HISTORY

OF

MASSACHUSETTS.

HISTORY

OF

MASSACHUSETTS

FROM JULY, 1775,

WHEN GENERAL WASHINGTON TOOK COMMAND

OF THE

AMERICAN ARMY, AT CAMBRIDGE,

TO THE YEAR 1789, (INCLUSIVE,)

WHEN THE FEDERAL GOVERNMENT WAS ESTABLISHED

UNDER

THE PRESENT CONSTITUTION.

By ALDEN BRADFORD,

AUTHOR OF THE VOLUME OF HISTORY OF MASSACHUSETTS
PUBLISHED IN 1822.

BOSTON:
PUBLISHED BY WELLS AND LILLY.

—

1825.

Research Reprints Inc. · New York

First Published 1825

Reprinted 1970

DISTRICT OF MASSACHUSETTS, TO WIT:

District Clerk's Office.

LIBRARY OF CONGRESS CATALOG CARD NUMBER:

71-124779

PRINTED IN THE UNITED STATES OF AMERICA

To JOHN ADAMS,

DAVID SEWALL, WILLIAM BAYLIES,

GEORGE PARTRIDGE, TIMOTHY PICKERING,

SAMUEL FREEMAN, THOMAS MELVILLE, DAVID COBB,

PELEG WADSWORTH, JOHN BROOKS,

PEREZ MORTON, JUDAH ALDEN, BENJAMIN PIERCE,

JOHN POPKIN, NATHAN RICE,

And Others,

WHO WERE IN CIVIL OR MILITARY OFFICE

IN MASSACHUSETTS IN 1775;

AND WHO,

AFTER A LAPSE OF FIFTY YEARS, STILL SURVIVE;

THE PATRIOTIC ASSERTERS, AND INTREPID DEFENDERS,

OF

AMERICAN FREEDOM,

IN THE CABINET AND IN THE FIELD; WITH GRATITUDE FOR

THEIR INVALUABLE SERVICES, AND ADMIRATION

OF THEIR UNDAUNTED HEROISM;

THIS VOLUME

IS VERY RESPECTFULLY DEDICATED,

BY

THE WRITER.

PREFACE.

In a volume, published in 1822, the record of events in Massachusetts was brought down to July 1775. The period embraced by that volume was one of uncommon political interest. It was from 1765 to 1775, that the controversy between the government of England and the people in the thirteen American colonies, then a part of the British empire, which issued in their independence, took place and was continued : and, as the dispute was more particularly and uniformly maintained by the Assembly of Massachusetts, than in any other colony, previously to a resort to arms in defence of constitutional rights, when petitions, remonstrances and arguments had failed, it was considered proper to give a full statement of it. Soon after the affair of Lexington and Concord, when it appeared that the British resolved to support their arbitrary measures by the sword, the Continental Congress concluded to make a common cause with Massachusetts; provided for an army to be raised by all the colonies unitedly; and appointed General Washington to take the command of it.

After this event, the contest having assumed a more military character, and being supported by the united strength of all the provinces, the history of Massachusetts becomes more connected with the general proceedings of the whole: and as the theatre of the war for many months after the epoch above mentioned, was in that province, a record of events which there occurred will include the important transactions of all the colonies in opposition to British usurpation. A principal part of the force opposed to the ministerial troops was also furnished by Massachusetts, for some time after the organization of the continental army.

In the subsequent periods of the revolutionary war, though the leading events which took place in the United States have been preserved by able writers, the particular efforts of Massachusetts have not been fully recorded. A faithful narrative will show, that her citizens did not relax in their exertions after the seat of war was removed to other parts of the continent; but that the same zeal was exhibited and support given, through the whole contest, which appeared in its early stages.

The writer of this volume has been sensible of the difficulty of doing full justice to Massachusetts, without referring to events of a general nature, in which all the states were concerned. It has been his endeavour, to give only a concise and rapid statement of transactions in other parts of the United States. A general and connected view seemed to be proper, in stating the particular efforts and services of Massachusetts; as these were rendered, in most cases, in compliance with the requisitions of the continental Congress, and composed a part of the united exertions of America for freedom and independence. He hopes he has not dwelt too much upon transactions, in which all the states were engaged; nor omitted to notice such as particularly regarded the state of Massachusetts.

It was asserted by some members of the convention in Massachusetts, January 1788, which adopted the federal constitution, that, for several years of the war, this state furnished nearly one third of the continental army. It will be seen in this volume, that the portion of troops required of Massachusetts, was very great, and that the number requested was usually raised. It will be recollected also, that general Washington acknowledged, on several occasions, that, but for the Massachusetts regiments, the regular army would have been insufficient for attack or defence. Although it had an extensive sea coast, of upwards of five hundred miles, to protect by its own militia, the most prompt measures were taken to procure the troops called for to join the continental army in distant parts of America. The state also advanced large sums to these troops, to induce them to engage in the public service; and when the accounts of the several states were adjusted, at the close of the war, it was found that Massachusetts had borne more than her just portion of the public burdens.

The history of Massachusetts, after the peace of 1783, during several succeeding years, is very important. The immense debt, for which it had to provide payment, and the embarrassments on trade, occasioned a general discontent and complaint among the people, which impeded the regular course of law and threatened to destroy all social order. It was a period of great public distress and alarm; and nothing but uncommon wisdom and firmness in the rulers saved the Commonwealth from the evils of anarchy.

The establishment of the federal government over the whole United States, which took place soon after the period just mentioned, was also an event of great interest in the country; and the proceedings in Massachusetts, relative to it, merit particular notice.

With a deep sense of the importance of accuracy, fidelity, and impartiality in those who profess to give a correct record of events, or a just character of public men, it is unnecessary, perhaps, to add, that it has been the constant endeavour of the writer, in this as in the former volume, to have the statements given strictly conformable to truth; and that he has been anxious not to advance any thing as fact, upon conjecture, or to give party representations as a substitute for prevalent public opinion.

BOSTON, 12*th February*, 1825.

CONTENTS.

CHAPTER I.

CHAPTER II.

CHAPTER III.

CHAPTER IV.

CHAPTER V.

CHAPTER VI.

CHAPTER VII.

CHAPTER VIII.

CHAPTER IX.

CHAPTER X.

CHAPTER XI.

CHAPTER XII.

CHAPTER XIII.

CHAPTER XIV.

CHAPTER XV.

HISTORY

OF

MASSACHUSETTS.

CHAPTER I.

Number and condition of troops at Cambridge, July 1775... Reasons for not attacking the British in Boston... Character of Washington... Generals in the army... Supply of men and powder by Massachusetts... The affair of Machias... Expedition to Lake Champlain... Defensive war *only* yet intended—Character of Hancock, T. Cushing, Samuel Adams, J. Adams, R. T. Paine, J. Warren.

WHEN General Washington, by appointment of the Continental Congress, took command of the American troops in the vicinity of Boston, the third of July, 1775, they were estimated at about 15,000. Of these, more than 9,000 belonged to Massachusetts; Connecticut, New Hampshire and Rhode Island furnished the residue. They had assembled at Cambridge and Roxbury, soon after the attack, by a detachment of the British army in Boston on the defenceless citizens of the province at Lexington and Concord. These troops, collected to oppose a large and disciplined army, were none other than the yeomanry of the country, with such arms as could be suddenly procured; though a small portion of them, denominated " minute men," had been occasionally trained to military duty, for a few months before. The whole colonial force had been under the command of general Ward, whose head-quarters were in Cambridge; general Thomas commanding the right wing at Roxbury, and general Putnam of Connecticut the left wing, on Prospect Hill, in the westerly part of Charlestown. On the arrival of Washington at Cambridge, as commander in chief, Ward was placed over the right wing in Roxbury; and Lee, then lately appointed a major general by Congress, had the command of the left, on Prospect Hill.

The American army did not consist of so many men, as had been represented to general Washington; or, as a short period before his arrival, were assembled in arms, in the neighbourhood of the metropolis. Several companies, which were marched at the moment of alarm, had returned to their respective homes. At one time, they had been estimated at 18,000. If it was in the design of Washington immediately to commence offensive operations against the British troops, and to drive them from the capital of Massachusetts, his plan must have been disconcerted on finding the Americans less numerous than he had expected; and his resolution for the attempt yet more shaken, by witnessing the deficiency of arms and the great want of discipline and subordination among the troops he was appointed to command.

To organize and discipline an army of such materials, of men who had seen little actual service
and who were unacquainted with military tactics;
and to render them formidable to regular troops;
was a work requiring time, intelligence and prudence. The yeomanry of Massachusetts and of the
other New England Colonies were, indeed, brave, resolute, and ready for any enterprize however hazardous. But they were the lords of the soil, and
they acknowledged no higher and lower grades
among them, in which some were entitled to command, and others bound to obey. To civil authority, they were certainly most obedient. But
happily they knew nothing of standing armies; and
officers of the militia, being chosen from the great
body of citizens, and usually retaining their commission only for a few years, acquired no peculiar
respect, by which their commands would be
promptly and uniformly obeyed. The first great
object of the commander in chief, therefore, was
to produce a spirit of subordination; and to persuade the people, both in and out of the American
camp, of the absolute necessity of military discipline and of strict obedience to superior officers.
With all his prudence and address, and enthusias-
tic as they were in the cause of freedom and of
their country, his wishes were but partially accomplished, until some time after the commencement
of the war. The subaltern officers frequently departed from the camp for several days, without
leave of absence : and whole companies, claiming
to have come as volunteers, left the army, contrary to the desires of the commander in chief.
At a subsequent period, though their term of enlistment had expired, but against the urgent re-

quest of Washington, as the army had become much reduced, the whole Connecticut line was disbanded and returned to their homes.

Another very serious difficulty prevented the plan of offensive warfare at this early period of the contest. The troops were deficient in good fire arms, for many which they brought with them were almost unfit for use. Nor was it possible entirely to remedy the deficiency, though great exertions were immediately made for that purpose. Of the necessary article of gun-powder, there was also a most alarming deficiency. And there were at this time, very few cannon in the American army, so essential in storming a fortified town. To the want of an efficient artillery corps may justly be attributed the defeat of the Provincial troops at Bunker's Hill, on the 17th of June.*

It was evidently, then, the dictate of sound discretion in the commander in chief, to refrain from an immediate attack on the British troops in Boston, who would probably have been provoked to retaliate upon the besiegers; and these would not have been able, in their unprepared condition, to repel the assault. It is matter of surprise, however, that the British general, with a regular army, so amply prepared for the contest, did not attempt to force the American lines, and disperse the provincial troops, who were so deficient in discipline and in military stores. These considerations are sufficient to justify general Washington, in not acting more decidedly on the offensive at this period. To which may be added, the reluctance of the opulent citizens of Boston to an attempt to

* There were only four *brass* field pieces in the whole American army at this time.

drive the British by force from the town, as a great destruction of property would probably be the consequence : and the system of opposition, deliberately adopted by the colonists, being then merely defensive, would not well consist with a more vigorous hostility, than preparations to prevent the ministerial army from marching into the country for plunder, and to meet it with a good face, at a future day, if a reconciliation should not be effected with the parent state. For even at this period, and for several months later, though the sword had been drawn, and the blood of Americans, wantonly spilt, called on the people for vengeance, there was still a hope that administration would recede from its despotic measures, and that the rights of Americans would be acknowledged without further hostilities. Many intelligent citizens also who were warmly opposed to the conduct of the British cabinet, were averse from the idea of Independence. And the language of the Continental Congress was in favour of reconciliation, upon the recognition of the civil authority of the Colonial Assemblies, as had been formerly exercised. When, nearly twelve months after this, the question of Independence was discussed, it was not without great reluctance, that several eminent patriots consented to the measure.*

The appointment of general Washington to command the American army was a most fortunate selection. Perhaps, no other individual in the colonies would have been competent to the place and the occasion. He possessed, in an emi-

* Mr. Dickinson, the celebrated author of the Farmer's Letters, was one of these.

nent degree, all the qualities necessary to a great general; particularly, to form and direct an army composed of men like the Americans. He came to the office with a high reputation for patriotism, intelligence and experience. In a former war between England and France, he had seen something of military plans and movements. And he had given proofs of great prudence and judgment, as well as of personal courage. Had he been impetuous like Putnam, or rashly bold like Arnold, the colonial army had probably been exposed to total defeat. But with great decision and energy of character, sufficient for the most daring enterprize, he united all the prudence and caution so important in the commander of a feeble and incipient army. His disposition and manners were such also as to win the affections of all ingenuous minds: and yet the disobedient and refractory were certain to receive that prompt infliction of punishment so requisite to military order and submission. He never exposed the lives of the soldiers unnecessarily; nor hazarded an attack on his enemy, where the prospect of success was very doubtful, except in cases where public opinion seemed loudly to call for action. If he was ever compelled to an act of apparent severity, it was a sacrifice of feeling to imperious duty; when the good of the country demanded it, and the rules of war rendered it justifiable.* Unprepared

* Extracts from his orders to general Arnold, who commanded the expedition to Quebec by the way of Kennebec, Sept, 1775, " You will observe the strictest discipline and order, by no means suffering any inhabitant to be abused, or in any manner injured, either in his person property, punishing with exemplary severity every person who shall transgress, and making ample compensation to the party in-

as the colonists were at first to meet the regular
troops of Britain in the open field, he was re-
markably fitted to direct their military movements; to restrain the resolute, to inspirit the
timid, and to create an army, adequate to the re-
pulsion of British mercenaries, and to the establishment of American freedom. His love of liberty was ardent and unextinguishable. In him, it
was a most elevated and holy sentiment, unalloy-
ed by selfishness or ambition. Had the British
troops been too powerful for the American army;
had they taken possession of the Atlantic settlements and planted the standard of despotism on
the cultivated lands of Anglo-Americans; he had
resolved to retire to the western mountains, with
the chosen sons of liberty who should adhere to
him; and there build up another empire of civil
freedom.

Charles Lee, Esq. then recently appointed major
general, by the Continental Congress, joined the
army at Cambridge at this time. He had been
several years in the English service, in which he
acquired a high reputation for courage, and dis-
played considerable military talents. But it was
supposed he cherished some feelings of rivalship
toward general Washington, and even aspired to
the chief command of the American army. At a
subsequent period, his conduct fully jutified this

jured. If Lord Chatham's son should be in Canada, and, by
any means, fall into your power, you are enjoined to treat
him with all possible deference and respect; you cannot err
in paying too much honour to the son of such an illustrious
character, and so true a friend to America. Any other prisoners who may fall into your hands, you will treat with as
much humanity and kindness as may be consistent with your
own safety and the public interest."

opinion. The citizens belonging to Massachusetts, who received commissions from the General Congress, at this time, were Artemas Ward, major general, Seth Pomeroy, John Thomas and William Heath, as brigadiers.*

The Provincial Congress of Massachusetts was in session, at this time, in Watertown, and on the arrival of general Washington at head-quarters in Cambridge, they appointed a committee to wait on him, with assurances of perfect respect and confidence, and of readiness to render him all the aid, which the resources of the province would admit. He had been instructed by the Continental Congress to consult the civil authority of Massachusetts; and, in his military operations, to conform, as far as possible, to its direction and advice. The most perfect harmony was maintained between them, while the American army continued within the province.

He had been at Cambridge but a few days, before he made a request for a reinforcement of the army of 3,000 men, to be raised immediately, within the province of Massachusetts, which already furnished about three fourths of the troops then collected. An order was promptly passed by the Provincial Congress for enlisting this number, and the several towns in Middlesex and the adjoining counties were required to raise their respective quotas, though, a few days after, a counter order was issued, at the suggestion of the commander in chief. The call was made when the movements of the British in Boston indicated an attack upon the American lines, and on finding that the

* Putnam of Connecticut and Schuyler of New York were appointed Major Generals in the continental army.

troops at Cambridge and Roxbury were not so numerous as had been represented. Some recruits arrived from the southern colonies in the mean time, even as far as Virginia;* and the fear of a sortie from the besieged in Boston subsiding, it was concluded to suspend the execution of the order, as to two thousand.

At the same time, a request was made by general Washington for gun-powder; an order was sent out, by the Provincial Congress, to all the towns within forty miles, to furnish a quantity from their regular stock, and a large amount was immediately collected.

Early in June, two large coasting vessels and a British tender went from Boston to Machias, a small settlement in the eastern part of Maine, to obtain lumber for the benefit of the enemy. The Provincial Congress of Massachusetts had forbidden the people to supply the British with provisions or lumber of any kind. The citizens of Machias were therefore determined to defeat the plan which the owners of the vessels had in view. They took possession of one of the coasters, and secured her at the wharf. The commander of the tender, with the other in his custody, moved down to the mouth of the river, intending there to load with lumber and return to Boston. A number of the people embarked on board a small vessel and dropped down to the entrance of the harbour, to prevent the British in their enterprize. A skirmish ensued. After a severe engagement of an hour, the tender was captured. The captain re-

* Eight companies of riflemen from Pennsylvania, Maryland and Virginia, consisting of 100 each : and were only twenty days on their march.

ceived a mortal wound, of which he died the next day, and two of his men were killed, and several severely wounded Six of the Americans also were wounded, and one was killed in this affray. Captain Jeremiah O'Brien, who commanded in the affair, conducted with great bravery.

In June, a committee* of the Provincial Congress of Massachusetts had been sent to lake Champlain for the purpose of causing such of the cannon and military stores, just before taken in the forts at Crown Point and Ticonderoga, as was practicable, to be transported to Cambridge for the use of the army there, and for concerting suitable measures for further military operations in that quarter and in Canada. It was early perceived, that it would be highly important to take possession of the fortresses on the lake, and thus prevent the British from penetrating into the western parts of the colonies, and also to engage the feelings of the Canadians in support of civil liberty, for which the colonies were contending.

The patriots of Connecticut, New York, Massachusetts and New Hampshire were early sensible of the great advantages of securing the northwestern passes from Canada to the frontier settlements. Soon after the affair at Lexington, when it was generally believed that the colonies must resort to force to maintain their rights, an expedition was planned in Connecticut† to seize the British forts on lake Champlain. A few resolute men immediately proceeded to the county of Berkshire in Massachusetts, where they were

* W. Spooner, J. Foster, and J. Sullivan.

† Mr. Hancock and S. Adams, then on their way to Philadelphia, were present at the consultation.

joined by Colonel James Easton, Major Brown
and others,* in the bold and arduous enterprize.
On the New Hampshire Grants, so called, (now
Vermont) the party was still further augmented
by a number of men collected by Ethan Allen, Esq.,
and Colonel Seth Warner. Benedict Arnold of
Rhode Island, who offered his services to the congress of Massachusetts for this purpose, was also
dispatched, in the early part of May, to that quarter, to assist in the undertaking. He was authorised to enlist 200 men for the service; but he
proceeded without raising any, and arrived at the
lake soon after the others had reached it, and
was engaged with them in the capture of Ticonderoga and Crown Point. Immediately after, he
proceeded to St. John's, situated at the northern
extremity of the lake, where he surprized and
took the fortress occupied by the British.

Arnold was a brave and resolute officer, but of
violent passions and unwilling to submit to the
command of others. A dispute soon arose respecting the chief command of the troops in that quarter; Arnold assuming the right, while Easton and
Allen were opposed to his pretensions. When the
committee from the Congress of Massachusetts
arrived, they gave an opinion unfavourable to the
claims of Arnold, in consequence of which he resigned his commission for that department. The
committee continued at the lakes several weeks,
for the purpose of organizing a military force sufficient to keep possession of the captured forts.
They provided for the reinforcement of the American troops by several companies from the county

---

* About 220 in the whole. Major Brown was a brave officer, and of great service in this expedition.

of Berkshire; and appointed agents to furnish them with necessary provisions, and such military stores as could be procured there. These troops were soon after augmented by a party from the province of New York, amounting to about three hundred.

Without this seasonable precaution, the British regular troops, assisted by the Canadians and Indians, would have harassed the western settlements in the New England Colonies; and so well secured themselves in the forts on lake Champlain, as to facilitate any future plan of a formidable invasion from that quarter. This seems to have been foreseen by men of intelligence in Massachusetts, as well as in New York, Connecticut, and New Hampshire. Joseph Hawley, Esq. of Hampshire county was most decided and zealous in favour of this expedition. He addressed a letter (June 4th,) to general Joseph Warren, then President of the Provincial Congress, and chairman of the committee of safety, urging immediate attention to the subject, and stating the great importance of maintaining a military force on the lake for the security of the country. He was then an influential member of the Provincial Congress, but was with his family at Northampton. In his opinion, it was equally important to prevent the British from regaining the forts on the lake, as to check them in their attempts to penetrate the province on the sea board. This letter, it is believed, induced the Congress of Massachusetts to appoint a committee to proceed to the lake and to take measures for strengthening the force of the Colonies in that region. This committee advised the Continental Congress of the great importance of holding the forts on the lake. It will also be seen, that, a few months after this period, Massachusetts raised a large number of men for the military service in Canada, although the capital of the Province was in possession of the British, and much more than half of the American army at Cambridge was composed of her brave citizens.

The public documents of the Continental and Provincial Congresses, at this time, afford evidence, that a defensive war only was yet waged against the British government; and that some hope was cherished of reconciliation on terms consistent with ancient charter rights and privileges. After referring to the arbitrary measures of the ministry towards the Colonies for ten years, the claims of Parliament to impose taxes on the people of America, who were not represented in that body, and the employment of military power to compel submission to oppressive and unconstitutional laws, they declared their resolution to stand in *defence* of their liberty, and to repel force by force. " Our fathers," they said, in an address to the people, " left their native land to seek, on these shores, a residence for civil and religious freedom; at the expense of their blood, at the hazard of their fortunes, and without the least charge to the parent state, by an unconquerable spirit and great enterprize, they effected settlements in the distant, inhospitable wilds of America, then filled with numerous and warlike nations of barbarians. Societies, or governments were formed, vested with *perfect* legislatures, under charters from the crown." They then stated the various claims and statutes of Parliament, which militated with their charter rights, and were subversive of constitutional freedom, as subjects and citizens of the British government; the transporting and stationing of an army in the Colonies to enslave the people; and the attacks already made by the military upon the innocent and defenceless inhabitants. " We are thus reduced," they added, " to the alternative of choosing an *unconditional* submission to tyrannical ministers, or resistance by force. The latter is our choice. We have counted the cost, and find nothing so dreadful as voluntary slavery. Honour, justice and humanity forbid us tamely to surrender that freedom which we received from our gallant ancestors, and which our innocent posterity have a right to receive from us.—We however, assure our fellow subjects in every part of the Empire, that we *mean not to dissolve that union which has so long subsisted between us, and which we sincerely wish to be restored.* We have not raised armies with *ambitious designs of separating from Great Britain and establishing independent States.* We *fight not for glory or conquest. In our native land, in defence of that freedom which is our birth right, and which we ever enjoyed until the late violations, for the protection of our property acquired solely by the honest industry of our forefathers and ourselves, against violence actually offered us,* we have taken up arms. *We shall lay them down when hostilities shall cease on the part of the aggressors, and all danger of their being renewed shall be removed; and not before.*"

There were several members of the Continental Congress, at this period, who were totally averse from the idea of Independence; believing that the Colonies were not equal to a successful resistance of the British government; and many were not even desirous of separation, if they could be restored to their former rights and authority.

The patriots of Massachusetts were not professedly aiming at Independence; nor was such their real ultimate object, at this period; and yet most of them were of opinion, thus early even, that a separation would be the result, as the British ministry were resolved to compel submission to their arbitrary and oppressive measures. They perceived the alienation which would arise from the contest; and believing, that the parent government would not recede, they came to the conclusion, that they must willingly submit to surrender up their liberty, or prepare to take their stand as an independent nation. The conduct of the British administration justified such an opinion. It declared its determination to prosecute the war it had begun until the colonies should acknowledge the entire and absolute supremacy of the British Parliament over them, though they had no voice in the laws they were required to obey. With a singular unanimity Massachusetts resolved to draw upon its resources to the utmost, to annoy the British troops and to strengthen the American army, collected within its territory. For several months after the Continental army was formed, this Province bore the chief burden of the contest.

The General Congress met again this year in May; the delegates to which from Massachusetts, were John Hancock, Thomas Cushing, S. Adams, J. Adams and R. T. Paine; the same persons who were appointed the year before, with the exception of Mr. Hancock in the place of Mr. Bowdoin, who declined. Mr. Hancock was early chosen president of that body in the absence of Peyton Randolph of Virginia; and on the death of Mr. Randolph, in October, he was again elected to that office, which he held as long as his health permitted.

Mr. Hancock was a man of great wealth, and possessed of showy and popular talents. On many occasions, he had given strong evidence of disinterested patriotism; and was aware of the destiny which awaited him, if the struggle should be unsuccessful. His conduct was so decided, and so obnoxious to the British ministry, that if the Colonists had been subdued, his opposition would have been followed by the forfeit of his life. Long before the British troops began hostilities upon the people in Massachusetts, he had taken his stand on the side of liberty and his country. For several years, he had been chosen one of the representatives of the patriotic town of Boston; and more than once a counsellor, but received the negative of the royal governor. When he pronounced the oration, before the inhabitants of that devoted place in 1774, on the anniversary of the massacre of March 1770, though the streets were full of British soldiers and some collected to hear the address, he denounced the conduct of the administration, in its various oppressive acts, and especially in sending an armed force to be stationed in the capital, in time of peace, with a boldness and an eloquence, which excited the astonishment alike of his friends and foes. He was president of the first and second Provincial Congress of Massachusetts, which set at Concord in October 1774, and at Cambridge in February 1775. He was also a member of the committee of safety for the

Province, which, after October 1774 exercised the powers of the Supreme Executive. And he was one of the first board of the Executive Council, in July 1775. Mr. Hancock was successively elected a delegate to the Continental Congress for Massachusetts till the year 1779. He was constantly devoted to the public service; and was ever ready to sacrifice property, as well as ease, to the good of the country. When the present constitution and frame of civil government of Massachusetts was adopted in 1780, he was chosen Governor, by a great majority of votes; and continued in the place, till his death in 1793, with the exception of two years 1785 and '86, when Hon. James Bowdoin was elected.

Thomas Cushing had long and justly sustained the character of a patriot, and had filled important public offices to the satisfaction of the people. He was elected Speaker of the House of Assembly for about twelve years; and he had the entire confidence of the friends of liberty. He was also one of the delegates to the General Congress from Massachusetts in 1774 and 1775. In 1775, 1776 and 1777, he was placed in the Supreme Executive Council; and in 1780 was chosen lieutenant governor of the Commonwealth.

In that band of firm and intelligent statesmen in Massachusetts, who so ably and resolutely opposed the plan of the parent government to infringe the liberties of the colonies, none was more uniform, and none more distinguished than Samuel Adams. James Otis was in the legislative assembly several years before him, and was more ardent and more eloquent; but Mr. Adams was not inferior to him in decision or in devotion to the sacred cause of civil liberty. He received his education at the university in Cambridge : and afterwards became well acquainted with history and politics. And the spirit of eminent English patriots as well as of the founders of New England animated his whole public conduct. Deliberation and judgment were predominant traits in his character. He was never rash or precipitate ; but most decided and persevering. And he was always careful to appeal to the constitution of England either to justify the conduct of the colonies, or to show the injustice of the British ministry. He possessed the happy talent of convincing the great body of the people, that the opposition was just and reasonable. He and Otis are believed to have been jointly concerned in preparing several publications, which have usually been attributed entirely to the latter. The British government marked him out with a few others,* for signal punishment. While a delegate to the Continental Congress, he was chosen a representative for Boston to the Massachusetts House of Assembly, July 1775; and in August following, was appointed secretary. At this time he was elected into the executive council. For several years following, he was chosen a delegate to the General Congress; and was there distinguished, among other eminent statesmen, for his industry, resolution and firmness. Upon the adoption of the constitution of Massachusetts, Mr. Adams was elected president of the Senate; over which he presided for several years with much ability and dignity. He was four years lieutenant governor : and in 1794, was elected governor of the state; in which

* Hancock, Bowdoin, Quincy, T. Cushing, W. Cooper, and Rev. Drs. Cooper and Chauncey.

office he remained, until admonished by old age and bodily infirmity to retire from the cares and duties of public life.

John Adams, one of the Massachusetts delegates to the General Congress, in 1774, 1775, 1776 and 1777, became distinguished, at an early age, for his ardent patriotism, and his decided opposition to the arbitrary policy of the British ministry. His public, political career was long and brilliant. No one of the colonies could ever justly boast a character more profound as a civilian, or more resolute and zealous as a patriot. In 1770, he was returned a representative from Boston to the General Assembly, at a time when governor Hutchinson was claiming the exercise of arbitrary power, under the colour of prerogative. In the disputes between the Governor and the Assembly, Mr. Adams took an active part ; and some able replies of the House were attributed to his pen. The following year he was chosen to the Council Board, but received the Governor's negative. In the General Congress, no member was more distinguished for legal talents and ardent patriotism. He was among the earliest advocates for Independence : and contributed by his ability and zeal as much as any other statesman in America, to vindicate that measure, and to raise the reputation of the country in foreign nations. He was appointed Envoy to France in 1778, and afterwards to Holland where he rendered essential service to his country, by shewing the resources and zeal of the United States, and procuring loans, so necessary at that period, to maintain the cause of liberty and the credit of the American Congress afterwards. He was afterwards minister at Paris, and had great influence in forming the treaty of peace in 1783. He then received the appointment of Envoy extraordinary to the English court; where he was distinguished as an able and faithful agent for the United States. In 1788, he returned to America, and was elected the first Vice President of the Union; and afterwards, on the retirement of Washington in 1797, he was chosen president. Decision and energy were his great characteristics. He was ardent and without disguise in his conduct, which sometimes subjected him to the charge of precipitancy; and his acquirements, as a statesman, were equalled by very few of his contemporaries.

Robert T. Paine held a high place in the public estimation, for intelligence, firmness and zeal. He took an early and active part in support of the rights of the colonies, when the claims of royal prerogative and of the supremacy of the British parliament were urged with great ability by Hutchinson and others; and the plan was laid to deprive Americans of the privileges secured to them by their charter. As a lawyer, he was considered among the most eminent in the province. On the failure of Mr. Sewall, the king's attorney, he conducted the prosecution on the part of government, in the memorable case of Captain Preston and his soldiers, for the massacre of several citizens of Boston, on the night of the fifth of March 1770. To this important duty, he was recommended by the selectmen and people of Boston. He was also chairman of the committee for the impeachment of Chief Justice, Oliver, by the House of Representatives in January 1773, on the charge of receiving his salary from England, contrary to the charter and the invariable practice in the colony. He was an active member of the House of Representatives in June 1774, when a decided posture was assumed, in opposition to the arbitrary measures of the British ministry, and to the requisitions of governor Gage, who had, a short time before, succeeded Mr. Hutchinson, as chief magistrate of the province. While he was a delegate from Massachusetts to the Continental Congress, which was four years, he was also a great part of that time a member of the House of Representatives, speaker, a member of the executive council, and attorney general.* He possessed great decision of character, and few men contributed more than he did, to the support of civil liberty in the country.

James Warren may justly be ranked among the leading patriots of Massachusetts. His early education was the best the country afforded. His talents were respectable; his decision and zeal equal to those distinguished men already mentioned. Soon after the death of major general Joseph Warren, he was chosen president of the Provincial Congress; and, in July, when a General Assembly was convened, he was elected speaker. In the year 1776, Mr. Warren was appointed a judge of the Superior Court, and in 1780, he was chosen lieutenant governor by the legislature, on the adoption of the constitution; but he declined both these offices.

---

* This being before the present constitution, there were no incompatibilites of office. All the delegates to the General Congress, from Massachusetts, for several years were also members of the Assembly or Council.

CHAPTER II.

On the 19th of July, the representatives from the several towns in the province, who had been chosen in pursuance of writs issued by the Provincial Congress in June, met at Watertown, where the latter body had been lately sitting; and proceeded to organize themselves, by the choice of a speaker and clerk, in conformity to former usage and the provisions of the charter, under which the legislature of the province had acted from 1692. Although the Provincial Congress did not materially differ from the House of Representatives, being chosen in like manner and by the same persons, yet it was an assembly not recognized in the charter, and had been substituted in the place of the latter, when governer Gage omitted to issue precepts for a regular General Court. As no new form of Government was prepared, and as a formal separation from Britain had not then taken place, nor any resolution been adopted to become Independent, it was the opinion of the intelligent civilians in Massachusetts, that it would be proper still to conform to the charter of 1692, which had hitherto been their constitutional political guide. They felt the difficulty of the situation, in which the people and the government they had assumed, were placed. They were too wise and too patriotic, to think of maintaining regular civil authority, necessary to the due administration of justice and to the support of good order, without a legislature, legitimately called and organized, an executive distinct, in some degree at least, from the legislative power, and a judiciary independent of both.

After the commencement of hostilities, when the authority of Gage, the royal govornor, and the counsellors appointed by the crown, contrary to the charter, was renounced, the anxiety increased in reference to the novel and dangerous state, in which the province was thus left, and the enquiry was often made, what remedy could be provided to prevent the evils which would probably ensue. It was true, that the Provincial Congress was composed of persons chosen by the people to legislate for them; or rather to advise to measures for their immediate protection. And this Congress or assembly had appointed a Committee of Safety from their number, who were to perform the executive duties of the government, except the appointment to office. But there were no courts of justice; for the commissions of the judges had been declared unconstitutional, and they forbidden to act under them. County conventions subsequently recommended to the people to suspend all demands and disputes of a private nature; and in public concerns, to submit to the directions of the Provincial Congress. A deep feeling of patriotism, and an anxiety for the freedom and welfare of the country absorbed all selfish considerations; and very few indeed were found to take advantage of the peculiar state of the government.

With this impression of the want of a regular government, the Provincial Congress of Massachusetts in May repeatedly applied to the Continental Congress for advice. They stated, that they were without a governor or deputy governor, without counsellors and judges, inasmuch as these, having refused to govern the Province agreeably to the charter, had been declared no longer fit, in their opinion, to hold and exercise their several offices; which, therefore, they considered vacant. In addition to the general reasons offered, which arose from the very necessity of the case, as all authority and government ought to be founded on certain principles, which had the approbation of the people, the source of all just power; they urged the danger which might soon arise from having a military force, and no civil power competent to direct and control it. In June, the Continental Congress recommended, that representatives be chosen, as formerly, who should elect counsellors, according to the provisions of their charter; and that this body act in concert with the House, as a part of the legislature; and separately, as the executive part of government. In giving this advice, it was assumed, that the places of governor, deputy governor and counsellors were vacated.

Agreeably to the recommendation of the general Congress, as well as to their own views, which had been given in their address to that body, on desiring its advice, when the representatives met, they proceeded to elect the same number of counsellors as had been appointed in years past, who were to have the powers given to that body in their charter, and also to exercise executive authority, in the absence of the governor. But a sufficient number to form a quorum were not present until the 27th of the month. The views of the Assembly on this subject will appear from the preamble to a resolve, which was passed the following day, in justification of their proceedings. " Whereas it is provided by the royal charter, that, when the governor and deputy governor of this province happen to die, be displaced, or be absent from the province, the council or assistants, or the major part of them, shall have full power and authority to do and execute all and every such acts, matters and things, which the said governor or deputy governor could lawfully do or exercise.—And whereas the late governor and deputy governor of the province have absented themselves and have refused to govern the province according to the charter: It is therefore resolved that, until the said governor or deputy governor shall be appointed to govern the province according to the charter, this House will consider the *constitutional* council of the province, or the major part of them, as governor of the province; and will acquiesce in whatever said council, or the major part of them, shall *constitutionally* do in said capacity."*

* Those counsellors, who immediately accepted and were present when the board was first formed, were Sever, Prescott, Lincoln, Gerrish, Fisher, Spooner, Foster, Taylor, Gill, Palmer, Holten, Otis, Winthrop, C. Cushing, Whitcomb.—S.

The legislative and executive departments of government, were thus established agreeably to the ancient charter, which still seemed to be acknowledged as the civil constitution of the province; and the consent and approbation of the people gave a sanction to the procedure. It was several months after this that the judicial courts were organized: and the attention, both of the legislature and of the people, was so occupied in providing for the general defence of the province, that no complaints were heard on account of this omission. The necessity for a more perfect constitution, however, was soon felt by the people of Massachusetts; and it will be seen, that efforts were early made to prepare one, although the perturbed state of society, which war occasioned, was not very favourable to such an undertaking.

Notwithstanding the previous measures of the Provincial Congress, it will be readily perceived, that the General Court had arduous and pressing duties to perform. To provide for the augmentation and continuance of the troops; to furnish arms and other military stores; to support the public credit, in a season of such uncommon expense—in a word, to call forth the resources of the province, in defence of the freedom and welfare of the people, demanded all the wisdom and zeal of this patriotic assembly. An emission of paper bills was ordered, on the credit of the province, amounting to 100,000*l.*; which had been previously recommended by the committee of safety. A tax of 40,000*l.* was voted; and the

Adams and J. Adams, soon after returned from Congress and took their seats at the Council Board.

Treasurer,* whose appointment was then confirmed by the General Court, though he had already
acted in that capacity by request of the Provincial
Congress, obtained a large amount by loans of patriotic individuals. It was but a short time after,
that the Continental Congress called for 3,000,000
dollars, 500,000, of which was raised by Massachusetts.

The public expenses were already great, and
still constantly increasing, while the former usual
sources of wealth were denied the people. A
great portion of the yeomanry from all parts of
the province had been in military service for
about three months, thus lessening the common
amount of productive labour in agriculture. In
some parts of the Province, particularly in Maine,
much distress prevailed among the people, and
appropriations were made, from the public treasury, for their relief.† On the request of general
Washington, who wished to annoy or check the
British in their probable plan of an attack, at this
period, the towns were again required to furnish
powder for the use of the American army; and
considerable quantities were accordingly collected.
Several fortifications were also built, at this time,
and soon after, in Charlestown, Cambridge and
Roxbury.

The powers of the General Congress were not
such as to authorize them to compel a compliance
with their requisitions. No such full power had
yet been given them; they could only recommend

* Henry Gardner, Esq.
† 1200*l.*, were granted for their relief in the month of
August.

and advise; but their advice was generally followed with great promptitude. They recommended
to the several colonies to raise men and money, to
collect provisions and provide fire arms and muni-
tions of war; and in most cases these were fully
complied with. They requested the legislature of
Massachusetts to call out such number of men as
general Washington might need, and to furnish all
articles of food and clothing, as well as military
stores, for the army at Cambridge. In August, the
troops there assembled were organized into a continental army, and received into the pay of the
whole united colonies. Many of the Massachusetts men had enlisted for eight months, and their
term of service would not expire till the first of
December. About three months of their service
therefore were to be compensated by Massachusetts alone.

At the request of general Washington, the legislature of Massachusetts provided whale boats
and experienced seamen to man them, for the purpose of bringing flour from Cape Cod for the use
of the troops; which had been forwarded to that
place from the southern parts of the continent.
These were very useful; and large quantities were
conveyed to the army at Cambridge, by way of
the southern waters of Boston bay; but at great
risk and danger. It was landed at Weymouth and
Braintree; and conveyed thence by land.* Provision was made at the expense of the colony for
erecting two powder mills, one at Stoughton, and
one at Andover; and establishments encouraged

* Captain Davis of Boston and captain Drew of Duxbury
were the commanders of this little fleet, which was of great
use to the American army.

for the manufacture of fire arms and cannon in several places. The people were also instructed as to the method of procuring saltpetre, and required to furnish it at an early period. Wood and hay were likewise provided for the whole army at Cambridge and vicinity, by the people of Massachusetts, on a requisition of the General Assembly. The people on the islands and sea coasts, including the district of Maine, were all prohibited from selling provisions or fuel to the British army in Boston. The militia from Braintree, and a detachment of men from Roxbury, landed on several islands in the harbour of Boston, in the night season, and took off the stock and hay to prevent them from falling into the hands of the English troops. Individual citizens of enterprize were permitted to fit out privateers; private voyages had been interdicted, except in cases of a special license; and several ships were purchased and sent to sea by the colony, to intercept the British transports on their voyage to Boston harbour. These were very successful; and contributed much to the welfare and strength of the American army; and to a supply for the people of many necessary articles of living.

The inhabitants of Boston, who remained in the town, were exposed to much suffering and gross insults. Provisions of all kinds were extremely scarce; and the little to be purchased was at very high prices. Numbers left the town occasionally, during the summer and autumn, as they could obtain permission of general Gage; but often they were denied the favour; and when granted, it was with the sacrifice of a large part of their moveable property. Through the influence of some malignant adherents to the British government, the people were treated with great severity. The small pox also raged among them; and added greatly to their distresses. Some of them, when they had this alarming disease, left Boston, and went into the country and in the vicinity of the American troops, who were thus exposed to its dreadful ravages. It was believed by many of the citizens, that there was a design in the British general to communicate this destructive malady to the Americans: but there was no direct proof of the fact.* The troops at Cambridge and Roxbury were justly alarmed by this disorder; and many made this an excuse for returning to their homes. The greatest vigilance and attention were necessary both in the commander in chief and in the House of Representatives to prevent the dispersion of a large part of the army, and to engage others to enlist, in the place of those who left it.

With all these difficulties, however, general Washington was able, by the prompt assistance of the Assembly of Massachusetts, to keep up something like a respectable army as to numbers, though greatly deficient in cannon, and in many military articles, which would justify any offensive operations. Several forts were also erected during the season, in advance of head quarters at Cambridge, for the purpose of preventing the enemy from executing any plan of attack on the provincial troops, as well as of annoying the enemy in Boston.†

* In one of general Washington's letters to Congress, at this time, he refers to several circumstances and reports which rendered such an intention in the British something more than conjecture.

† In a letter to Congress. Nov. 1775, he says, " The trouble

Prospect Hill, lying north west from Boston, about two miles, but a less distance from Bunker's hill, then possessed by the British troops, was early fortified. Soon after, works were erected on Winter hill, situated north from the former place, and at a short distance ; and easterly of the latter place, towards Mystic river, redoubts were thrown up, to prevent the passage of the enemy up that river, in their rear, or their landing opposite the fort. On a less elevated eminence, called Ploughed hill, but much in advance of Prospect hill, and within about half a mile, on a direct line of Bunker's hill, a breast-work was thrown up, while the

I have in the arrangement of the army is really inconceivable. Many of the officers sent in their names to serve in expectation of promotion, and some who had declined have sent in their names to serve. So great has been the confusion arising from these and other perplexing circumstances, that I found it absolutely impossible to fix this interesting business exactly on the plan agreed in conference with the committee of Congress, though I have kept to the spirit, as near as the nature and necessity of the case would admit. The difficulty with the soldiers is as great, and indeed more so, if possible, than with the officers. They will not enlist until they know their Colonel, Lieutenant Colonel, Major, Captain, &c. You can much more easily judge than I can express, the anxiety of mind I labour under on this occasion ; especially at this time, when we may expect that the enemy will begin to act on the arrival of their reinforcements. I have other distresses of a very alarming nature. The arms of our soldiers are so exceedingly bad, that I assure you, Sir, I cannot place a proper confidence in them ; and our powder is wasting fast, though the strictest care, attention and economy are paid to it." " I fear I shall be under the necessity of calling in the militia and minute men of the country to my assistance. I say, I *fear* it ; because, by what I can learn from the officers in the army belonging to this colony, it will be next to an impossibility to keep them under any degree of discipline, and that it will be very difficult to prevail on them to remain a moment longer than they choose themselves."

enemy were constantly cannonading the provincial troops. But they completed the work, and afterwards extended the fortifications, so as to render the spot perfectly secure. At a later period, and sometime in November, general Putnam was ordered to erect fortifications on Cobble hill,* about the same distance from the British works on Charlestown heights, as Ploughed hill, but nearer to the town of Boston. When the Americans were perceived to be fortifying this place, the British ships of war, then lying in Charles river, between West Boston and Charlestown, as well as the forts on Bunker hill, opened a severe fire upon them, but without checking the enterprize. The fort was soon built. Putnam bestowed much time and labour upon it; and it was called "Putnam's impregnable fortress."

Soon after, strong fortifications were erected on Lechmere's point, a little south of Cobble hill, and near the margin of Charles river, where it was considered the British would probably land, if they meditated an attack on the American army. They had indeed, a short time before, landed 300 troops at this place, but they were soon driven back to their boats by the Americans. These also were planned and completed in an able and judicious manner; and the remains are now (1824) as little injured, as to the form and appearances of the ground, as any works erected by the American troops in the vicinity of Boston. The high land in Roxbury was also fortified, and made a place of considerable strength; and some works were thrown up on the peninsula which connects

* The Asylum for the Insane is now standing on the spot.

that town with Boston, near the boundary line of these places, being the advanced post of the American troops, stationed there under general Ward.

In addition to the troops furnished by Massachusetts to the Continental army at this time, which amounted to about 9,000, many towns in the province bordering on the sea, and exposed to visits from the British ships, were required to guard their respective harbours, for the safety of the people. At Plymouth, a company was ordered out for the defence of that town, and of the *Gurnet*, so called, a promontory at the northern entrance of the harbour. At Weymouth, Hingham and Braintree, towns lying on the southerly part of the bay of Boston, four companies were constantly in service for many months, to prevent depredations threatened by the British whose fleet was in the harbour. The inhabitants of Marblehead, Salem, and Gloucester, by direction of the Provincial legislature of Massachusetts, and at their own urgent request, had a portion of the citizens employed in military service from June 1775 to April 1776. In several instances, requests were made from these towns for some companies of the Continental army at Cambridge, for protection; but general Washington did not think it consistent with his duty to weaken the main army by granting the request. Some works were thrown up at Cape Ann, however, at the expense of the colony.

In September, the legislative assembly were so desirous of the frequent and early advice of the Continental Congress, that they requested that body to hold its meetings in the vicinity of Cambridge, where the American army was then stationed. General Washington, in his great prudence and from regard to the civil power, was unwilling to engage in any hazardous enterprize without the immediate consent and knowledge of Congress; and he was frequently calling for aid and advice from the general assembly of Massachusetts. New troops were also to be raised; and the army provided with clothes, provisions and money. Many injudicious people were impatient for Washington to make an attack upon the British in Boston. The legislative assembly of Massachusetts was unwilling to take all the responsibility attending the crisis; and it was suggested to the Congress at Philadelphia, through their members, that it might be of great advantage to the cause, if it could hold its meetings near the seat of war.

This request was not complied with; but a committee was sent from the General Congress to Cambridge to confer with the commander in chief, and with the Provincial Assembly of Massachusetts, which were desirous of advice, and believed also, that the other colonies should be called upon to contribute more equally to the support of the Continental army. The celebrated Dr. Franklin was one of this committee. And an arrangement was made, by which Congress should provide for raising an army of 24,000, for the next year; and for calling upon the several colonies for their respective portions of the amount necessary to meet the expenses; instead of requiring each province to raise its own quota of troops. These men were not raised without much difficulty and delay: and the militia of Massachusetts were called out in the mean time to recruit the continental army under general Washington. The provincial troops assembled at Cambridge in the spring and summer of 1775, were engaged only for a few months; and none for a longer term than to the last of December. It was necessary therefore to provide for raising more troops by the first of January 1776.

The assembly of Massachusetts appointed a committee* to confer with the members of the Continental Congress and the commander in chief; and the governors of Connecticut and Rhode Island, and the president of New Hampshire, were also present at the convention. During this visit of Franklin at Cambridge on public business, the legislature of Massachusetts ordered payment to be made him for his faithful services to the interests of the province, while their agent for several years in England, which amounted to about 800*l.* sterling. A large portion of this sum he immediately appropriated for the relief of those unfortunate persons who had suffered at the battles of Lexington and Charlestown. The constitutional society, and some individuals in England also contributed to their support.

Specie, as the common medium of business, disappeared at this period; and paper bills, both provincial and continental, came into general circulation. Congress said, " they had very little money, to support and pay an army; that there was no regular government to levy and collect taxes; that they could not borrow of any nation, and that they had no other resource but the natural value

* Bowdoin, Sever, J. Otis and W. Spooner

and worth of this fertile country—*That on the credit of such a bank*, they had emitted bills, and the faith of the continent was pledged for their redemption."

The legislature of Massachusetts, as well as the general officers of the American army, addressed both the people and the soldiers then in the camp at Cambridge, urging them to engage in the military service. "Happy will be the man," they say, "who shall be able to boast, that he was one of those, who assisted in this arduous but noble work! In serenity shall he pass his future days; and when satisfied with life, he will have the proud satisfaction of bequeathing the inestimable patrimony to his grateful children." Washington also addressed the country in the following style. "We have taken up arms in defence of our liberty, our property, our wives and our children; and we are determined to preserve them, or die. We look forward to the day, we hope not far remote, when the inhabitants of America, will have but one sentiment, and the full enjoyment of the blessings of a free government." Committees were appointed in each county in the province, and the field officers of militia were required to forward the enlistment of men for the continental service for the coming year, by the time for which those then engaged should expire.

Although Congress were resolved on vigorous measures of defence, they had not yet determined to separate from the parent country. The following is part of their address to the king, in August 1775.

"Attached to your majesty's person, family and government, with all the devotion which principle and affection can inspire, connected with Great Britain by the strongest ties which can unite societies and deploring every event which tends in any degree to weaken them—we solemnly assure your majesty, that we not only most ardently desire the former harmony between her and these colonies may be restored; but that a concord may be established between them, upon so firm a basis as to perpetuate its blessings uninterrupted by any future dissensions, to succeeding generations in both countries; and to transmit your majesty's name to posterity, adorned with that signal and lasting glory, which has attended the memory of those illustrious personages whose virtues and abilities have extricated states from dangerous convulsions, and, by securing happiness to others, have erected the most noble and durable monuments to their own fame. We beg further to assure your majesty, that, notwithstanding the sufferings of your loyal colonists, during the course of the present controversy, our breasts retain too tender a regard for the kingdom from which we derive our origin, to request such a reconciliation, as might in any manner be inconsistent with her dignity or her welfare. These, related as we are to her, honour and duty as well as inclination induce us to support and advance: and the apprehensions, which now oppress our hearts with unspeakable grief, being once removed, your majesty will find your faithful subjects on this continent ready and willing at all times, as they have ever been, with their lives and fortunes, to assert and maintain the rights and interests of your majesty, and of our parent country."

General Gage continued to treat the people of Boston, and particularly some persons of distinction,* who were favourable to the liberties of the

* James Lovell, Esq. was among them. He was kept in close confinement till March following, and then carried to Halifax.

Letter of James Lovell to general Washington, dated

Boston, Provost's Prison, Nov. 19, 1775.

" May it please your Excellency, I wish, at this time, to waive the expression of my veneration of your character, in a still lively hope, that Providence will bless me with an opportunity of attempting it by the united sincere language of my eyes and lips, though even that too must prove inadequate.

" Personally a stranger to you, my sufferings have yet affected your benevolent mind, and your exertions in my favour have made so deep an impression upon my grateful heart, as will remain to the period of my latest breath.

" Your excellency is already informed that the powers of the military government established in this town have been wantonly and cruelly exercised against me from the 29th of June last. I have, in vain, repeatedly solicited to be brought to some kind of trial for my pretended crimes. In answer to a petition of that sort presented on the 16th of October, I am directed by captain Belfour, aid-de-camp to general Howe, to seek the release of colonel Skeene and his son, as the sole means of my own enlargement.

" This proposition appears to me extremely disgraceful to the party from which it comes, and a compliance with it pregnant with dangerous consequences to my fellow citizens. But while my own spirit prompts me to reject it directly with the keenest disdain, the importunity of my distressed wife and the advice of some whom I esteem have checked me down to a consent to give your excellency this information. I have the fullest confidence in your wisdom; and I shall be perfectly resigned to your determination, whatever it may be. I must not, however, omit to say, that should you condescend to stigmatize this proceeding of my enemies by letter, the correction might work some change in favour of myself, or at least of my family, which must, I think, perish through want of fuel and provisions in the approaching winter, if they continue to be deprived of my assistance.

I have the honour to be, &c.

James Lovell."

After this, general Washington requested the exchange of Mr. Lovell, but without effect.

country, with great cruelty. Several were confined in the common jail, in company with the most vile and abandoned characters. General Washington wrote him on the subject, and assured him, that he should feel himself obliged to subject some prisoners in his custody to similar treatment, unless the American citizens in confinement in Boston should be released. Gage was not easily dissuaded from this dishonourable conduct: but finding that Washington was decided in his purpose, after some time, he treated his prisoners with less severity.*

* Extract from a letter of general Washington to governor Gage, dated head-quarters,

CAMBRIDGE, AUGUST 11, 1775.

"I understand that the officers engaged in the cause of liberty and their country, who by the fortune of war have fallen into your hands, have been thrown indiscriminately, into a common jail, appropriated for felons; that no consideration has been had for those of the most respectable rank, when languishing with wounds and sickness; and that some of them have been amputated in this situation.

Let your opinion, sir, of the principle which actuates them be what it may, they suppose they act from the noblest of all principles, a love of freedom and their country. But political opinions, I conceive, are foreign to this point. The obligations arising from humanity and claims of rank are universally binding and extensive, except in case of *retaliation*. These, I should have hoped, would have dictated a more tender treatment of those individuals, whom chance or war had put in your power. Nor can I forbear suggesting its fatal tendency, to render that unhappy breach, which you and those ministers under whom you act, have repeatedly declared you wish to see forever closed.

My duty now makes it necessary to apprize you, that for the future I shall regulate my conduct towards those gentlemen, who are or may be in our possession, exactly by the rule you shall observe towards those of ours now in your custody.

If severity and hardship mark the line of your conduct.

In October, general Gage embarked for England; and sir William Howe succeeded to the

painful as it will be to me, your prisoners will feel its effects; but if kindness and humanity are shewn to ours, I shall, with pleasure, consider those in our hands only as unfortunate, and they shall receive from me that treatment to which the unfortunate are ever entitled.

I beg to be favoured with an answer as soon as possible; and am, sir, your very humble servant,

GEORGE WASHINGTON.

HIS EXCELLENCY GENERAL GAGE."

The following is the answer of general Gage,

BOSTON, AUGUST 13.

" Sir,—To the glory of civilized nations, humanity and war have ever been compatible: and compassion to the subdued is come almost a general system.

Britons, ever preeminent in mercy, have outgone common examples, and overlooked the criminal in the captive. Upon these principles, your prisoners, whose lives by the laws of the land are destined to the *cord*, have hitherto been treated with care and kindness, and more comfortably lodged than the king's troops in the hospitals; indiscriminately, it is true; for I acknowledge no rank that is not derived from the king.

My intelligence from your army would justify severe recrimination. I understand there are of the king's faithful subjects, taken sometime since by the *rebels*, labouring like negro slaves to gain their daily subsistence, or reduced to the wretched alternative to perish by famine, or take arms against their king. Those who have made the treatment of the prisoners in my hands, or of your other friends in Boston a pretence for such measures, found barbarity upon falsehood.

I would willingly hope, sir, that the sentiments of liberality, which I have always believed you to possess, will be exerted to correct these misdoings. Be temperate in political discussion, give free operation to truth, and punish those who deceive and misrepresent; and not only the effects, but the causes of this unhappy conflict will be removed.

Should those, under whose usurped authority you act, controul such a disposition and dare to call severity retaliation, to God who knows all hearts be the appeal for the dreadful consequences. I trust, that British soldiers, asserting the

chief command of the British troops in Boston. In his conduct towards the citizens of Boston, he was as arbitrary and severe as his prede-

rights of the state, and the laws of the constitution, will meet all events with becoming fortitude. They will court victory with the spirit their cause inspires; and from the same motive, will find the patience of martyrs under misfortune.

Till I read your insinuations in regard to ministers, I conceived that I had acted under the king, whose wishes, it is true, as well as those of his ministers, and of every honest man, have been to see this unhappy breach forever closed: but unfortunately for both countries, those who long since projected the present crisis, and influence the councils of America, have views very distant from accommodation.

I am, sir, your most obedient humble servant,
THOMAS GAGE.
GEORGE WASHINGTON, ESQ."

On the 19*th* general Washington addressed a second note to general Gage, which follows—

HEAD QUARTERS, CAMBRIDGE, AUGUST 19*th*.

" Sir,—I addressed you on the 11*th* instant, in terms which gave the fairest scope for the exercise of that humanity and politeness, which were *supposed* to form a part of your character. I remonstrated against the unworthy treatment shewn to the officers and citizens of America, whom the fortune of war, chance or a mistaken confidence, had thrown into your hands.

Whether British or American mercy, fortitude and patience are the most preeminent; whether our virtuous citizens, whom the hand of *tyranny* has forced into arms, to defend their wives, children and property, or the mercenary instruments of *lawless* domination, avarice and revenge, best deserve the appellation of *rebels*, and the punishment of the *cord*, which your affected clemency has forborne to inflict; whether the authority under which I act is usurped, or founded upon the genuine principles of liberty, were altogether foreign to the subject. I purposely avoided all political disquisition; nor shall I now avail myself of those advantages, which the sacred cause of my country, of liberty and human nature *give me over you;* much less shall I stoop to retort an invec-

cessor had been. He refused them the liberty of leaving Boston; and obliged them to form into companies and to procure arms, for the purpose of

tive. But the intelligence you say you have received from our army requires a reply. I have taken time to make a short inquiry, and find it has not the least foundation in truth. Not only your officers and soldiers have been treated with a tenderness due to fellow citizens and brethren, but even those *execrable parricides*, whose councils and aid have deluged their country with blood, have been protected from the fury of a justly enraged people. You advise me to give free operation to truth, to punish misrepresentation and falsehood. If experience stamps value upon council, yours must have a weight which few can claim. You best can tell how far the convulsion, which has brought such ruin upon both countries and shaken the mighty empire of Britain to its foundations, may be traced to these malignant causes.

You affect, sir, to despise all rank not derived from the same source with your own. I cannot conceive one more honourable than that which flows from the uncorrupted choice of a brave and free people, the purest source and *original fountain* of all power. Far from making it a plea for cruelty, a mind of true magnanimity and enlarged views would comprehend and respect it.

What may have been the ministerial views, which have precipitated the present crisis, Lexington, Concord and Charlestown can best declare. May that God, to whom you there appealed, judge between America and you. Under his providence, those who influence the councils of America and all the other inhabitants of the united colonies, at the hazard of their lives are determined to hand down to posterity those just and invaluable privileges which they received from their ancestors.

I shall now, sir, close my correspondence with you, perhaps forever. If your officers, our prisoners, receive a treatment from me different from what I wished to shew them, they and you will remember the *occasion* of it.

I am, sir, your very humble servant.

GEORGE WASHINGTON."

assisting the British in opposing the American troops, if they should make an attack on Boston.*

* *Letter of general Washington to general How.*

CAMBRIDGE, DECEMBER 18*th*, 1775.

" Sir,—We have just been informed of a circumstance, which, were it not so well authenticated, I should scarcely think credible. It is, that colonel Allen, who, with his small party, was defeated and taken prisoner near Montreal, has been treated without regard to decency, humanity or the rules of war. That he has been thrown into irons and suffers all the hardships inflicted upon common felons. I think it my duty to demand, and do expect from you an eclaircissement on this subject. At the same time, I flatter myself, from the character which Mr. How bears, as a man of honour, a gentleman and a soldier, that my demand will meet with his approbation. I must take the liberty also of informing you, that I shall consider your silence as a confirmation of the truth of the report; and further assuring you, that, whatever treatment colonel Allen receives, whatever fate he undergoes, such exactly shall be the treatment and fate of brigadier general Prescott, now in our hands.

The law of retaliation is not only justifiable in the sight of God and man, but absolutely a duty, which, in our present circumstances, we owe to our relations, friends and fellow citizens.

Permit me to add, sir, that we have all the highest regard for your great personal qualities and attainments, and that the Americans in general esteem it not as the least of their misfortunes, that the name of *How*, a name so dear to them, should appear at the head of the catalogue of the instruments employed by a wicked ministry for their destruction.

With due respect, &c.
GEORGE WASHINGTON."

The following is the answer of general How, to the foregoing.

BOSTON, DECEMBER 21, 1775.

" Sir,—In answer to your letter of the 18*th* instant, I am to acquaint you, that my command does not extend to Canada, nor, having received no accounts wherein the name of Allen is mentioned, can I give you the smallest satisfaction on the

It was considered an object of importance, by the legislature of Massachusetts, as well as of New York and Connecticut, that a treaty should be attempted with the Mohawk and the other Six nations of Indians. An agent for this purpose was appointed in Massachusetts, Joseph Hawley, Esq. who was to join with those designated from the other two colonies. They met at Albany, and succeeded in conciliating the friendship of many of these savages of the wilderness, who, if united to the British, would be able to do much injury to the Americans in the western settlements. Some of them continued friendly. But many afterwards proved treacherous; and, instigated by the British generals, and by individuals disaffected to the cause of liberty, they often fell upon our defenceless borders and murdered the people in cold blood.

In the month of August, a large American ship, with a valuable cargo, arrived off the harbour of Gloucester, and several of the inhabitants went to her in boats, to assist in bringing her into the port, as a British frigate was known to be in the bay, at no great distance; and it was apprehended she might take possession of the merchant vessel and carry her to Boston. On perceiving the Ameri-

subject of your letter. But trusting major general Carleton's conduct will never incur censure upon any occasion, I am to conclude, in the instance of your inquiry, that he has not forfeited his past pretensions to decency and humanity.

It is with regret, considering the character you have always maintained among your friends, as a gentleman of the strictest honour and delicacy, that I find cause to resent a sentence in the conclusion of your letter, big with invective against my superiors and insulting to myself, which should obstruct any further intercourse between us.

I am, sir, with due respect, &c.

WILLIAM HOW."

can ship going for the harbour of Gloucester, the captain of the frigate sent his boats with thirty men and took her. But the merchant ship was grounded near the entrance of the port, where the frigate could not safely approach. The inhabitants made a vigorous attack upon her, and soon obliged the enemy to surrender. The vessel was then conducted safely into port, and the British marines lodged in Ipswich jail. The captain of the British frigate was greatly mortified and enraged; and bombarded the town of Gloucester for several hours, but without effecting any material injury to the place.

Although no affair of great moment took place between the American and British troops during the autumn of 1775, constant vigilance was necessary in each; and several slight skirmishes happened near the lines and in the vicinity of the two armies. Soon after the works were erected at Ploughed hill, a small advanced party of the provincials were attacked by the British near Charlestown neck; several of the enemy were killed and taken; and one of the Americans was shot by a cannon ball from Bunker's hill, from which place the British fired on the occasion. Some time in the month of August, a party from the Roxbury division also advanced to the extreme southern fort of the enemy on the peninsula leading from Boston to the former place, drove the guard within the lines and burnt their guard house.* When the American troops were discovered, a heavy fire commenced against them; but none were killed or wounded. About the same period, some armed men went down the harbour of Boston, under

* Formerly the house of Mr. Brown

command of major, afterwards colonel, Vose; who cut and carried off all the barley and grain at Nantasket, amounting to upwards of a thousand bushels. They proceeded to the lighthouse near Nantasket, placed at the entrance of Boston harbour, and destroyed the lanterns. Those of Plymouth and Cape Ann were taken away or destroyed, about the same time, in pursuance of orders from the legislature of Massachusetts. The British attempted to repair the Boston lighthouse and lanterns soon after; when a party of the Americans, of about two hundred, from the army at Roxbury, under major Tupper, were ordered to dispossess them. They went down the harbour in light boats, in the evening; and after a short resistance from the men employed in making repairs, they overpowered them and brought them to the camp at Roxbury. Several of the British were wounded and killed in this affair, before the party surrendered.

In the month of October, two floating batteries were prepared at Cambridge, and dropped down Charles river, whence they fired on the town of Boston; which occasioned great alarm, and injured several buildings. Liberty tree, so called, growing in the southerly part of Boston, was cut down, about this period, by the British, or some of the tory inhabitants, with great parade and exultation. But it was observed by some of the patriotic citizens, " that the American tree of liberty was too strongly rooted in our soil to be destroyed by all the power of Great Britain."

A British frigate and several transports with troops, were dispatched from Boston, in the month of October, to compel the inhabitants of Falmouth, in Maine,* to furnish spars for the fleet at the former place, and other articles which could be obtained in that quarter, if desired by the British; with directions, on a refusal, to destroy the town. The captain of the frigate, on arriving in that harbour, sent word to the inhabitants to furnish the articles, and to submit quietly to all his requisitions, or to expect an immediate cannonade from his ship, and the landing of marines from the transports, for the threatened work of destruction. A meeting of the people was called forthwith, who requested leave to remove their families and furniture, and desired the suspension of the intended attack until the following morning. They resolved not to comply with the requisition, and only desired a few hours to save their families from ruin. The haughty Briton so far yielded, as to allow them until the next morning to retire from the town. A heavy bombardment immediately after took place, and almost the whole of this flourishing seaport was destroyed by the British troops. About 140 dwelling houses and 250 stores were burnt; besides much wanton destruction of other property.

About this time, Bristol, in the State of Rhode Island, but formerly within the colony of Plymouth, was invaded by a British naval force from Newport, consisting of three large ships of war, and several tenders and transports. Some of the principal citizens were ordered to come on board the commodore's ship; but they declined, and a heavy cannonade immediately ensued against the town. The meeting house, court house, and many dwell-

* Since called Portland.

ing houses were much injured. The people were in great jeopardy and attempted to make some terms with the British. Sheep and cattle were offered, which were supposed to be their object; these were accepted, and other articles of provisions taken away by force. The conduct of the British commodore was severely censured; and it was certainly a deviation from that of an honourable enemy.

The inhabitants of Boston, who had left the town, were authorised by the legislature to meet at Watertown, in September of this year, and chose a representative in the place of S. Adams,* who was then attending the continental Congress at Philadelphia. The other delegates from Massachusetts this year, were John Hancock, John Adams, and Robert T. Paine. Congress was in session the greater part of the year, after April. The last of July they adjourned for a few weeks, but assembled again the first of September. Mr. Hancock was elected president of that patriotic and truly respectable assembly, in October, in the room of Peyton Randolph of Virginia, who died suddenly in Philadelphia, while attending on the public service.

The general congress provided for the establishment of a continental Post Office at this period, and placed Dr. Franklin at the head of the department. The plan was soon put into operation from Georgia to Maine, and greatly facilitated the early communication of important intelligence from one end of the colonies to the other.

The legislative assembly of Massachusetts,

* Mr. Adams was chosen Secretary of Massachusetts in July, and Perez Morton deputy Secretary.

which met and organized on the 19th of July, had various important duties to perform, and many serious difficulties to meet, in establishing civil authority through the Province, and drawing forth its resources for the protection of the country. They had to provide for the regular administration of the laws, for paying a large body of troops, who were in the service of the colony nearly four months, previously to the day they were taken into the pay of the continent. New recruits were to be collected in a few months, and clothing and fire arms would be necessary for immediate use. The persons selected for the Executive Council were justly entitled to the confidence of their fellow citizens. They were known to be patriotic, intelligent, firm and prudent. Great harmony subsisted between the Council and the House of Representatives. One instance only is mentioned of the contrary. The Council supposed they had the sole right to appoint to civil and military office; but the House claimed a voice in the selection. The Council yielded to the wishes of the Representatives, " for the sake of peace ;" and it was possible, that, in some cases, the members of the House had a knowledge of characters, which the Council did not possess. But it clearly belonged to the executive part of government to make the appointment of civil and judicial officers. The military officers were at this time generally designated by a committee of the Assembly, though the council signed their commissions. Afterward the officers of the army were appointed by the commander in chief. All the commissions of persons who had been appointed by the Governor and former council, were by law declared to be vacated and null. New judges of courts of common pleas and justices of the peace were now appointed ; the oath formerly taken by public officers was dispensed with, and another provided and required, which expressed allegiance only to the existing authority of the Province. Judges were appointed for the Superior Court of Judicature in November, being John Adams, William Cushing, N. P. Sargent, William Reed, and Robert T. Paine. Sargent, Reed and Paine declined ; and Jedidiah Foster and James Sullivan, were appointed in their stead, a few months after.

Vessels were sent during the autumn to the West Indies by individual adventurers, with the encouragement of the legislature, for the purpose of obtaining a supply of gun-powder. The American army was long deficient in this necessary article, to a most alarming degree. It was not to be obtained to any large amount in any part of the United Colonies. The people were prohibited by the General Court, from firing at birds, or other game, or at marks, and for sport, under a heavy penalty. As yet, the plan projected sometime before of having powder mills, had not been completed. The object was not relinquished ; but it required time to obtain the desired fruits of their labours.

The General Assembly of Massachusetts applied to the Continental Congress, in October, for a reimbursement of a part of the great expenses incurred by the province for the common welfare, after the battle of Lexington. The colony had paid 10,000l. for provisions and necessary military articles for its troops, during the period which elapsed from April 19th, to the first of August. The wages due to the Massachusetts troops for the same period, being from 9,000 to 12,000 the greater part of that time, amounted to upwards of 65,000*l.* Their clothing, to 16,000*l*; and one hundred and seventy barrels of powder had been purchased and distributed through the towns on the sea coast exposed to the enemy, and who had requested the means of self defence. The colony had 2,000 men in their service, the greater part of the season, at different stations on the Atlantic shores, as the people were constantly exposed to plunder, and it was wished to prevent the British from collecting supplies for the army in Boston. A large amount was advanced for these purposes : and the public treasury of the colony was also frequently drawn upon, to supply the wants of the unfortunate inhabitants of Boston, who were obliged to leave their homes and all their property, and to depend upon the contributions of the country for immediate support. Their services and zeal in the cause of liberty were justly appreciated ; and their distressed condition deeply commiserated. The Continental Congress advanced to Massachusetts, at this time, the sum of 133,000*l.*

CHAPTER III.

Views of the Colonies September 1775 ... Expedition to Quebec by way
of Kennebec ... Unsuccessful ... Armed Vessels ... British ships captured ... Captain Manly ... Treachery ... Church ... Militia called
out ... Colonel Knox brings cannon from Tyconderoga ... Resolve of
Representatives justifying a resort to arms ... Meditated attack on Boston ... Dorchester heights fortified ... Conduct of Washington approved by Congress ... Militia organized ... Nantucket ... Suspension
of civil suits ... Refugees ... Regiment raised for Quebec.

ALTHOUGH the people of Massachusetts and of
the other colonies had now become exasperated
by the arbitrary plans of the British ministry, and
the resort to force, to carry their plans of oppression into execution; and although they were determined to defend, to the utmost, the constitutional liberties of the country, they had not yet
given up all hope of reconciliation with the parent state : They had not yet absolutely resolved
upon Independence. They had some belief that
administration would retract of its despotic purposes of coercion; that public opinion in England
would be in their favour; and that the determination already manifested to defend themselves by
force, would induce the British government to
change its infatuated councils, and to listen to the
claims of justice and humanity. It was not their purpose to yield, or to relax in their efforts; but they
were still willing to supplicate for redress, and to desist from all opposition upon sufficient assurance of

the restoration of their ancient charter rights. They were not desirous of separation; nor could they but foresee the possible and not improbable failure of success in their resistance, and anticipate the punishment which awaits defeat in a civil contest. They had indeed, resolved, deliberately resolved, never to abandon their liberties; but they were not so desirous of independence, as to refuse all offers of reconciliation, if consistent with the enjoyment of the privileges which they claimed as their birth-right. Public addresses and resolutions both of the General Assembly of Massachusetts of the Continental Congress fully justify these remarks. They still professed to be acting on the defensive, and called themselves subjects of the crown of Great Britain. Had the plan of Pitt, and other friends of civil liberty in Parliament been adopted, of recalling the ministerial army, and repealing the late arbitrary laws, the colonies would not have urged a separation.—But the conduct of the British government gave little hope of a reunion, indeed, upon conditions compatible with the liberties of America. It seemed to have been the opinion of the ministry for several years, that the people in the colonies were subjects of the British Empire, for the purposes of obedience, and of submission under any burdens it might impose; but not entitled to all the rights and privileges of Englishmen. The colonists were too wise and too much attached to civil freedom to admit, that there existed a right to govern, without the consent of the people by their representatives, and according to the principles of the constitution. It was true, that many eminent statesmen in England, were opposed to the claims set up by administration of an absolute authority over the Americans, without their being represented in parliament; and who contended that the colonial legislatures had power to a great extent, for all the purposes of self government, so their laws were not repugnant to the constitution and laws of Great Britain. But men of such just sentiments were comparatively few in the parent state; and their voice was scarcely heard in the councils of the nation. The men then in power, and in favour with the king, were resolved that the colonies should submit "in all cases whatever," to the requisitions and laws of the British parliament.* They had not indeed expected such a formidable opposition to their measures as appeared; for they supposed the colonies without resources for a serious resistance to the government; and they had been deceived by the representation, that it was only a *few* ambitious men who were opposed to the conduct of administration.

The affair at Concord, and still more, the desperate resolution manifested by the provincials at Charlestown to resist force by force; and the formation of a continental army at Cambridge; must have convinced the British administration, that the Americans would not yield, while they had ability to resist; and that an immense physical force was necessary to subdue them. The measures of the ministers were now, more than ever, condemned by the friends of constitutional liberty. And a few, who had not expected so much union among the colonists nor so much courage in opposition to go-

* A Petition from the General Congress of July 1775, presented to the king in September, he refused even to hear.

vernment, were in favour of allowing some of the claims preferred by them. The ministry were not prepared to yield, in any part, the authority they had assumed over the people of America; and it was determined to augment their forces, in the hope that the colonies would be discouraged, and that some, under apprehensions of defeat and subjugation, would return to their allegiance to the parent state. Aware of this determination of the British cabinet, the colonies had no alternative presented to their choice, but servile submission, or resolute resistance.

An expedition was projected by the northern colonies in the summer of 1775, with the approbation of the Continental Congress, to invade Canada, in the expectation of meeting with the general support of the inhabitants of that province, of making an easy conquest of Montreal and Quebec, of securing the military stores in that quarter, and of guarding the settlements in the northwestern parts of New England from the ravages both of the English and Indians. This was considered an important object, at an early period. Soon after the affair at Lexington and Concord, when it was found the British would attempt to bring the colonies to submission by an armed force, the Provincial Congress of Massachusetts adopted measures to take possession of the forts on Lake Champlain, and to prevent the incursion of the British in that quarter. The people of Connecticut, of New York, and those on the New Hampshire grants, so called, (now Vermont) agreed in the importance of the measure; and united, with Arnold, Easton and Brown from Massachusetts, in an attack upon the British posts in that quarter. The success which attended the enterprize has been already mentioned. At a later period, and some time in the month of August, the Continental Congress was impressed with a conviction of the policy of taking possession of Canada, or of sending a force to the lake sufficient to awe the British. General Schuyler was appointed commander in chief in that region; and the brave Montgomery was made second in command. Massachusetts furnished a number of troops for the department; and colonels Easton and major Brown from Berkshire county were among the chief officers. They had acquired a high reputation for military skill and bravery in the first expedition, in May; and it was not forfeited by any neglect or inattention, at a later season, when the American forces were increased and put under the command of the heroic Montgomery.* Fort Chamblee was taken by a detachment under major Brown, in October; and a large quantity of military stores was found in the place, which was a great acquisition to the American army. Soon after this, the fortress of St. John's was captured by Montgomery; and the city of Montreal also surrendered to his victorious arms. A committee of Congress was sent to inquire into the state of the northern army at this time; one of whom was R. T. Paine of Massachusetts.

Massachusetts assisted in this expedition against Canada, not only by furnishing a portion of the troops under Montgomery and Schuyler in September and October, on lake Champlain; but a

* Montgomery was really the chief in command; general Schuyler was sick the greater part of the campaign.

party of 1200 men was sent from the camp at Cambridge in the month of September, by the way of Kennebec river, to co-operate with those already at Montreal, in an attack upon Quebec, the capital of the province. These men belonged chiefly to Massachusetts. Some, indeed, were from New Hampshire and some from Connecticut. Arnold of Rhode Island, lately appointed a general, who five months before, had been sent to lake Champlain by the Provincial Congress of Massachusetts, to act in concert with some troops from the county of Berkshire and from Connecticut, was selected to command them. They embarked at Newbury, and sailed up the Kennebec river, about fifty miles. Their baggage was conveyed in boats still higher on the river; when they forced their way through an untrodden wilderness one hundred and twenty miles farther, to the British settlements in the vicinity of St. Lawrence. About three hundred of the men returned from Kennebec, on account of the difficulty of the passage, and the scarcity of provisions. Nine hundred persevered, amidst severe sufferings and appalling obstacles. Montgomery had notice of this detachment from Cambridge, and pushed on to Quebec, with only a few troops, expecting more would soon follow, and hoping that the inhabitants of Quebec would not make a formidable resistance to the Americans, who went to them rather as friends than as enemies. He was too brave and too sanguine of success to suffer any delay, by such preparations as prudence might have dictated. Being joined by the party under Arnold, though the men were much fatigued, and the whole American force insufficient to justify an attack upon a place so strongly fortified as Quebec, he hesitated not to make an assault upon the city. The attempt was unsuccessful. He fell soon after the attack began; Arnold also was wounded; and the Americans were obliged to retire from the siege as the only means of saving any part of the American troops. The only fault which could attach to the conduct of Montgomery in this unfortunate affair, was a degree of imprudence, in not waiting for a reinforcement and making more efficient preparations for the assault. He died gloriously in the cause of America, and her citizens will never forget to honour his memory with their warmest admiration. The troops from Massachusetts suffered severely in this defeat. A series of misfortunes followed in Canada; and in the spring following the British regained most of the places which had been taken from them by the colonial army.

The citizens of Massachusetts soon perceived the advantages which would probably arise in employing armed vessels on the coasts, to prevent the British in Boston from collecting provisions at any places accessible by them, and to capture the enemy's ships loaded with military articles. As the besieged army in Boston could not obtain provisions from the country by land, they were obliged to fit out small vessels, which committed depredations on the people in several towns on the coast. Transports were also frequently arriving from England with provisions, men and military stores. The General Court voted to build or purchase ten vessels, and appropriated 50,000*l*, for the purpose. Some enterprizing individuals also, with the consent of the civil authority of the province, fitted vessels, at their own charges, to engage the enemy's ships. And in the following year, the Continental Congress ordered several frigates to be built for the service of the country. Some of the armed vessels belonging to Massachusetts were very successful in their first cruises. During the months of November and December, (1775) several large and valuable ships were captured within a short distance of the harbour of Boston: and some smaller vessels which had sailed from that port to collect articles of provision, were taken, as they were returning with the fruits of their depredations. Captain Manly, in a provincial brig, took three very valuable vessels bound into Boston harbour, in the course of a few weeks: one of which had a full cargo of ordnance, fire arms, and other military stores, of which the American troops were in great need: and one loaded with various kinds of provisions, which were at once acceptable to the provincials, and a severe loss to the British. This enterprizing and patriotic naval hero, with some others who engaged in similar pursuits of almost equal intrepidity, rendered important service to the colony, and to the continent. During the residence of the British troops in Boston, these nautical adventurers were very vigilant, and captured a great number of vessels bound to that place, which occasioned much distress to the besieged army. In several instances they discovered uncommon spirit and courage; and, on meeting a vessel of equal force, were always victorious. Captain Manly was so much dreaded by the British, that an armed vessel of superior force was sent out from Boston to seize him. On coming out of the harbour of Plymouth, in January 1776, he was watched and pursued by the British ship; and he ran his vessel, ashore near the mouth of north river in Scituate, to avoid capture. The British fired upwards of 300 guns, after he was on shore; and sent two boats filled with men to burn the American brig. But the crew and the people in the vicinity defended her. She was removed the next day, without receiving much injury; and was soon fitted for useful service.

In October of this year, an act of treacherous intercourse was discovered, in Dr. Benjamin Church, who was a member of the General Court, one of the committee of safety, and who had long been esteemed as a most zealous friend of the liberties of America; which excited much surprise and indignation. He was a representative from the town of Boston: and the treasonable conduct, of which he was accused, and finally convicted, was holding correspondence with a British officer in Boston, and communicating information by letters written in characters known only to each other, respecting the weakness of the American army and its deficiency in military stores. There was, indeed, no direct attempt or promise, on his part, to betray the army or to introduce spies into the American camp; but the correspondence was altogether unjustifiable. The manner in which it was conducted afforded proof, that his views were friendly to the British; and there was no doubt, that, had he not been detected, he would have proceeded to real acts of treason. A short time before his letter was intercepted, which gave evidence of his improper intercourse with the enemy, he had been into Boston, on pretence of some urgent family concerns; and it was known that he had a private interview with general Gage.* Dr. Church was arrested by order of general Washington, and kept in confinement for several weeks, until the General Court should again meet. After some time, the letter which had been intercepted, but which no one could interpret to whom it was first shown, was decyphered by the learned and reverend Dr. West of Dartmouth. A court of enquiry, instituted by general Washington, found him guilty of a criminal correspondence with the enemy; but inflicted no punishment upon him. When the assembly was in session, he was brought before the House of Representatives; was accused and convicted of improper conduct, inconsistent with the character both of a patriot and of a member of the House; and was thereupon deprived of his seat. He was kept in confinement for some time, but was afterwards released by advice of the Continental Congress: when he went to the enemy at Newport, and thence to some part of the West Indies.

The general Court of Massachusetts was in session the greater part of the year, after it was organized in July. There was an adjournment of a few weeks in September, and another for a short time in November. The Executive Council was sitting the whole season, with the intermission of a

* Soon after Lexington battle, when the committee of safety were sitting in Cambridge at the house of J. Hastings, Dr. Church said he was determined to go into Boston the next day, the president, Dr. Warren, interrogated " are you serious? they will certainly hang you, if they catch you." Church replied, " I am serious; I am determined to go, let the consequence be what it may." He was to pretend to be after medicine for the wounded men. He went into Boston, accordingly; and visited general Gage, without restraint.

very few days. General Washington, in his letters to the Continental Congress, bore testimony to their zeal and activity in complying with all his requests. Particularly, when calling for the militia of Massachusetts, as he had occasion to do several times in the course of December 1775, and January and February 1776, he said, he had many proofs of the patriotism and promptitude of the assembly, and of the alacrity of the people, in fulfilling his requisitions. On one occasion, general Lee accused the Council of want of promptness in furnishing some men which had been called for; but there appeared to be no reason for the charge. When the term for which the American troops had engaged was about to expire, in the month of December, most of which at this time belonged to Massachusetts, Connecticut, and New Hampshire, and little progress was made in recruiting for the ensuing year, general Washington applied to the civil authority of Massachusetts for 5000 of the militia; and the number was called in, at very short notice.* Afterwards, they were retained beyond the time for which they were first required, as a considerable number of men from New Hampshire had gone home, and the new recruits were but comparatively few. In the month of January, six other regiments of militia in Massachusetts were raised, to strengthen the army at Cambridge, under general Washington;

* The critical situation of the American army at this time, will appear, by an extract from a letter of general Washington to Congress. " It is not in the pages of history, perhaps, to furnish a case like this—To maintain a post for six months within musket shot of the enemy, without ammunition, and at the same time to disband an army and to recruit another, within that distance of 12,000 regular disciplined troops."

for he was at this time meditating an attack upon the British in Boston, and the regular troops for the year's service amounted to scarcely 9,000. These were enlisted for the term of three months; and without them he would have had little confidence either for offensive or defensive operations. The companies in the particular service of the colony, stationed at various places on the sea coast, were also marched to the camp at Cambridge or Roxbury, by the special request of the commander in chief. Fortifications were likewise built at Cape Ann, at the expense of the province. During a great part of the winter, Massachusetts had nearly 10,000 men in military service, either as a part of the continental army, or as provincial troops, to guard and protect the sea coast.

A small party of the Americans, under major Knowlton of Connecticut, passed from Cobble Hill, across the mill dam, to Charlestown, in the month of January, and attacked the advanced guard near the western base of Bunker Hill. They made prisoners of several of the British, and set fire to the guard house; and retired without receiving any injury from the enemy.

In January '76, the Council and House of Assembly of Massachusetts issued a proclamation, referring to the oppressive acts of the British parliament and ministry for several years before, and to the petitions and remonstrances of the people and representatives of that and of the other colonies; in which they observe, "that in every government there must exist a supreme and sovereign power, and that such power was justly vested in the great body of the people; that when rulers became oppressive, and attempted to impose unconstitutional burdens upon the people, they had a right to resist, and the rulers forfeited all just claim to exercise authority : that they had adopted all peaceable measures in the constitution to obtain justice, which had been denied, and that a resort was at last had by the British government to compel submission by force, to unjust and oppressive measures, which they had felt to be their duty to themselves and to posterity to resist." "It was the will of Providence," they said," "for wise and righteous ends, that this colony should be singled out, by the enemies of America, as the first object, both of their envy and their revenge ; and after having been made the subject of several merciless and vindictive statutes, one of which was intended to subvert our constitution by charter, it is made the seat of war. No effectual resistance to the system of tyranny prepared for us could be made without either instant recourse to arms, or a temporary suspension of the ordinary powers of government. To the last of these evils, in hope of a speedy reconciliation with Great Britain upon equitable terms, the General Congress advised us to submit. And we have seen a large and populous colony subsisting, for more than a year, in great harmony and order, under such suspension of the powers of government." They then referred to the measures adopted to establish and maintain the civil authority, and urge the people to obedience, order, industry, patriotism, and piety. "An army, they said, was raised for the protection of the liberties of the country ; but civil power was essential to the maintenance of regulated freedom, and should always be paramount to all military force."

Colonel, afterwards General Knox, the principal officer in the artillery, belonging to Massachusetts, with the spirit and enterprise for which he was justly characterised through the whole war, engaged in an expedition of great labour and fatigue: but which was of important service to the American army. By order of general Washington* he went to Lake Champlain, in the month of November, and conveyed to Cambridge the cannon and other military articles and stores, to a large amount, which had been taken at Tyconderoga and Crown point, the summer before, by a small party of Americans under Arnold, Allen, Easton, and Brown. The two latter officers were from the county of Berkshire in Massachusetts, and the former was employed and commissioned by the

* *Instructions from general Washington, to H. Knox, Esq.* Nov. 16, 1775.   HEAD QUARTERS, CAMBRIDGE.

" You are immediately to examine into the state of the artillery of the army, and take an account of the cannon, mortars, shells, lead, and ammunition that are wanting. You will then proceed in the most expeditious manner to New-York; and there apply to the President of the Provincial Congress and learn of him, whether Colonel R. left any orders respecting these articles, and procure such of them as can possibly be had. If the President cannot provide immediately for sending them on here, you must put them in a proper channel to be transported with the greatest dispatch, before you leave there. After you have procured as many of these necessaries as you can, you must go on to general Schuyler and get the remainder from Tyconderoga, Crown-point, St. Johns—and if it should be necessary, from Quebec, *if in our hands.* The want of them is so great, that no trouble or expense must be spared to obtain them. I have written to general Schuyler; and he will give every necessary assistance that they may be had and forwarded to this place with the utmost dispatch. I have given you a warrant upon the paymaster general for a thousand dollars, &c."

Provincial Congress, then sitting at Watertown. Colonel Knox did not return with these heavy stores till the first of February, and it was a matter of surprise that he should have accomplished his purpose, even so soon; as the way, for a great distance, was new and extremely difficult for teams and sleds to pass. When, at Albany, on his route to the lake, he received a letter from the Continental Congress, requesting him to examine the grounds near the Hudson, between those places, with a view to the erection of a line of forts, to prevent the access of the British at any future time.

The ordnance and military stores furnished for the American army by this arduous enterprize of colonel Knox, and by the capture of some British store ships by captain Manly, a short time before, encouraged general Washington in his long meditated plan of an attack upon the ministerial troops in Boston. He had been desirous of offensive operations against the besieged army in that place for some months. He wished to drive them from the capital of Massachusetts, and hoped so to weaken them, if he could not succeed in the capture of the whole army, as to convince them of the desperate nature of the enterprize in which they were engaged, of subjugating the colonies; and to prevent their falling upon any other part of America with a sufficient force to cause danger or alarm. But he had too much prudence to engage in an enterprize, glorious as its issue promised to his ardent and patriotic mind to be, when there was so much hazard, which might be highly injurious to the country, and when the general opinion was against such an attempt. Some, indeed, were of opinion,

that he ought to have made an attack upon the
British in Boston. And there was a time, when
many members of the Continental Congress expressed a hope that he would storm the town of
Boston, where the English troops were quartered,
at every hazard. Aware of these expectations,
and sensible of his great responsibility, Washington was resolved to make the attack; but the officers of the army, to whom he submitted his plan,
convened as a council of war, solemnly decided
against the expediency of the measure. He too,
it appears, had some doubts as to the prudence of
the attempt. The most of the troops under his
command, after December, were new recruits: in
reality they were mere militia, and without proper
discipline. And he was long destitute of the cannon necessary for such an attack, as well as of the
article of powder, without which the infantry could
not be expected to maintain the onset, except for
a few hours. The hope of success must have
been founded upon a calculation of miracles, or of
utter weakness and despondence in the British.
The regular troops in the American army were
not so numerous as those of the British in Boston:
and most of these, though forming part of the Continental army, had engaged in the service within a
very short period; and the residue of his force
were militia-men called out in the exigency, and not
to be relied on for a formidable attack on regular
and disciplined troops. But with all his prudence
and caution, Washington sometimes thought it proper to yield to public expectation. And in this
case, sensible of the general feeling through the
continent, he was resolved to make an attack upon
the strong hold of the enemy, if circumstances

should favour such an enterprize. After the arrival of Knox from lake Champlain, with the cannon and military stores, he became more fixed in this purpose. The militia were called in from the distance of twelve miles, at his request, by an order of the legislature of Massachusetts, of the last of February; although there was then nearly five thousand with the army at Cambridge and Roxbury, besides a large portion of the continental troops then lately enlisted for the year. Fire arms and powder had also been collected by the Provincial Assembly, a short time before, for the American army, at the urgent call of the commander in chief.

The execution of the plan depended upon the severity of the weather, in the event of which the attack was to be made by the American troops passing over on the ice from Cambridge and Sewall's point in Brooklyne, across Charles river and landing west of the Common. The cold was not sufficiently severe after the month of January, to make a safe way for the passage of the troops: and there was no other avenue to the capital, which was believed to be practicable. A small part of the British troops in Boston could have easily prevented the entrance of the Americans by the way of the peninsula through Roxbury. The plan was matured, had the season favoured its execution, for the Americans to make an attack upon Boston in two divisions under generals Sullivan and Greene, the whole to be commanded by major general Putnam. This intended expedition failing, it was determined to take possession of the highlands in the northeasterly part of Dorchester, opposite to the south side of Boston, and distant, in a direct course, not more than one mile. This was accordingly done, in the night of the fourth of March, being Monday; after a heavy cannonade against Boston for three days, successively, probably with the design to divert the attention of the enemy.

Major general Thomas had the command of the troops detached for this arduous service. They passed from the camp at Roxbury to the highlands in Dorchester with great caution, under cover of the night; and when the light of day exposed them to the view of the British in Boston, they had thrown up a sufficient breast work for protection and security in prosecuting the object of their enterprize. The enemy were surprised at the spectacle: and there seems to have been some infatuation in their councils, that they had not previously taken possession of such an important post. For general Bourgoyne and the British admiral had often observed, " that, if the *rebels* should possess themselves of those heights, the British must leave the port and harbour of Boston."

Immediately after this event, the British general resolved to quit his situation in the metropolis of Massachusetts. He had been shut up within very narrow limits for about ten months. He had acquired no glory; he had been kept in fear by the undisciplined troops of the colonies, which he and his colleagues had affected to despise; and his men had suffered all the evils of a protracted siege. General Clinton left Boston some time before; and proceeded to New York, where governor Tryon, an advocate for the British ministry, resided and retained a degree of civil authority; and thence he sailed to Carolina, where he hoped to be joined by those who were friendly to the cause of royalty. Bourgoyne returned to England in November preceding, to state the disasters of the ministerial army in Massachusetts, and to form the plan of attack in some other part of America.

The conduct of general Washington during his command near Boston, was fully approved by the Continental Congress, in a letter which was addressed to him after the British evacuated that place, and by a resolution which they ordered to be published. They commended his caution and prudence, and his great attention to the organization of the army; and expressed their entire satisfaction, that he had not hazarded the welfare of the country, by attacking a large and disciplined army, with a body of men, however brave, who had seen little military service, and were in a great measure destitute of arms and ammunition. There was a period, however, during the siege, after he was furnished with additional means which justified an attack, and Washington was resolved to strike a blow on the enemy, powerful as they were, if circumstances had favoured the plan. While he meditated an attack, every facility was afforded him by the legislature of Massachusetts, wh h their resources would supply. They granted h m a loan of 50,000l., when he was without continental funds in his hands, to enable him to pay the troops, who would otherwise have left the service. They ordered large bodies of the militia at three distinct periods between December 1775 and February 1776, to strengthen the American army, before the new recruits were engaged for the ensuing campaign. For a part of the winter, a full moiety of the men in the continental army belonged to Massachusetts. The sea coasts in many places being exposed, the General Court raised several companies, also, for their protection. Marblehead was furnished with military stores, and with one hundred men, at the expense of the province. The people of that town had early thrown up batteries for their defence, as the harbour was accessible by the ships of the enemy; but their great losses and privations, occasioned by the war, left them without the ability to furnish and man their forts. In February the General Court ordered that twenty field pieces be procured, and a large quantity of powder and fire arms should be purchased for the use of their troops, wherever they could be obtained. Some of these articles were procured soon after from Connecticut and Rhode Island.

The militia of the province were arranged anew by order of the general assembly at their winter session; and Massachusetts proper parcelled into three divisions. John Hancock, James Warren* and Azer Orne were appointed major generals. Officers of brigade, and field officers also, were commissioned through the colony. A new emission of paper bills was ordered, to a large amount, to meet the expenses of the province, with a promise of being redeemed by the taxes for 1777, 1778 and 1779. Various sums were allowed and paid to persons who suffered losses at Lexington, Concord and Charlestown; and grants were made to such as were wounded, as well as to the widows and children of those who were slain in the battles at those places. A proposition was made during

---

* General Warren declined,—B. Lincoln was appointed in his place.

this session of the assembly for the payment of the representatives out of the public treasury of the province; but it did not meet the support of the majority of the House. They considered it most proper, that each town should pay for the attendance of its deputies. It was also recommended to every town to choose a committee of correspondence, inspection and safety, distinct from the selectmen, for the purpose of attending exclusively to political concerns; to consult for the welfare of the province, to watch the conduct of those who were disaffected to the cause of liberty; and to be ready to act in concert, in great exigencies, for the defence of the country. A law passed in February, not however without some discussion and alterations of the bill first reported, prohibiting the commencement of civil suits for the space of three months; and ordering the justices of the county courts to continue actions of that kind, to a distant day. Laws of this nature are often indeed in prevention of justice; but if ever they were proper, it was at the period, when the statute of Massachusetts was adopted in February 1776; for there had been no commercial enterprise for a year; the demands upon the people for public purposes had been most extraordinary, and many were entirely unable to meet the payment of their just debts.

Complaint was made to the General Court, about this time, that some of the inhabitants of Nantucket were in the practice of furnishing the enemy with provisions from that island. Most of the people undoubtedly were innocent of such criminal conduct; but some of them were proved to be guilty. They had abused the license given

them to carry provisions from the main to that
island for the necessary supply of its own population; and had furnished the British army in Boston with many vessel loads. One Dr. G—— was
confined at Cambridge, by order of the general
assembly, for assisting the enemy in this manner.
Their location was such, that it was proper for
them to decline all directly hostile movements
against the British; but those who aided the
enemies of the country, from motives of gain, or
from attachment to the ministerial cause, were
justly deserving of censure and punishment.

It was at the same session of the legislative assembly of the province, that a law was made for
confiscating the estates of those citizens who had
put themselves under the protection of the ministerial party, and whose conduct gave evidence of
their hostility to measures adopted for the defence
of American liberty. The law suffered some alterations at a subsequent period, but was continued
substantially the same; and all who remained with
the British army, or retired from America to
England, forfeited their estates to the province.

After the unfortunate affair at Quebec, though
the Americans remained in the country, they were
not in a situation to act on the offensive against
the British. And there was an apprehension, that
the governor of Canada would avail of the occasion to collect a powerful force of Canadians and
indians and make a descent upon the northern
frontiers of New England. It was the opinion of
general Washington, as well as of many intelligent
public men in Massachusetts, that a reinforcement
of the American troops in that department should
immediately be made. It was therefore voted by

the general assembly to raise a regiment for that specific purpose, from the counties of Hampshire and Berkshire for the term of one year. This was in addition to the men already enlisted for the continental army, in pursuance of resolves of Congress of November 1775. And the expense incurred by the colony in raising this regiment, was very great, on account of clothing and the means of conveyance at such a severe season of the year. Specie was borrowed by individuals for the purpose, as they were going into the province of Canada, where paper would not pass. Elisha Porter Esq.* was appointed to the command of this regiment: all possible dispatch was given to enlist and organize them; and early in March they proceeded to join the American forces under general Arnold near Quebec. The Continental Congress acknowledged the zeal and promptness of Massachusetts, in furnishing these troops for such an important expedition.

The intelligence received from England at this time respecting the policy and purposes of administration towards America, was not of a nature to justify any hope of reconciliation, but upon terms of submission, to which the patriots of Massachusetts and of the other colonies could never accede. The king, in a speech from the throne to the two houses of Parliament, had declared " his subjects in America to be in a state of rebellion," and recommended measures " to reduce them to unconditional obedience." A large majority of the members approved of the recommendation of his

* Alner Morgan, Esq. major of the regiment is now living, 1825.

majesty. A respectable minority, indeed, protested against the system adopted by ministers and sanctioned by the crown; and the people of London, Bristol and of some other places in England petitioned the king to recal his troops from Massachusetts, and to consent to the claim of the colonists to their ancient charter rights and privileges. But it was evident, that administration would not restore America to the enjoyment of civil liberty formerly exercised, but would pursue the policy already begun of forcing the people in the colonies to abject submission. The king and his ministers supposed the Americans were resolved on independence. And, although many truly patriotic statesmen were averse from such a measure, in the hope that a reconciliation would be effected, yet more imbibed the opinion, that the arbitrary conduct of the parent state would oblige them to adopt it. An arduous struggle was therefore to be expected; and all the resolution and effort of the country they perceived would be demanded for the crisis. In no other colony, were there so many of the intelligent and influential citizens, as in Massachusetts, who were early and decided in favour of this important step.

CHAPTER IV.

If the British had not previously determined to leave Boston, where they had suffered so much, and where they had little hope of success in their object of subduing the Americans, they were soon convinced of their critical situation, after the fortifications were thrown up at Dorchester neck; and in a few days they accordingly prepared for embarking on board their fleet. The British admiral gave it as his opinion to general Howe, that his ships could no longer remain in safety, in the upper part of the harbour; and that all vessels passing to or from the town would be greatly exposed. Howe was not many days in coming to a resolution to convey his troops to some other part of America: and he prevailed on the selectmen of Boston, who were in the town, to request general Washington to suspend the cannonade, which had been kept up for several days, with an assurance that the British army was preparing for their departure. A threat was more than intimated, also, that if the cannonade continued, acts of retaliation might be expected, by destroying the property of the inhabitants. But neither the request nor the threat was regarded; and the British general was convinced, that his safety depended on a speedy departure. He formed a plan, however, to dislodge the provincials from the heights of Dorchester, but was not successful in the attempt. A large body of British troops left Boston in boats, the day after the Americans began their fortifications, with the intention to land at the easterly point of Dorchester and attack the works newly erected. But a heavy storm ensued and the plan was relinquished. Such a project had been expected by Washington; and he had made arrangements to invade Boston from Cambridge in the event. He had selected four thousand troops for the purpose, which were to land on the westerly side of the town, when a part of the British was engaged in the meditated assault upon Dorchester. His plan was so well matured, and promised so glorious an issue, that many regretted the storm which interrupted the British troops in their project of surprising the forts on Dorchester neck.

The day after the Americans took possession of the heights of Dorchester, and when an attack from the British was apprehended, general Washington visited the fortifications, for the purpose of inspecting the works and giving directions in person. To inspire the troops, he observed to them, "that they should remember that it was the fifth of March."* The remark was quickly circulated

* The anniversary of the Boston massacre on the 5th of March, 1770, was observed this year at Watertown, by a

through the whole detachment, who appeared eager for the expected encounter.

The American troops now at Cambridge and Roxbury, including five thousand militia, were estimated at about fifteen thousand. The British were supposed to be less than ten thousand. On the 13th of March, it was perceived that active preparations were making by the ministerial troops for embarking on board their fleet in the harbour of Boston; and on Sunday, the 17th they left the town, to the great joy of the inhabitants of that place and of the whole province. The evening preceding, a party from Dorchester heights, had entrenched themselves on Nook-hill, an eminence still nearer to Boston; which probably hastened their departure. A detachment from the American army, under major general Putnam, took possession of the metropolis the same day.*

The joy of the occasion, however, was mingled with much grief and regret, to witness such destruction of buildings and property, in that formerly flourishing capital. Some of the churches were essentially injured, having been used as stables for the British cavalry; and many houses and stores

great number of the inhabitants of Boston and other patriotic citizens. The Rev. Peter Thacher delivered an oration on the occasion.

* When Boston was evacuated by the British, a large quantity of medicine was found in their hospital; and on inspection by Dr. John Warren, it appeared that arsenic was mixed with it. At the request of the General Court, he gave his affidavit to the fact. It excited great horror and indignation in those who believed it was intended to poison the sick among the Americans. Many however, were inclined to the more candid supposition, that the design was to injure the whole stock of medicine and render it unfit for use.

were razed to the foundations, and the materials used for fuel: ornamental, and fruit trees were cut down for the same purpose. The streets were filled with dirt and filth, which had been accumulating for nine or ten months; and the small pox was raging in various parts of the town. This gloomy scene formed a most striking contrast to the appearance of the place twelve months before.* The British embarked in such haste that

* Extract of a letter from a citizen of Boston, of March 23d, 1776, who left that town just before the siege, and returned a few days after the British troops left it.

"Yesterday I returned from my exile after an agreeable journey, and arrived in this once flourishing but now solitary town. Once more I tread the streets of Boston, and with a sad and pensive feeling, view the havoc of civil war. Were I to give you a particular detail of its situation last winter and its present state, it would exceed the limits of my time and paper. You will excuse me, therefore, if I only give you a hasty view of some occurrences which the little time I have been here has furnished.

The face of the town is, indeed, very little altered; excepting that the shops are shut and many old wooden buildings have been demolished. When we enter the houses there are seen the marks of violence and outrage—scarcely any that are not robbed and plundered by the merciless *bandit* Nor have public buildings and houses devoted to the worship of God escaped the outrage. The old south meeting house presents a melancholy spectacle. The pulpit and galleries were taken down; the floor strewed with dirt and made the receptable of beasts. The old north, that venerable edifice, fell a sacrifice to the importunity of the tories, and was appropriated to their use, though the officer who ordered it taken down, is said to have done it with reluctance. The steeple of the west meeting house is taken down and otherwise damaged.

After the tories had embarked, the soldiers and sailors vied with each other who should commit the greatest violence; and I am told, whig and tory suffered indiscriminately.—The small arms belonging to the town, which had been delivered up, they have left behind, but they are entirely useless.

they were obliged to leave behind them several large cannon; but the most of these they rendered unfit for immediate use. They also dismantled the fort at Castle island; and it required much time and expense afterwards to put it in a state sufficient to afford protection to the town. The enemy's fleet only proceeded to the lower harbour of Boston, at this time: and a considerable part of it remained till the month of June. A number of their ships proceeded first to Halifax, and there taking some new recruits, sailed for New York, and landed at Staten island in June following.

At an early day, after the British army left Boston and Charlestown, the body of general Joseph Warren was discovered near the fort on Breed's hill, where it had been buried, the day following the memorable battle of 17th of June 1775. The legislature gave directions for a public funeral to be attended in Boston.* An immense concourse of the inhabitants were present, on the solemn occa-

They have demolished most of the pictures in the Court house and Faneuil hall. The latter place hath undergone a strange metamorphosis, was changed into a play-house, and is now in a very disordered state. The distresses of the inhabitants last winter were very great, being without fuel, and provisions very scarce and dear.

'The tories were sanguine that the British troops would beat the rebels, until they returned from their design against Dorchester hills. Their countenances then gathered paleness; in their distress they applied to those whom they had just before affected to despise. Their distractions and distortions could be described only by the pencil of Hogarth. They are charged with being the instigators of all the mischiefs which happened."

* Perez Morton, Esq. pronounced an eulogy on his character, on the occasion.

sion, as well as a committee of the council and representatives then in session at Watertown, and many other public characters, both civil and military. His memory was cherished with great respect and gratitude : for he was one of the most illustrious patriots of Massachusetts, as well as one of the earliest victims which were offered on the altar of freedom.

A few days after the British troops left Boston, general Washington, having dispatched several regiments of the continental forces for New York, for which place he supposed general Howe was destined, visited the metropolis, and there remained for a few days, giving directions respecting the military stores left by the enemy and making arrangements for the defence of the town, when he should leave the colony for New York.* A committee of the inhabitants delivered him an address, congratulating him on the departure of the British army from the province, and expressive of their high sense of his patriotic and judicious conduct while commanding the American army in the vicinity. An address was also made to him by the General Assembly of Massachusetts, at this time; which was as follows.

" When the liberties of America were attacked by the violent hand of oppression, when troops hostile to the right of humanity invaded this colo-

* On the 28th, the public Thursday lecture was again attended in Boston and Dr. Eliot preached from Isaiah xxxiii, 20. General Washington and several other military officers of high rank were present on the occasion, with the members of the council, committee of the House of representatives, selectmen of Boston and others. A public dinner was also given to the commander in chief, this day, in the Capital.

ny, seized our capital, and spread havoc and destruction around it; when our virtuous sons were murdered and our houses destroyed by the troops of Britain; the inhabitants of this and of the other American colonies, impelled by self-preservation and the love of freedom, forgetting their domestic concerns, determined resolutely and unitedly to oppose the agents of tyranny. Convinced of the vast importance of having a gentleman of great military accomplishments to discipline, to lead and conduct the forces of the colonies, it gave us the greatest satisfaction to hear that the Congress of the United Colonies had made choice of one thus qualified; who, leaving the pleasures of domestic and rural life, was ready to undertake the arduous task. And your nobly declining to accept the pecuniary emoluments annexed to this high office fully satisfied us, that a warm regard to the sacred rights of humanity and sincere love to your country solely influenced you in the acceptance of this important trust.

" From your acknowledged abilities as a soldier, and your virtues in public and private life, we had the most pleasing hope; but the fortitude and equanimity so conspicuous in your conduct; the wisdom of your councils; the mild yet strict government of the army; your attention to the civil constitution of this colony; the regard you have at all times shewn for the lives and health of those under your command; the fatigues you have with cheerfulness endured; the regard you have manifested for the preservation of our metropolis; and the great address with which our military operations have been conducted; have exceeded our most sanguine expectations, and demand the warmest returns of gratitude.

" The Supreme ruler of the Universe having smiled on our arms and crowned your labours with remarkable success, we are now, without that effusion of blood we so much wished to avoid, again in quiet possession of our capital : the wisdom and prudence of those movements, which have obliged the enemy to abandon our metropolis will ever be remembered by the inhabitants of this colony.

" May you still go on approved of heaven, revered by all good men, and dreaded by those tyrants who claim their fellow men as their property. May the United Colonies be defended from slavery by your victorious arms. May they still see their enemies flying before you. And the deliverance of your country being effected, may you, in retirement, enjoy that peace and satisfaction of mind, which always attend the great and good. And may future generations, in the peaceable enjoyment of that freedom, the exercise of which your sword shall have established, raise the highest and most lasting monument to the name of WASHINGTON."*

To this address, general Washington made the following reply—" Gentlemen, I return you my most sincere and hearty thanks for your polite address; and feel myself called upon by every principle of gratitude, to acknowledge the honour you have done me in this testimonial of your approbation of my appointment to the exalted station I now fill, and what is more pleasing, of my conduct in discharging its important duties.

* Sever, Hawley, Spooner, Cushing and Sullivan, were the committee of the Council and House of Representatives, to prepare and present the address to general Washington on this occasion.

" When the councils of the British nation had formed a plan for enslaving America and depriving her sons of their most sacred and invaluable privileges, against the clearest provisions of the constitution, against justice and truth; and, to execute their schemes, had appealed to the sword, I esteemed it my duty to take a part in the contest; and especially when called thereto by the unsolicited suffrages of the representatives of a free people; wishing for no other reward, than that arising from the conscientious discharge of the important trust, and that my services might contribute to the establishment of freedom and peace upon a permanent foundation, and merit the applause of my countrymen and of every virtuous citizen.

" Your acknowledgments of my attention to the civil constitution of this colony, while acting in the line of my department, also demand my grateful notice. A regard to every provincial institution, when not incompatible with the common interest, I hold a principle of duty and of policy, and shall ever form a part of my conduct. Had I not learned this before, the happy experience of the advantages resulting from a friendly intercourse with your honourable body, their ready concurrence to aid and counsel whenever called upon in cases of difficulty and danger, would have taught me the useful lesson.

" That the metropolis of your colony is now relieved from the cruel and oppressive invasion of those who were sent to erect the standard of lawless domination and to trample on the sacred rights of humanity, and is again open and free for its rightful possessions, must give pleasure to every virtuous and sympathetic heart; and being effected without the blood of our fellow citizens, must be ascribed to the interposition of that Providence, which has manifestly appeared in our behalf through the whole of this important struggle, as well as to the measures pursued for bringing about the happy event.

"May that Being who is powerful to save, and in whose hands is the fate of nations, look down with an eye of compassion upon the whole of these united colonies ; may he continue to smile upon their councils and arms, and crown them with success, while employed in the cause of virtue and of mankind. May this distressed colony and its capital and every part of this wide extended continent, through his divine favour, be restored to more than their former lustre and once happy state, and have peace, liberty and safety secured upon a solid, permanent and lasting foundation."

The corporation and overseers of Harvard College conferred on general Washington, the third of April, when he was preparing to leave the colony and to join the army near New York, the honorary degree of Doctor of Laws, not only on account of his great intelligence and sound judgment, but in consideration also of his civic virtues, and his patriotic, disinterested services in the cause of liberty. During the whole period of nine months, which he passed in the colony, at the head of the continental forces, arduous and difficult as were the various duties which devolved on him, his conduct received the applause and admiration of all classes of people.

General Washington left Massachusetts for New York, where it was believed the British intended to make an attack, early in the month of April.

The greater portion of the continental troops who had composed the army at Cambridge and vicinity, were sent on to that colony, at the time the British embarked from Boston, under the command of generals Sullivan and Heath; and major general Putnam followed, in a few days after, to resume the chief command, until Washington should arrive. Three regiments were left at Boston, under major general Ward, for the protection of that place and vicinity; to whom Washington gave particular instructions to consult the civil authority of the colony in all his movements within their territory. The General Assembly requested that six of the continental regiments might be permitted to remain for some time ; as a part of the British fleet was still in the lower harbour, and they feared an attack, unless they could command a formidable force. And it was found necessary, soon after, to raise three additional regiments for the protection of the coast, at the expense of the province.

A part of the American troops at Cambridge and Roxbury were also ordered to Canada, immediately on the departure of the British from the metropolis of Massachusetts. Though general Arnold remained in the neighbourhood of Quebec through the winter, and some fresh troops from Massachusetts and New York had been sent on to reinforce him, the Americans were not sufficiently strong to effect any great object : but it was still considered highly important, if not to take possession of that whole province, to prevent the British from recovering the forts on lake Champlain, by which any future plans of attack on the western and northern parts of New England would be more easily accomplished. Major general Thomas, of Massachusetts, was entrusted with the command in that department; and many of the continental forces which marched into that quarter belonged to the province. These troops endured great privations and sufferings in travelling through a new country, partly covered with snow, and almost destitute of provisions. The British were reinforced by fresh troops from England early in May, and the Americans near Quebec were obliged to retreat soon after general Thomas arrived there. The men were so worn down by sickness and fatigue, that no offensive operations were attempted. A council of war gave an opinion for retiring from that place. The whole number of American troops was less than 2000; and not more than 300 were fit for active service. The time for which a large part of them had enlisted, had then also expired. Indeed, it was not without great judgment and unremitting effort, that the Americans were prevented from falling into the hands of the British, who opened the campaign with great force, consisting of regulars, Canadians and Indians.

On their return to Montreal and Crown Point, the Americans were subjected to the severest sufferings, from sickness and a want of suitable provisions. At the latter place they made a stand; but general Thomas died before they reached that station. His conduct was approved as able and judicious, under the many difficulties he had to encounter. He was attacked by the small pox, which prevailed among his troops, and survived only a few days; and general Sullivan succeeded him for a short time in the command of the troops in that quarter, when general Schuyler of New York was ordered to that department.

The death of general Thomas was deplored as a great public calamity. He was distinguished by great prudence and judgment, as well as resolution and intrepidity. He was appointed a major general on the continental establishment in March; but had been second in command in the provincial army in the summer of 1775, till general Washington arrived at Cambridge. He had also served with reputation as a field officer, in the war of 1756, between England and France, and was descended from one of the most ancient and respectable families in the county of Plymouth.

While the General Assembly was in session, on the 10*th* of May, they passed an order, which was published, by which the people of the several towns in the province were advised to give instructions to their respective representatives, to be chosen for the following political year, commencing the last of the month, on the subject of Independence; which, at that time, was more generally contemplated, than it had been at any former period. A reconciliation with Great Britain was now expected by very few of the intelligent patriots of America. The British ministry had not moderated their claims, nor relaxed in their measures of coercion. On the contrary, they breathed a more threatening spirit, and had resolved to prosecute the war with new vigour. The people of Massachusetts had now also experienced too much of the vindictive disposition of the ministerial party, to expect any thing at their hands but cruel oppression and utter subjugation. Even the recent pretended conciliatory plan of lord North was too flimsy to deceive the most ignorant. It required absolute submission, upon a specious province of mercy, to be shewn in such way as the crown might see fit to grant. They spurned the proposed pardon, when they had committed no fault, unless it was one to defend their charter rights; and they rejected the offer of peace, upon terms degrading to them as freemen, and dishonourable to them as patriots. It was the prudent suggestion of the assembly, however, that the people, in their primary meetings should give their opinions upon this most important subject. The citizens of Boston and of some other towns expressed themselves in favour of such a measure; declaring, however, their perfect confidence in the patriotism and wisdom of Congress, in whose decision they were determined to acquiesce.

Some of those citizens of Massachusetts, who disapproved of the opposition made to the measures of the British ministry, and who had repaired to governor Gage for protection after the battle at Lexington, remained in Boston when the English troops left that place in March; and some, who went to Halifax with the fleet, were dissatisfied with their reception there; and, returning to the province soon after, threw themselves upon the mercy of the government. They were immediately taken into custody; and most of them were kept in confinement several months. Those who had rendered themselves most obnoxious did not return. The conduct of the others, after they came back, was closely watched; and it was a long time before they gained the confidence of the people.

In April, the General Court voted to erect a powder mill at Sutton. There were already two in the province, built under the patronage of the legislature. A bounty was offered for manufacturing salt-petre;* and a committee appointed to superintend the casting of cannon and making of fire arms. Beacons were ordered to be erected in Boston, Cape Ann, Marblehead, and on the Blue-hills in Milton; for the purpose of giving an alarm to the people whenever the British should attempt to land near those places. An additional number of armed vessels, in the service of the province, were fitted out; and an offer was made to aid in completing a continental frigate, then building at Portsmouth, as a British ship of war was making havock near the coast. Hulks were also ordered to be sunk in the harbour of Boston: and two vessels were employed to keep a watch in the bay and give seasonable notice of the approach of the enemy. The assembly of Massachusetts, at the request of general Knox, provided for conveying a large quantity of cannon and military stores to New York by land; where the main body of the American army was now stationed.

It was during the session in April, that they passed a resolve to alter the style of writs and other legal processes; substituting " the people and government of Massachusetts" for George the Third: and, in dating official papers, the particular year of the king was omitted, and only the year of our Lord mentioned.

The General Court, at this session, ordered the militia to make use of a system of exercise prepared by Timothy Pickering, Jr. Esq. This was an improved edition of a book published by him

* In one week, in the month of May, 37,000 pounds were deposited with the public agent, at Watertown; and large quantities besides carried directly to the powder mills.

in May 1775, and then recommended, by the Provincial Congress, to be observed by the minute companies and others.

The new General Assembly for 1776 was organized at Watertown, on the last Wednesday in May; and the same gentlemen were elected to compose the executive council, who were members the preceding year, with the exception of six, who declined the trust.* That body then consisted of twenty eight members. The town of Boston elected twelve representatives for this year. The year before, the number was only five. The small pox, then raging in Boston, probably prevented the court from sitting there, at this time.

Although the enemy had quitted the town of Boston, and the greater portion of them had left the province of Massachusetts, neither the citizens nor the General Court could promise themselves much intermission in arduous service for the public welfare. They had not only much to restore and to repair, after a siege of more than ten months, when their constant attention had been given to measures for preventing the utter conquest and desolation of the province; but some of the enemy were still within the harbour of the metropolis, intercepting the scanty commerce which remained to them. There was also reason to fear, that the British might soon return with additional force; and New York at the south, and the settlements at the north west were so much exposed as to induce Congress to call on Massachusetts, struggling

* Mr. Bowdoin was again president of the council. Those who declined, were J. Otis, the elder, John Adams, Jedidiah Foster, &c. Mr. Adams was a member of Congress, and Mr. Foster a judge of the Superior Court.

as she was with her own wants and dangers, for aid in the common cause. General Washington thought it consistent with his duty, as commander of the continental army, to leave but few regular troops for the defence of Boston. Before he left the province, he gave directions for repairing the works on fort hill, so called, in Boston; and soon after his departure, the General Assembly ordered fortifications to be erected on Noddle's island, and the cannon left by the British in an injured state on Castle island, to be fitted for use. They also made immediate provision for raising two regiments, to be stationed within and near the harbour of Boston; and, in May, another was called for, together with six companies of artillery; all at the immediate expense of the province.

These were soon organized, and placed some of them at the castle, some at Nantasket, and some at Noddle's island. General Lincoln was chairman of the committee appointed to direct in the accomplishment of these objects: and, under his judicious management, the forts were built, and the vessels of the enemy driven from their position at the mouth of the harbour. The General Court, at this time also, provided for fortifications at Salem, Marblehead, Cape Ann, Plymouth, and Falmouth on Casco bay. Cannon and other military stores were furnished, and men were stationed at these places, for the greater part of the summer following. These towns were exposed to the British ships, which were hovering on the coasts for a great distance. Some of these were large sloops of war and frigates, which rendered the coasting business extremely hazardous. The private armed vessels and those in commission of the province and of the continent, were of essential benefit to the country at this period. They were numerous, and constantly on the watch for the enemy. Scarcely a week past, but they captured a valuable prize; while only one of them was taken by the British for a long period. This was an armed brig called the Yankee Hero, belonging to N. Tracy of Newburyport. She was captured near the coast by an English sloop of war, which had greatly annoyed the commerce and coasting trade of the province. But the American brig did not surrender, until she had made an obstinate resistance of nearly two hours and lost about half her men.

Captain Mugford of Marblehead, in a continental schooner, called the Franklin, achieved a brilliant exploit (April 17th,) but eventually became a victim of British vengeance. The Franklin had twenty men, and she engaged a large ship from Ireland with eighteen men, mounting six guns, and loaded with provisions, cannon and other valuable military articles. This was just at the entrance of Boston harbour, and in full view of the British ships then lying in Nantasket roads: and he carried her up to the town of Boston, through the northern passage. Three days after, captain Mugford went down the harbour, intending to put to sea on a cruise. His vessel run aground in the gut. The British were informed of his situation, and they sent ten boats filled with men, in number about two hundred, to attack him. They approached the Franklin in the evening, and when they were hailed, pretended to be from Boston. But he suspected they were enemies, and ordered them to keep off. They did not regard him; and perceiving them pulling for his vessel, he fired into the boats with great spirit. Two boats were sunk, and the others were soon obliged to sheer off. But the brave commander was shot dead in the contest. Several of the enemy were slain in the boats; among whom was the first lieutenant of the British ship of war. About this period three large transport ships from England and Scotland were captured by privateers from Marblehead; each having about one hundred highlanders and thirty marines for the British fleet. One of these ships engaged the privateers some hours before she surrendered, and lost seventeen men, besides major M. an officer in the British service. A colonel Campbell was on board one of the captured vessels.

There were frequent alarms in the months of May and June, and fears were entertained of another visit from the British, which gave much uneasiness to the inhabitants; although there were some continental troops at Boston, and several regiments had been called into the colonial service in the vicinity. It was not believed, that the British fleet would remain long at Halifax; and whether Massachusetts or some southern colony would be attacked, was very uncertain. It was, therefore, determined by the General Court, early in June, to throw up fortifications at Nantasket, and on several islands in the harbour of Boston, and, if possible, to drive all the enemy's vessels from its waters. There was already some provincial troops at Nantasket, at the Castle, and at Noddle's island; but they had hitherto acted only on the defensive. On the 14th of June, two years from the time of the odious "Boston port bill," a large party of men went down the harbour, consisting of two provincial regiments, a battalion of artillery and some continental troops; and took post, at Nantasket, Long island, Pettick's and Moon Islands, where they threw up entrenchments, and immediately began a heavy cannonade upon the British vessels lying in the channel. These were then about twenty in number. Their situation was found to be too hazardous to remain; and they soon got under way and left the harbour, excepting two or three which were taken by the Americans. They suffered some from the forts before they departed; and on leaving the outer harbour, they blew up the lighthouse, the only injury which was in their power to commit.

It was considered prudent to retain the two regiments and the battalion of artillery in the service of the province through the season : and to keep guards at the fortifications, which had been erected in various parts of the harbour. Several other companies were also retained, at populous places on the coast, which were most liable to be approached by the enemy's ships. But there were still greater demands upon Massachusetts in June and July for men to recruit the army at New York, and at the northward, on lake Champlain, where attacks were threatened by formidable forces of the British, who had lately been victorious, in that quarter, over the Americans.

On the arrival of the British at New York in June, general Washington called upon Congress for an additional force, to enable him to prevent their landing, or to check them in any plans of ravaging the country. The regular troops under his command were but few, compared to the numbers with which it was expected the British would open the campaign in that quarter.* Many of the continental regiments belonging to Massachusetts were in the northern department, where a large force was also deemed necessary. General Bourgoyne had arrived in Canada with fresh troops, and was driving before him the Americans, who were worn down with fatigue and sickness. Congress addressed the legislature of Massachusetts, as well as of some other colonies, and urged them to send on the militia with the greatest possible dispatch. On the 25th of June, the general assembly resolved to raise five thousand militia for six months, to reinforce the continental army. This must have been a great effort and have required great sacrifices, when it is recollected, that the province had already furnished more than its portion of regular troops for the year's service, and had also a great number of men doing duty at Boston and other places on the

* On the 20th of June, an attack was made upon some British soldiers at Sandy Hook near New York, by a party of Americans of about 300, commanded by colonel Tupper, with major Brooks as second in command, all belonging to Massachusetts. The British retreated to the light house, which served them as a shelter; and two ships of war, lying in the offing kept up a fire upon the Americans for nearly two hours, which prevented them in the pursuit of the English soldiers. But the party under colonel Tupper received no injury. Major Henly, aid to general Heath, a brave and meritorious officer, was killed soon after, in an engagement with some British troops at Harlem, near New York. Heath had then recently been appointed a major general in the continental army. In October, a party of the Americans chiefly from Massachusetts, under colonel Shepherd, attacked some British at New Rochelle, near New York. and a severe skirmish ensued, when the enemy fell back to the main army. It was said by one of the officers, "that the Massachusetts boys fought the regulars bravely for some time in the open field."

sea coasts. The preamble to the resolve for raising these men is indicative alike of the sense they had of the danger to which the country was exposed, and of their resolute purpose to sacrifice every thing for the preservation of their liberties. It is as follows :

" As the unrelenting spirit, which possesses the king and Parliament of Great Britain, has pushed them on to leave no measures unessayed to accomplish our destruction, and with infinite disgrace to themselves are about to pour in upon us a number of foreign troops, with intent this year to decide the contest and to enslave us forever ; and as such a manly and brave resistance, as with the smiles of heaven we are able to make, will, we trust, utterly defeat their haughty and unrighteous designs, and establish our liberty ; the American Congress have called upon this colony for five thousand of its militia to co-operate with the continental troops at Canada and New York, and it is absolutely necessary that a proper number of men should be reserved for the defence of the sea coasts against the attacks which may be made upon them, it renders it unavoidable that the levies should be made on the towns least exposed to invasion from the sea ; and although the numbers are large, yet the exertions now called for are not to be regarded when compared to the great and noble objects for which we are contending; this court, therefore, have the fullest assurance that their brethren, on this occasion, *will not confer with flesh and blood,* but being convinced of the necessity of the measure, will without hesitation and with the utmost alacrity and despatch, fill up the numbers proportioned on the several towns, in which case we shall have the highest prospect of defeating the bloody designs of our unjust and cruel adversaries. We derive the greatest confidence from the spirited and distinguished part our constituents have taken upon all important occasions, and we flatter ourselves that a noble defence this campaign will put an end to the contest. Every thing, therefore, calls for our united exertions; not only the safety of our property, children and families, but the security of the rights of the present and future generations."

These men were raised at great expense to the province; and committees were employed in every county to assist and encourage the enlistments. A bounty and a month's pay in advance were allowed as an inducement to the people to engage in the public service. The sum of 50,000*l.* was appropriated for the purpose. Three thousand of these militia were ordered to the northern department, and two thousand for New York. Before the whole were enlisted, the legislature proposed to general Washington to take two regiments of the continental troops stationed at Boston, for the defence of that place, and offered to call out the inhabitants in the vicinity as a guard, till they should be able to relieve them by others which should be enlisted.

The first of July several additional regiments were ordered to be marched to New York; together with a large number of light-horse, and several companies of artillery. The British had landed a great force, and threatened to subdue the whole country. Two more regiments were required to be forwarded to Canada, the tenth of July; and the legislature ordered a levy of every 25th man for the purpose. These were raised principally in the western parts of the province, and in Middlesex and Essex; while those which marched for New York were from Suffolk, Plymouth and Bristol. For although several of the continental regiments were hurried off immediately from the Boston station, and some of the militia repaired thither to take their place, others of them hastened directly from the towns where they were mustered to the southern and northern departments.

Such exertions as these could not have been made without great patriotism and zeal, both in the General Court and in the people of Massachusetts. To those who live in peaceful times and pass their days in ease and quiet, it appears almost incredible, what sufferings were endured and hazards met by the brave men of that eventful period. Few persons in any age have made greater efforts for the enjoyment of any earthly blessing. In communicating the resolves of Congress at this time, Hancock urged the General Court and people, by every consideration which could influence honourable men and freemen, to assist in the great work of saving the country from tyranny and oppression. Many others were equally decided and zealous: and without such characters to animate and rouse the people, brave and attached to liberty as they were, they would have been discouraged, and have sunk under the increasing difficulties which surrounded them.

Under all these difficulties and threatened as they were with ministerial vengeance, the delegates of the several North American colonies, in General Congress assembled, after much deliberation and mutual consultation, on the fourth of July (1776) declared themselves INDEPENDENT of the crown and government of Great Britain. But it was not without some opposition, that this declaration was adopted and publickly made. Some highly patriotic citizens were not then prepared for such a serious measure; nor were they willing to relinquish entirely the hope of a reconciliation with the parent country. But a large majority of the members were decidedly of opinion, that no reconciliation could be effected, and that the period had arrived, when it was necessary to declare the colonies a separate government from England. The British ministry might be incensed. But their vengeance was already in exercise, to its utmost extent; and by becoming an independent nation, the governments of Europe might be induced to assist them against an unnatural foe. The resolution of Congress was zealously advocated by all the delegates from Massachusetts; and was approved by a vast majority of the people, in this and the other twelve colonies; which, from this memorable period, were called and known as the thirteen United States of America. On the eighteenth of July, this Declaration of Independence was publickly read from the balcony of the State House in Boston, in presence of a vast concourse of the citizens, of several military companies, of the officers of the militia and of the continental army on the station, of the selectmen and other municipal officers of the town, and of many members of the executive council and General Assembly of Massachusetts. There was great parade and exultation. The king's arms were taken down, and a public dinner given on the occasion. And afterwards, the declaration was read in the churches on the Lord's day, after the religious service had closed.

The several states were now considered *sovereign*, as well as independent. The supreme civil authority resided in the legislature in each state; and each claimed the right to exercise sovereign power, within its own jurisdiction, yielding due respect to the advice and recommendations of the General Congress. It soon became an important question in Massachusetts, what should be the particular form of civil government. Some gave an opinion in favour of one branch for the legislature, others prefered two branches, as in the British parliament. There was indeed no necessity for an immediate decision on the subject. For the government was then such as had long existed in the colony, except a vacancy of the office of governor, the duties of which were performed by the executive council. It was proposed however, at this session of the General Court, to appoint a committee of their own body, to prepare a form of government; but they did not proceed to the business, as the opinion was generally expressed, that the subject ought to originate with the people, and that they should elect delegates for that specific purpose : and accordingly, it was only recommended by the House of Representatives to their constituents, to choose their deputies to the next General Court, with power to adopt a form of government for the state. This advice was first given in September 1776 : and afterwards more formally, in April 1777. Between these dates, the committees of safety from a majority of the towns in Worcester county assembled, and voted that it would not be proper for the (then)

General Court to form a constitution; but that a convention of delegates from all the towns in the state should be called for the express purpose.

In the month of August, a day was set apart by the General Court of Massachusetts for public humiliation and prayer. The situation of the state and of the country was very critical. The enemy had two large armies, commanded by able generals, resolved, if possible, to overrun the continent. The one at New York consisted of nearly 20,000 men; and that on Lake Champlain at the northward, was estimated at 12, or 14,000. Many of the American troops, though probably almost as numerous as the British, were militia called out for only a few months. And the resources of the country were too limited to furnish all needful means of defence against such a formidable enemy. But no efforts were spared to oppose a sufficient force to the invaders, for defending the United States; and no part of the country afforded more ready assistance than Massachusetts.

Another requisition for men was made on Massachusetts in September by Congress, who had been solicited by general Washington to furnish a fresh supply of troops; and the legislature ordered every *fifth* man to march to the neighbourhood of New York, the quarters of the commander in chief. The towns on the sea coast were excepted, in this order of the General Court, as their service would probably be required for the defence of the state. Major General Lincoln was appointed to command this detachment; and they marched immediately to Fairfield in Connecticut, with directions to report themselves to general Washington. They were raised to remain in service until such time as the General Court should determine, though an assurance was given, that they would probably be discharged within three months. In the terms of enlistment, it was also stated that they were to serve in the New England States, or in New York and New Jersey. Before the whole of these were ready to march, two regiments were ordered to Rhode Island, which was now attacked by a British squadron, and whale boats were furnished to convey them from Falmouth, Dartmouth and Buzzard's bay. The residue were discharged in two months, as the British near New York discovered no disposition to penetrate into the country, and part of their fleet sailed to Newport. General Lincoln soon after took command of the troops raised for the defence of Rhode Island. The General Court of Massachusetts, in the same month, employed a large number of ship carpenters to repair to the army on Lake Champlain, where it was considered important to have a fleet of small vessels to check the enemy ; and, at the request of general Schuyler, they furnished him with powder, nails, &c. in that quarter. Misfortunes still attended the American army in the northern department. The British took several important posts there in August and September; and were also victorious in a naval engagement on the lake.

With very short intervals, the General Assembly was in session the whole of this year. The one formed in July 1775, was together until the middle of May 1776: and afterwards, there were only three adjournments of the court for a few weeks for the residue of the year: in November they sat in Boston. And when the House of Representatives adjourned, the council had power given them to provide all necessary measures for the defence of the state, and for calling out the militia to recruit the continental army. This body was usually in session; or a committee remained to act in any sudden emergency. Their attention and advice were almost constantly required. Scarcely a week elapsed, in which there was not a call upon the civil authority of the state for the militia to march to head quarters near New York, to lake Champlain, or to Rhode Island; and frequently there were alarms within the state, which rendered it expedient to increase the forces at Boston, or station men at other parts of the extensive sea coasts.

The General Court had, also, much legislative duty to perform, respecting the internal regulation of the State. At one time, they found it expedient to suspend the ordinary execution of the laws, which regarded merely pecuniary disputes between the people. And the interruption which took place in the common business and pursuits of life, and the difficulties occasioned by great taxes and heavy drafts of men for the military service, produced so much distress and discontent, that the prudence and wisdom of the most intelligent patriots were called forth, in adopting means of relief for the people and of protection to the country. The paper currency had now depreciated: many, who had demands upon the state, were unwilling to receive it in payment; and the soldiers and their families complained, not without reason, that before their wages were paid, the bills were far less valuable than the nominal sums purported to be. The General Court appointed a committee, about this time, to meet others from Connecticut, Rhode Island and New Hampshire, for the adoption of some measures to restore the credit of paper money, or to prevent its further depreciation; and to check a spirit of monopoly, speculation and extortion, which was manifested in many places; and in consequence of which the poorer classes, especially the soldiers, were subjected to great injustice and sufferings. This committee was to have met at Providence; but that place was occupied by the military, and no meeting was held. The following spring, another committee was appointed for the purpose, to meet at Springfield; and New York was also represented on the occasion. A plan was reported, chiefly for the relief of those who were in the public service, by which the articles of food and clothing furnished their families were fixed at certain prices; and the evil to which they were before liable was in some measure checked. But it was found difficult to prevent all speculation and monopoly. And whenever such an attempt has been made, it has generally been found ineffectual.

CHAPTER V.

Continental army for 1777 . . . Slavery forbidden . . . Several calls for militia . . . Invasion of Rhode Island under general Lincoln . . . Military stores from France . . . Monopolies and depreciation . . . Additional State troops, and drafts of militia.

In the month of September of this year, (1776)* in order to prepare seasonably for a powerful army for the next campaign, Congress recommended that 70,000 men be raised by the States for the term of three years, or during the war; and apportioned to the several States their respective quotas. Massachusetts was first required to raise fifteen battalions; and soon after there was a requisition for two additional regiments, and a battalion of artillery; being in the whole about thirteen thousand, and nearly one fifth of the whole continental establishment. The term for which those then in service had engaged would expire with the present year, and they had been enlisted directly by continental agents and officers, without the special intervention of the individual States. It was now concluded to have each State raise a certain number of troops, but when enlisted, to form, as before, a continental army. The time for which they were to enlist, was to be so long

* Members of Congress for 1776, from Massachusetts, S. Adams, J. Adams, J. Hancock, R. T. Paine, and E. Gerry.

as the war might continue; or at least for the period of three years. This was certainly a wise and judicious plan; but some of the States were averse to it, as the people objected to an engagement in the service for more than a year. Nor will this appear strange, when it is recollected that most of the soldiers were the yeomanry and citizens of the country, who were unwilling to devote themselves to a military life.

A committee of the Legislature of Massachusetts was chosen in October, to go on to the head quarters of general Washington, and if necessary, to Philadelphia, to consult with Congress upon the subject of bounty and wages for the soldiers. They waited on the commander in chief, and having made known the object of their mission, desired to learn if an enlistment for one year would not meet his approbation. He was very decided,* that during the war, or three years, should be the term of the enlistment; and expressed a strong apprehension of the final success of the British, unless the States would consent to raise an army for a long period, so that the men could be taught the military discipline. He had already suffered much for want of regular troops, on whom he could rely for a long period of service. Many of his men were militia at that time; he saw that he must depend upon the militia also at the close of the

* Hon. Mr. Partridge, one of the committee, related afterwards, that he never saw Washington discover any thing but perfect self-command, except on that occasion. When a year was mentioned for the time of service, he started from his chair, and exclaimed, " Good God, gentlemen, our cause is ruined, if you engage men only for a year. You must not think of it. If we ever hope for success, we must have men enlisted for the whole term of the war."

year, while a new army should be forming; and he was determined to guard against such an evil at any future period.

During this month, an estimate was made of the sums expended and advanced by Massachusetts, for the service of the continent, in addition to the amount for various services in the State, and was found to be 150,000*l.*, after a former calculation, towards the close of the preceding year. Application was soon after made to Congress for a reimbursement of that sum, or the greater part of it. 100,000*l.* was ordered to be paid, and was accordingly sent on to the treasurer of the Commonwealth, the beginning of 1777.

On several occasions, before this period, the General Court of Massachusetts had expressed a disapprobation of the slave trade, and a disposition to put an end to the practice of retaining the Africans in the degrading condition, in which they were held in many parts of the country. Several of these unfortunate persons were brought into Salem, at this time, who were found on board a British prize ship from Jamaica, and they were publicly advertised to be sold; but the Legislature forbid the sale, and ordered them to be set at liberty.

A board of war was appointed in October, for the purpose of providing military stores, cannon and fire arms, for the men stationed within the State, as well as for those to be enlisted for the service of the continent. Several detachments of the militia were called for, at this time, to strengthen the army near New York, and on the lake; and in December many were marched to Rhode Island, for the defence of Newport. All these were to be furnished with arms and ammunition; and though there were some of these in the public stores, many were to be collected to meet the great demand made for them. Some military articles were also loaned to the governor of Connecticut for the militia of that State, a great number of whom were in service at Rhode Island, with general Washington, or in the northern department.

During the months of November and December, large detachments of the militia were ordered out to reinforce the continental armies, and to assist in protecting Rhode Island, which was attacked, in the latter of these months, by a party of the British from New York, estimated at 6000, with a large fleet. Within the same period, committees of the legislature were sent on, both to the head quarters of Washington at the south, and of Gates at the north, to urge the men belonging to Massachusetts, whose term of service would soon expire, to enlist, on the new establishment, for three years, or during the war; and to prevail with those who chose not to engage for that time, to remain in service till the new recruits should join the army. A few consented to remain; but many returned home as soon as their time was out. At this time, likewise, arms were furnished to all the militia in the county of Berkshire, who were destitute; as it was believed they might be called out *en masse*, to strengthen the army on the lake. In November, the two regiments stationed at Boston, and around the harbour, whose time would soon expire, were engaged to continue in service several months beyond their former enlistment; and some additional regiments were marched to New Jersey to join the army under general Washington, who was pursued by a powerful enemy, and whose already scanty forces were daily diminishing.* Towards the close of the same month, the militia of Plymouth and Barnstable counties, were ordered to Rhode Island; and a part of them were transported by whale boats from Dartmouth, Falmouth, and from some other places on Buzzards Bay. Two regiments from Worcester county were also marched to Providence for the protection of Rhode Island; and the militia lately ordered to be raised in Berkshire and Hampshire counties were directed to proceed to Albany, to act as the public service might require. The latter were permitted soon to return home; for the British retired into Canada, and it was concluded by the American general only to maintain his station at Ticonderoga for the winter.

The detachment of British troops from the main army at New York ordered to Newport, at this time, was estimated to be nearly 6000; and were commanded by several distinguished officers; general Clinton, lord Piercy, major general Prescott, and others. A large number of the militia from Connecticut and Massachusetts were immediately collected there, to act with those of Rhode Island, and some few continental troops, for the defence of the country. Besides those already ordered from Plymouth and Barnstable, an additional number was sent in from the former county, and from

* Two regiments from Worcester were among them; and a large company of volunteers of respectable citizens marched from Salem, though the people of that town, being on the sea board, were not required to furnish men at this time.

Bristol, Suffolk, and the southern parts of Worcester county. Major general Lincoln, who had been sent on some time before with the militia of Massachusetts to reinforce the continental army near New York, was ordered to take command of the troops at Rhode Island and Providence. A part of those ordered for Rhode Island, were directed to proceed to New Jersey, and join general Washington, whose situation was now become very critical, being pursued by a British army of regular troops estimated at 15,000, while he had scarcely one third of that number, some of which were temporary recruits. Boston being thus left unprotected, two regiments were immediately raised in the vicinity for its defence. All these various establishments amounted to more than one half of the militia in the counties above mentioned, besides a great number from all the other counties in the state.

The aspect of public affairs was, at this period, most gloomy and alarming; and but for the resolute efforts and brilliant successes of general Washington at Trenton and Princeton, the country would have sunk into a state of despondence. With a handful of men, whom the British general thought scarcely worth immediate pursuit, as he concluded they could not again become formidable, Washington fell upon a detached division of the enemy at each of these places within a short period; and destroyed and captured almost the whole, to the utter astonishment of the British, and carrying conviction to their fears, that they were opposed by a man whom difficulties could not appal, nor numbers overpower. Many Massachusetts troops were with the commander in chief in these important attacks; for, though their term of enlistment was about to expire, they had been prevailed upon to remain till some fresh troops should arrive for the ensuing year.*

Among the officers of high rank, then with general Washington, were Green and Knox, who urged the pursuit of the enemy immediately after the affair at Trenton; which probably would have been attended with the happiest effects to the American arms. General Washington was in favour of the plan; but the majority of the officers were opposed to it.

In January (1777) a plan was laid to re-take fort Independence, near King's bridge in the vicinity of Hudson's river; which was to be executed by the militia from Massachusetts and Connecticut, to the number of about 4000. Major general Heath had the command, and Lincoln, Wooster, and Parsons, were brigadiers in the detachment. But nothing important was effected; and it was believed that the general in chief did not discover all that energy and promptness which some others might have exhibited; and which could not have failed of success.

The call for aid upon Massachusetts by the governor of Rhode Island in December, was so urgent, that almost the whole of the militia in the southern counties, and many from Worcester, Mid-

* Extract of a letter from general Washington, January 1777. " It is painful for me to hear such illiberal reflections upon the eastern troops, as you say prevail in N——. I always have, and always shall say, that I do not believe any of the states produce better men. Equal injustice is done them in other respects : for no people fly to arms more promptly, or come better equipped, or with more regularity into the field."

dlesex, and Suffolk, were ordered for the defence of that state. It was believed also to be the plan of the enemy to march through the country to Boston. The two continental regiments stationed in the capital of Massachusetts were ordered to Providence. The corps of artillery, and an independent company soon followed;* and several field pieces and military stores were sent on to Rhode Island at the same time.

The troops required of Massachusetts for the continental service, for the whole period of the war, or three years, to be enlisted the beginning of this year, (1777,) were raised with great difficulty. A similar delay, indeed, attended the efforts to engage them in all the other States. In the preceding campaign, the Americans had been generally unfortunate. Many were desirous of remaining at home to provide for their families. They had suffered much for want of sufficient clothing; and the bills by which their wages were paid had depreciated nearly one half. The General Assembly of Massachusetts proposed to offer an additional bounty; but Congress disapproved of the plan, as it would render it necessary for other states to do the same, and it was believed that some of them would not consent. Indeed, twenty dollars and land were promised by Congress; but this was a very distant good, and not valued as it ought to have been. The enlistment was so slow, that Massachusetts engaged to pay the men raised for her regiments, in addition to the offer by Congress, 20l. to be paid in two equal

* One of these was commanded by Thomas Melvill, and one by Henry Jackson.

instalments, and promised that the depreciation of paper, received in payment of their wages from the continent, should be made up to them by the state. In many cases, also, they were furnished with clothing at a fixed price, by which they were saved from the loss to which they would have been subjected, if they had received their whole compensation in the bills of the continent.

Four of the fifteen regiments were raised with all possible dispatch and ordered to the northward, in January, where the British movements now indicated the renewal of offensive operations.* The American army in that department, which in October preceding was estimated at 13,000, including militia, had been reduced to a number so low as to be scarcely adequate to the maintenance of the fort of Tyconderoga. The regular troops had gone home, as their term of service expired with the year just past; excepting the few who had been induced to engage upon the new establishment. The militia, also, who had been forwarded at different times during the summer and autumn of 1776, for reinforcing the army in that quarter, had been dismissed. The above number of regiments had been requested by the commanding officer in that department; and great efforts were made by the General Court to raise this portion at an early day. All the other regiments were not filled until the months of May and June; although the people were frequently urged to enlist, by all the powerful considerations, which could operate with free and patriotic citizens. The General

* These were commanded by Brewer, Francis, Bradford, and Marshall.

Court prepared an address to be read in the churches and at the head of the militia companies, soliciting the enlistment of soldiers for three years or during the war. "We entreat you," this was their language, "for the sake of religion, for the enjoyment of which our ancestors fled to a wilderness, for the sake of freedom and social happiness, to act vigorously in this critical state of our country; and we doubt not that your exertions will be crowned with that success which is due to the brave, the wise and patriotic." There was a public Fast this year in January, by advice of the General Court. Officers of militia and selectmen of the several towns in the state were enjoined to make constant exertions for raising the men required. The proportion for each town was determined, and a resolve passed, that they should provide the number fixed. In some places, the citizens were taken by lot or drafted; and all such were obliged to enter the service or to engage soldiers in their stead.*

In January, as the new levies came in very slowly, general Washington called again upon several states for the militia, for a short period. Massachusetts furnished 2000, which joined the continental army in New Jersey in the month of February. They were forwarded under command of general Lincoln, who was succeeded as the chief officer at Providence, by major general Arnold. But general Spencer of Connecticut soon after had the command on that station. On this occasion, as well as many others, the militia were of great

* Every seventh man was called for at this period; and the towns were also required to furnish 5000 blankets.

service in the war of the revolution. Lincoln was created a major general in the continental army, in 1777, and he possessed in a peculiar degree the esteem and confidence of the commander in chief.*

A greater part of the British left Newport in March, without effecting the object of their expedition, except it was merely to find winter quarters for a large portion of their troops, who could not procure support at New York. They excited great apprehensions, indeed among the inhabitants of Massachusetts, Rhode Island, and Connecticut; and the exertions made to collect a military force to prevent any scheme of conquest or plunder, occasioned much distress to the citizens of these states, already nearly exhausted by other and previous sacrifices for the public welfare. General Clinton, left Newport for England at an earlier day; and it was supposed that there was a serious misunderstanding between him and Lord Piercy, who was second in command in this expedition. When it was known, that the British fleet was preparing to sail from Newport, there was an apprehension that they were destined for Boston. This circumstance induced the General Court to order the forts in the harbour of Boston to be repaired and manned, and to call in the militia to aid in the defence of the capital. As the enemy did not proceed to Boston from Newport, the militia were soon dismissed. But two regiments were ordered to be raised for that place, and several companies in the service of the state

* Glover, Patterson, Learned and Nixon of Massachusetts, were this year appointed brigadiers, and Knox, general of artillery.

were stationed in many towns on the sea board, during the year. In the spring of 1777, general Ward resigned his military commission, and was elected one of the council. He was succeeded on the Boston station by general Heath.

The private and public armed vessels belonging to Massachusetts, as well as the larger ships commissioned by the continent, were still successful in their cruises near the coast, and even in the latitudes of the West Indies. Richly laden English ships bound from those islands to Europe, and others on their voyage from Great Britain to New York, to furnish the enemy with military stores, provisions and clothing, were captured by the Americans; and thus the continental troops were supplied with necessary articles, which it would have been impossible, perhaps, to collect elsewhere. A calculation was made in England, that in eighteen months, from July 1775, to January 1777, the Americans had captured English merchant ships to the amount of 1,500,000*l.* sterling; besides a great number of transports, and provision vessels destined for the British troops.

Early this season, in the months of March and April, several ships arrived from France with woollen and linen goods, hardware, and large quantities of fire arms and military stores. This was supposed to be in consequence of the applications of the American agents, Franklin and Dean, then at Paris. One of these vessels, which arrived at Portsmouth, had about 5000 stands of arms, and various other articles for the American army. The General Court of Massachusetts applied for the fire arms to equip their troops just then preparing to march to Ticonderoga. Aware of the necessity of the case, the continental agent furnished them; and the new recruits were therefore able to join the northern army immediately; many of whom had been delayed for want of this necessary article. Further efforts were required, indeed, to complete the battalions alloted to Massachusetts for the continental establishment. The towns from which the requisite number had not been furnished were again addressed; and an order of the General Court was issued for drafting them, if they could not be persuaded voluntarily to enlist. The regiments were not entirely filled after all these efforts.* But the militia were frequently employed, at different times, and for different periods, during the season, by which the regular army was greatly strengthened.

The General Court ordered a new emission of paper in February (1777) to the amount of 125,000*l.*; and a tax of 100,000*l.* At the same session, they consented that general Ward should order a part of the continental troops to Providence, who were stationed at or near Boston; and the citizens of the metropolis, to the number. of 350, were embodied for its defence. At this time, 400 additional militia were sent on to the former place, to complete the quota of 2000, which had been before required from Massachusetts. The inhabitants of Boston had a large meeting, during

* The commanders of the Massachusetts regiments were Vose, Bailey, Greaton, Shephard, Putnam, Nixon, Francis, Brewer, Alden, M. Jackson, Wesson, Marshall, Bradford, Smith, Bigelow, H. Jackson, and Crane, of artillery. Francis was killed early this year, and Sproat had command of the regiment. Brewer left the service, and Tupper took command of his regiment. Brooks was lieutenant colonel commandant of M. Jackson's.

this month, to take into consideration the complaints of the poorer classes, respecting monopolies, and the high prices on articles in common use. The conduct of some individuals was censured for extortion, and more public spirit was recommended ; and it was voted that the names of all who should offend in this way, in future, should be made public. There were a few persons in the state, also, who refused to take the bills issued either by the General Court or by Congress, which tended to lessen their value in the estimation of the common people. This was severely condemned, as injurious to the public welfare and credit ; and many patriotic citizens of distinction made great personal sacrifices and efforts for the good of the community. But the debt of the state was so great, and the resources so inadequate to provide for immediate payment, that public paper of all kinds continued to depreciate, which was the occasion of great distress to many of the people.

Lead and flints to a considerable amount, were again furnished the state of Connecticut, for the supply of their troops. Nor was this done because of a great quantity in Massachusetts ; for at this time the people were requested to take *the weights from their windows for the public use.*

In March, companies were ordered to be raised at the expense of the state, and stationed at Falmouth, Cape Elizabeth, Kittery, Newburyport, Gloucester, Salem, Marblehead, Plymouth, and Dartmouth. There were already several companies raised by the state at different places round the harbour of Boston, besides the two continental regiments, generally on this station, when not ordered away to head quarters on some sudden emergency. They were so ordered to Rhode Island, on two occasions; once to the head quarters of Washington, and once to the northern department. And in all these instances, the militia were embodied for the public service, until the troops enlisted by the order of Congress could relieve them. In the same month, when there was an alarm at Boston, after the continental regiments had marched, by consent of the legislature, to strengthen the main army, and general Washington was requested to furnish some regular troops, he could not prudently comply with the request, and the state was obliged to call out the militia for its own protection.

In April, 1500 of the militia from the counties of Hampshire and Berkshire were ordered to Tyconderoga. The regular regiments of Massachusetts were not yet even entirely full; and the British had commenced hostilities with a force much superior to that employed by them in that quarter, the preceding year. A regiment of artillery, in addition to the one raised for the continental service, was ordered to be enlisted for the particular defence of the state; but liable, however, by direction of the General Court, to do duty in any part of the Continent. And upon an urgent request of the governor of Rhode Island, an additional number of the militia of Suffolk and Bristol were marched to Providence. At this period, there still remained a large body of the enemy at Newport, and several ships of war were in the waters in that vicinity; by which the people were kept in a constant state of alarm; and the principal force which could be had to oppose them was the militia of that state and of Massachusetts and Connecticut. Each of these, especially the two last, had several regiments of this description of troops employed in other places. General Spencer of Connecticut commanded on that station; and the great object was to defend the country and to prevent all attempts at further invasion. The British were too powerful, especially as they had command of the bay and river, to justify the Americans in an attack; though at a subsequent period, it was supposed they might have acted with more effect and with success, if the commander had been more resolute and energetic. It was important in the opinion of judicious individuals, that the enemy should be driven from their station on Rhode Island, and that an attempt should be made for that purpose. The General Court of Massachusetts sent a committee to Providence, to consult with the governor of Rhode Island, for such an expedition, as well as for the defence of that state; and they were authorised to promise 5000 men, in addition to 2000 already there from Massachusetts. But no plan was settled for the purpose at that time; though a considerable force was kept up through the season. The militia of Massachusetts, who had been on that station for two months and some even for a longer time, were relieved by 1500 others, early in June. And these again, after a short period, were permitted to return home, two regiments being raised for six months, to take their place. At this session of the legislature, a resolve was passed, requiring all the militia of the state to be equipped, and ready to march at the shortest notice.

CHAPTER VI.

General Court 1777 ... Expedition to Nova Scotia ... Constitution pre-
pared by General Court, and rejected by the people ... 4th of July
... Militia to reinforce northern army ... Secret expedition to Rhode
Island ... Bourgoyne checked and captured ... Affairs at the south ...
Capture of captain Manly.

WHEN the General Court was organized in
May, this year (1777) it assembled in Boston.
The representatives from that ancient town were
not so numerous as the preceding year; there
being only six returned, when for the former year
there were twelve. The members of the supreme
executive council, with the exception of a small
part, who declined a re-election, were the same
as the year before. A board of war was again
chosen, to attend to the pressing demands for
military stores; and committees appointed, for furnishing clothing and provisions for the great body
of troops, which the state had to support. They
were estimated at about 12,000, besides militia,
and those engaged on the sea coasts within its own
jurisdiction.

The state incurred considerable expense in the
month of June by projecting an expedition for the
defence and relief of the people of St. Johns and
other places on the bay of Fundy, who were friendly
to the United States and called for assistance, as
they were harassed and oppressed by the British

in Nova Scotia. The expedition was proposed with the consent of Congress; but it was prepared by the government and people of Massachusetts. A regiment was raised in Maine, and a naval force, such as was supposed would be necessary, was procured for the purpose. But unexpected difficulties arose in the prosecution of the plan; and after much delay, it was abandoned, in the form first intended. Some months after, however, a single company from Maine without exciting alarm in the British at Halifax, proceeded up to the head of the bay of Fundy, took a small fort there situated, and brought off several families, who were attached to the cause of American liberty, and obnoxious to the English government. It had long been meditated to afford assistance to the inhabitants of Nova Scotia, many of whom were supposed to be friendly to the rights of America. When general Washington was at Cambridge, and during the winter of 1776, it was represented to him, that an expedition to that province would afford relief to some well disposed citizens, and be of advantage to the other colonies. He sent two gentlemen at that time to learn the views and situation of the people in Nova Scotia. But they proceeded only to the lines of the province; and found it would be very hazardous to go further, as the British authority there was suspicious of all intercourse between the people of that province and Massachusetts. The Indians in that quarter manifested a friendly disposition. Some of them were taken into the pay of the state, and served with a battalion raised in the course of this year, for the defence of the settlements in the eastern part of Maine.

During the session in June, the House of Representatives and the Council formed themselves into a convention for the purpose of preparing a constitution, or frame of civil government for the state; and a committee of twelve was chosen to consider the important subject. The former General Court had advised the people to elect their next representatives for such an object. The majority of towns in the state, it would seem,* chose their representatives with this view, and gave, at least, an implied assent to this mode of forming a constitution; although Boston and several other towns were opposed to such a proceeding, and expressed an opinion, that a Convention ought to be called, to be composed of delegates for the express and sole purpose of preparing a form of civil government. This committee reported a draft of a constitution in January 1778, which the General Assembly submitted to the people; but which they did not approve.†

The fourth of July 1777, being the first anniversary of the declaration of the independence of the United States, was publicly celebrated in Boston, by order of the General Court, which was sitting at that time. A sermon was delivered by the chaplain before the representatives, councillors,

---

* It is presumed the representatives would not have proceeded to prepare a constitution, unless the greater part of the towns in the state had authorised the measure. No document can be found in the secretary's office, to determine how many towns voted for it. The committee was composed of the following gentlemen:—I. Powell, T. Cushing, D. Davis, I. Taylor, of the council; and J. Warren, R. T. Paine, A. Orne, J. Bliss, J. Prescott, J. Pickering, G. Partridge, J. Simpson, representatives.

† See Appendix.

and other public characters, military and civil.
There was also a military parade on the occasion,
a public dinner, and other demonstrations of gratitude and joy.

At this session, the legislature ordered specie, to
a considerable amount, to be sent to persons in
prison at New York, belonging to the state, whose
privations and sufferings were represented to be
very severe. It was forwarded to general Washington, with a request that he would send it into
New York by a flag of truce, and take suitable
precaution, that is should be safely delivered.

At this period, more of the militia were ordered
from Hampshire and Berkshire counties, to reinforce the northern army. And a few weeks subsequently, the enemy having taken Ticonderoga,
an additional number was required to proceed to
that quarter, not only from those two counties, but
from Worcester, Middlesex, York, and also from
Suffolk and Essex, except from Boston and the
regiments in Essex on the sea coast. This was an
urgent call; and every seventh man was ordered
to be marched off with the greatest dispatch.*
General Heath was specially desired by the House
of Representatives to ascertain what deficiencies
there were in the regular regiments ordered to be
raised by the state, and to use every effort to complete the battalions which were not already full.
Large sums were also appropriated for purchasing
provisions and clothes for the troops on the lake;
and for rendering the road passable through the

---

* In the address of the General Court to the people, on this
occasion, they said, " we rely upon that public virtue, and
that unbounded love of freedom and of their country, with
which the militia of this state have always been inspired."

the western part of the state, and over the green mountains in Vermont. In this month (August) a day was observed for fasting and praying, on account of the distresses of the people and the alarming prospects of the country.

The repeated successes of the British in the northern department, under general Bourgoyne, had justly excited great apprehensions, that he would make his way to Albany, unless soon checked by a strong reinforcement from the militia of the New England states. Should he succeed in such a plan, he would be joined, it was believed, by the British forces near New York, a part of which was then already endeavouring to ascend the Hudson, for the purpose of a junction with the troops under Bourgoyne. The southern and northern states thus separated, it would be comparatively easy to subdue them. No time, therefore, was to be lost, in preparing to prevent the execution of such a project. It was seen, that all possible effort was demanded to save the country, and to defeat the bold schemes of the enemy. Although there had then been a large portion of the militia of the state, not in service at Providence and on the sea coast, ordered to reinforce the army under general Gates, who had then recently been appointed to the command in that quarter, it was immediately resolved to send on an additional number; and one *half* the residue in all the western counties, (excepting the south part of Worcester, from which large drafts had then lately been made for Rhode Island,) and in Middlesex and Essex. In the absence of the continental troops from Boston, who had also been ordered to join the army under general Gates, several companies of the militia from Suffolk and Middlesex were called out to protect the capital, and to guard the military stores in that place, in Cambridge and Watertown.

An expedition was planned in September, by the General Assembly, with the knowledge and at the request of the governors of Rhode Island and Connecticut; the object of which, though not publicly known at the time, (for it was called a *secret* expedition,) was to make an attack upon the enemy at Newport, in the hope of forcing them to retire from that place. It was ordered that 3000 troops be raised, immediately, from Bristol, Plymouth and Barnstable, and the southern parts of Suffolk, Middlesex and Worcester. The state regiment of artillery, under colonel Crafts, was also to make a part of the detachment. Two brigadiers were to be in the command; and the whole of the Massachusetts militia to be under major general Hancock, who was then absent from Congress, and resident in Boston. General Spencer of Connecticut commanded the whole force. After great exertions, the most of the men called for were raised, and marched to Providence and vicinity. But the British troops on Rhode Island, at this period, were numerous, and no attack was made upon them. Much blame was attached to the brigadier generals, and to Spencer, the commander in chief, and there was probably some foundation for the complaints against them. But the expedition was projected at a time when there were great demands upon the state for troops to reinforce general Gates, and it was impossible, perhaps, to furnish a force sufficient to have justified a descent upon Rhode Island. It was of great service to the country, at that critical period, to have prevented the enemy on the Island, from extending their conquest to other places in the vicinity. There was a court of inquiry soon after; but both Spencer and Palmer, a brigadier of Massachusetts militia, who had been censured, were acquitted. There was evidence of some want of promptness on the part of Palmer; but it was excused, because of the difficulty of collecting the militia at the time appointed.

The affairs in the north, where the attention of the New England states was particularly directed, at this time, were now fast approaching to a crisis. Bourgoyne, who had been driving the American army before him for months, and capturing post after post, had penetrated so far into the country from Canada, that he could not retreat, without subjecting himself to disgrace, and his army to great loss, if not to total defeat. His hazardous situation was seen by the American general, and he meditated the capture of the conquering enemy. The militia were called for, and they marched with great spirit and dispatch. Those from New Hampshire and the grants, (afterwards Vermont,) were early assembled, and first taught the British regular troops, that the hardy yeomanry of the soil could oppose formidable obstacles to their progress. A detachment of the enemy, of about 1000 men, sent by general Bourgoyne to scour the country, to collect provisions, and to prepare for the reception of the whole British army, which, in the moment of success, was supposed could subdue the country, wherever it might choose to proceed, was attacked near Bennington by a party of the militia, under the brave and intrepid general

Stark, and totally defeated. He took 300 prisoners and two valuable field pieces, in the first attack. The enemy retreated, and were pursued by the Americans; and, though reinforced by 1000 fresh troops, Stark, with a small additional number who joined him, again gave them battle, and obliged them to retreat with great slaughter. Several other field pieces fell into the hands of the Americans, and upwards of 300 more of the British party were taken; making in the whole 650, besides nearly 300 killed and wounded. The total loss of the enemy was 930. This brilliant affair, while it convinced general Bourgoyne that the country would not be so easily subdued as he had imagined, gave great encouragement and confidence to the American troops.

The British army continued, indeed, to advance still further into the country, in the direction of Albany, in pursuance, probably, of an understanding with general Clinton, who was in the neighbourhood of New York, that he would pass up the Hudson and join Bourgoyne in that quarter. But the progress was slow, and every day's march manifested to the wary chief, the necessity of caution and circumspection. When he had advanced some distance south of lake Champlain, the Americans, under general Lincoln of Massachusetts, who had then lately joined the northern army,* made a diversion in his rear, and cut off all communication between the British camp and the fortresses which they had left. It remained now, that the British general must press forward, op-

---

* Lincoln was first selected by general Washington for this department, when Schuyler had the command there; "because of his great decision and energy of character."

posed as he was by a very powerful force under general Gates, or attempt to return to his forts on the lake, which would be almost equally hazardous. Leaving a number of men at fort Independence, on the southern border of the lake, Lincoln joined the main army under Gates, to act in concert against the enemy. On the 19th of September, a severe and almost general action took place between the two armies, near Saratoga. The advanced guards of the Americans were attacked by three regiments of the British, about a mile in front of their main body, when, after an obstinate resistance, the latter were obliged to retire with considerable loss. But they were soon reinforced, and resumed the attack. The advanced party of the continental troops received support from Arnold's division; and thus united, they were able to check the enemy, the greater part of whose whole force was soon brought into action, for the safety of the party first engaged. The Americans maintained their position, although not more than half the troops under general Gates was on the field. The loss of the British was reported to be about 1000, in killed, wounded and taken; and the Americans did not exceed 320.

Another attack took place on the 7th of October, by the right wing of the British attempting to take post on the right of the Americans. The scouts of the latter were driven in, and the former advanced rapidly. Three regiments of the Americans were ordered to receive them, who met them when they had approached within a mile of their lines. Each party pushed for an eminence, which was situated between them; and the Americans had the good fortune to gain it. The engagement continued through the afternoon without intermission. The enemy soon fell back, and were closely pursued a distance of nearly two miles. The continental troops entered one of the British entrenchments sword in hand. The evening being very dark, they could not with prudence attack any other posts. They halted for the night within half a mile of the main body of the enemy. Bourgoyne moved off silently during the night to a distant position, which was more strongly fortified. On the following day, there were frequent skirmishes, between the advanced parties of the two hostile armies; many were wounded on both sides, and some of the British were made prisoners. In reconnoitering the enemy's movements, general Lincoln was wounded in the leg; which obliged him to retire from the public service for several months. It was supposed he must have submitted to the amputation of his limb; but he recovered without so great a loss; and soon after joined the continental army in the southern department.

Among the many American officers who were distinguished in these several engagements, were colonel Brooks of Massachusetts and major Dearborn of New Hampshire. On the 19th of September and the 7th of October, they conducted with great spirit and bravery: and Brooks was the last who left the ground on the evening of the 19th after the enemy retired. Colonel Colburn of the Massachusetts line, who was killed in the battle of that day, was much lamented. Colonel Francis, a highly meritorious officer of the Massachusetts line, was killed at an earlier period of this campaign. He had command of the rear of the American troops on the retreat from Tyconderago in August, when St. Clair was general in chief in that quarter. He was overpowered by a superior force of the pursuing enemies; and received a mortal wound, while bravely attempting to protect his men from their avenging arm. The British lost many officers of high rank and great merit. General Frazer, who was killed on the occasion, was considered one of the first military characters in their army. And he was also beloved for his accomplishments and virtues as a man.

General Bourgoyne, receiving no reinforcements, and surrounded by a numerous army, found himself obliged on the 19*th* of October to surrender his troops as prisoners of war to the Americans. They were marched to the vicinity of Boston; and barracks were provided for their reception, on Prospect and Winter Hills. The greater part of the continental army, after the capture of Bourgoyne, was ordered from Saratoga to join general Washington near Philadelphia; and soon after went into winter quarters at Valley Forge.

General Stark of New Hampshire, who commanded the militia in the brilliant affair of Bennington, presented to the legislature of Massachusetts several military articles taken from the British on that occasion. A letter of thanks was written to general Stark by order of the assembly; and it was voted " that the trophies should be preserved in the archieves of the state." They have a conspicuous place in the spacious room occupied by the Senate.*

* A present was ordered by the legislature to general Stark, of a suit of clothes and a piece of linen. At the present time, it may appear an insignificant gift; but it should

The greatest portion of the British troops in America were, during this year, in the vicinity of New York, in New Jersey and on the Delaware near Philadelphia, under general Howe, the commander in chief of all the English forces on the continent.* To watch his motions, and to protect that part of the country from depredations, was the arduous and responsible duty of general Washington. He had not a sufficient force, at any time, to justify him in seeking a general engagement with the British; and one unfortunate battle, on his part, would have put the country in imminent danger of an entire and speedy conquest, by the enemy. In his situation, it was the dictate of patriotism as well as of prudence, to act chiefly on the defensive. Yet there were occasions, when Washington thought it necessary, as in the affairs of Trenton and Princeton the preceding year, to engage in more decisive operations. Towards the close of August, lord Howe landed a large force from New York, near the mouth of Elk river, of about 25,000. General Washington marched from the vicinity of Philadelphia where he then was, to Wilmington, a few miles from the position which the enemy occupied. Congress called upon the militia of Pennsylvania and New Jersey, who collected under generals Cadwallader and Dickinson; and general Sullivan with his division was

rather be considered as proof of their poverty, than as want of gratitude or of a just appreciation of his great merits.

* The whole number of British troops in America, before the capture of Bourgoyne, was estimated at 50,000. From the beginning of 1775 to October 1777, inclusive, their loss was said to be as follows, 9,000 killed 11,000 wounded, 10,000, prisoners; making about 30,000 in the whole.

directed to join the main army under Washington. The British approached the Americans within two miles; but soon filed off, with a view to possess themselves of a fort on the heights of Brandywine. Washington, aware of their intention, detached general lord Sterling with a division to anticipate them. The following morning, September 11*th*, a general action commenced, which continued, with different degrees of intenseness through the day. The British were greatly superior to the Americans in number. But through the skill and activity of general Washington, and the gallantry of the officers and men under his command, the Americans maintained their position during the whole day; and in the night, retired in good order, without being pursued by the enemy. General Washington had almost 1000 men killed and wounded; and the loss of the British was reported to be double that number. The marquis de Lafayette, a French nobleman of great merit, who had a short time before joined the American army, and was acting as a volunteer, received a severe wound in this action. Captain Bryant, a brave officer in the Massachusetts line, from Boston, was slain in this battle : and in November, a captain Treat of Boston was killed in the attack upon Fort Mifflin on Mud Island, who was highly esteemed for his intrepidity and courage. On the fourth of October another action took place between the continental troops and general Howe, at Germantown, within eight miles of Philadelphia. The enemy were then stationed in that city, of which they took possession a few days after the affair at Brandywine. The British general, having detached a part of his troops, with a view to reduce some posts on the Delaware possessed by the Americans, general Washington, with advice of his officers concluded to make an attack upon the British force stationed at Germantown. In the first attack, the Americans were successful; but the morning was very foggy, and the plans of Washington were interrupted; so that the result was not such as was promised by the good fortune of the morning. Two separate divisions of the continental troops mistook each other for the enemy, which was the occasion of much embarrassment and misfortune. The British gained nothing in this affair; and the Americans lost neither reputation nor stores. Their loss of men was not great, though several brave officers fell in the battle; among whom was brigadier general Nash of Carolina. Sullivan and Greene distinguished themselves on this occasion; and were particularly applauded by the commander in chief, who was in the field through the whole engagement.

In the summer of 1777, captain Manly in the Hancock, a public ship of thirty two guns, was taken by a British forty gun ship, commanded by sir George Collier. A few days before this unfortunate affair, Manly captured a sloop of war of twenty eight guns. He was exchanged the next year, and appointed to the command of a larger frigate.

CHAPTER VII.

AFTER a short recess the first of November, (1777) the General Court met in the latter part of that month and found several important subjects demanded attention. Congress had then recently recommended to the states to raise by tax, five millions of dollars; and the amount required of Massachusetts was 820,000, a quarter more than any other state. The legislature, soon after, resolved to raise 75,000*l.* immediately by loans, and laid a tax also of 240,000*l.* Massachusetts was, at this time, much in advance to the United States, and appointed agents to request an adjustment of its claims. The period, for which the militia at Rhode Island and the companies on the sea coast had engaged was about to expire; and it became necessary to provide for the enlistment of others to supply their places. It was accordingly ordered, that two regiments be raised for a year, to serve in Rhode Island or in any of the New England states. Some of the militia were also called out for the defence of the sea coast, at the same places as had been guarded the year past; but in some towns, a less number was provided. Detachments were ordered, likewise, on the request of general Heath, still commanding on the Boston station, from the militia nearest to the metropolis, amounting to about a regiment in the whole, to serve as guards for the public stores, and for the defence of that place and harbour. The court loaned general Heath, at this time, $30,000, for the continental service: and to do this, they were obliged to borrow it of individuals.

In February 1778, a committee was sent by the legislature of Massachusetts to confer with general Washington upon the expediency of raising more men than the quota before required, and to consult him as to the time, for which it would be necessary to engage them. This committee were particularly instructed "to assure him that this state, in testimony of their peculiar affection and respect for him, which he had so highly merited by his incessant and unwearied exertions in behalf of the country, as well as from what they owe to the common cause, will cheerfully co-operate with him, as far their ability will admit, in endeavours to expel the enemy, and to free America from thraldom and slavery." Soon after, the assembly voted to furnish, gratis, a full suit of clothes to every soldier from Massachusetts in the continental army. The field and other officers who had been some time in the service, and engaged still to continue, had an additional sum granted them; the former 150 dollars, and the latter 120. Many of the officers had then recently resigned their commissions and returned to their families; which were in such destitute circumstances, as to induce even those who were truly patriotic to return home.

Soon after the return of the committee from their visit to general Washington, the legislature of Massachusetts issued fresh orders to those towns which were still delinquent in raising their respective quotas of men for the three years' service, and subjected such as did not immediately comply, to a heavy fine; and the attorney-general was directed to prosecute them. As it was difficult to prevail on men to engage for so long a period, it was resolved by the General Court, a few weeks after, to raise 2000 men for eight or nine months, to fill up their sixteen regiments in the continental establishment. For this purpose, a particular number was required of each town in the state; and committees were also appointed in every county to hasten the enlistment, and to send on the men to the army under general Washington. All those towns which should have their respective numbers raised by the first of May, were promised a bounty. The board of war in Massachusetts was also required to furnish arms, and such other accoutrements as should be necessary for their equipment. The same week that this order issued, the Assembly resolved to raise 1500; 1300 of which were to be stationed on the northern frontier, for eight months, and 200 for the defence of Rhode Island. These men were called out by particular and urgent request of Congress. The force of the enemy was still great at that place; and it was thought necessary to keep a number of troops in that quarter, to prevent their predatory incursions into the surrounding country.

To animate the people to patriotic exertions at

this critical period, when the country was as much exposed as in any former season, and when extraordinary efforts were necessary to justify any hope of success, addresses were prepared and published by Congress, and by the legislatures of several of the States, as well as by many individuals, who were deeply impressed with the danger which impended. Language such as this was used:—" Act like yourselves. Arouse at the call of Washington and of your country, and you will soon be crowned with glory, independence, and peace. Present ease and interest we must part with for a time; and let us rejoice at the sacrifice."—" What words can paint the solid joys, the delightful recollections, which will fill the patriotic mind hereafter. He who wishes for permanent happiness, let him now put forth all his strength for the immediate salvation of his country, and he shall reap immortal pleasure and renown. It is good for us to anticipate the joy that will fill our minds, when we shall receive the reward of our labours; when we shall see our country flourish in peace; when grateful millions shall hail us the protectors of our country, and an approving conscience shall light up eternal sunshine in our souls."—" Considering the noble ardour which has been heretofore manifested in the common cause, we feel confident that the virtuous yeomanry will take particular pleasure in complying with the call of Washington and of Congress. It is hoped that the ensuing campaign will make the enemy repent their execrable purpose of enslaving a free people. For the sake of liberty, let not our expectations be disappointed for want of men and means, which we are still able to furnish. We are convinced you will exert yourselves. Your country calls : and to the call of your country you were never deaf."

The authority of Congress had hitherto been only advisory, though the legislatures of the several States had such confidence in the wisdom and patriotism of that respectable body, as almost invariably to comply with its requisitions. The importance of a general and consistent course of policy for the whole country was, indeed, very evident to every intelligent citizen; and the advice of Congress was accordingly received with a regard, little less than could be given to the most perfect authority. This was particularly the case for the two first years of the revolutionary war. But difficulties arose in this unsettled state of the powers of Congress ; and the country suffered from its want of authority to enforce obedience to orders calculated for the common welfare. In December, 1777, a plan was proposed by that body, " of confederation and perpetual union between the thirteen United States," embracing a number of articles, defining the power to be exercised in future by the delegates from the several States, in Congress assembled. These articles were submitted to the legislatures of the respective States in the Union. Boston, and some other towns in Massachusetts, expressed an opinion in favour of the adoption of this plan of confederation. The General Assembly, at a session in the following year, declared its approbation of the articles submitted by Congress, and authorized their delegates to ratify them on the part of the State. Maryland did not consent to the plan till 1781.

In February, 1778, the Hon. John Adams was appointed by Congress an envoy to the court of

Versailles; and soon after embarked at Boston in a continental frigate, which was prepared to convey him to France. Mr. Adams remained sometime at Paris, and afterwards resided in Holland, as minister to the United Provinces. He was an able negociator, and rendered essential services to his country while in Europe. The delegates to Congress from Massachusetts for this year, were Samuel Adams, Elbridge Gerry, Francis Dana, James Lovell, and Samuel Holten. William Cushing, Foster, Sargeant, Sullivan, and Sewal were Justices of the Superior Court of Judicature at this time, and R. T. Paine, attorney-general of the State. The General Court was prorogued, early in March, to the month of April; and it was ordered then to be convened in the town of Roxbury.* The small-pox was then raging in Boston: many of the representatives were alarmed on this account, and a vote was therefore passed for meeting at the former place. Before the adjournment, power was given to the Council to provide for the defence of the State, should the exigency demand any particular expense. They were also authorized to call out the militia, to any number, not exceeding 3000, should they be required by general Washington. He did not call for any; but two large detachments were ordered to be enlisted soon after, during the months of April and May.

The committee of the General Court reported

---

* When the General Court was in session in April, their chaplain, Rev. Dr. Gordon, was dismissed, for some free remarks written by him, and published in the newspapers, in in which the court was charged with *intrigue*, in their conduct respecting the newly proposed constitution. Gordon was a zealous whig, and an active politician. He was the author of the history of the American war.

a draft of a Constitution, in December, 1777, but it was not considered by the whole Court till February following; it was then approved by the legislature, and in March, ordered to be submitted to the people. Two thirds of the votes given in were to decide in favour of its adoption: all free males of the age of twenty-one were allowed to vote; and for any alteration, it required two thirds of the inhabitants. It did not receive the approbation of the citizens;* and a very general opinion prevailed, that a convention should be called, consisting of persons to be chosen for that particular purpose.† There were many objections to the constitution prepared by the General Court. That it contained no declaration of rights which belonged naturally to the people, was considered an essential defect. The principle of representation was said to be unequal, because the smallest towns were allowed to have one deputy; and others, if not containing more than 300 polls, to be confined to that number. But a rule not very different from this was admitted in the Constitution afterwards adopted. The governor and lieutenant-governor were to be members of the Senate; the former to preside over the deliberations of that body. The senate was to consist of twenty-eight members; Suffolk, Essex, and Middlesex were to elect ten; Plymouth, Bristol, Barnstable, &c., six;

* There were 10,000 votes against it, and only 2000 for it: and 120 towns made no returns.

† The citizens of Boston voted unanimously against this constitution. They were also for a convention for the sole purpose of preparing a new one: and they were further of opinion, that a thing of so much importance should not be hastily decided, but be postponed to a period of more tranquillity.

Worcester, Hampshire, and Berkshire, eight; York and Cumberland, three; and Lincoln, one. The Judges, Secretary, and Treasurer, to be chosen annually, by the General Court; and other officers, civil and military, by the governor and senate. The Protestant religion to be professed by all officers and legislators; but full toleration to be enjoyed by all religious denominations. The powers and duties of the legislators and of rulers, it was also objected, were not accurately defined.*

The British troops evacuated Philadelphia in June, after having been in possession of that city for six months, and began their march through New Jersey, for New York. General Washington immediately resolved to pursue them, and if a favourable occasion should present, to attack the rear of the army. The march of the enemy was unusually rapid, for they had the precaution to send on most of their heavy baggage before they left Philadelphia. By great efforts, however, an advanced party of the American troops came up with a division of the British, near Monmouth court house, and immediately attacked them. In the mean time, other troops, detached for the purpose by Washington, arrived, and the action soon became very general between the two armies. The judicious plans of the commander in chief were defeated, through the criminal neglect or the mistaken judgment of general Lee, who had been early sent on to take command of the advanced troops. A great portion of the men engaged in this battle were from Massachusetts. General Knox, who commanded the artillery, received the particular approbation of Washington.

* The constitution prepared in 1778, and rejected by the majority of the people, is printed at the close of this volume.

General Wayne, of Pennsylvania, greatly distinguished himself in this affair. The enemy suffered severe loss. The killed, wounded, and missing, were upwards of 2,000; while those of the Americans did not exceed 350; many of whom perished through fatigue, on account of the intense heat of the weather.

A large British force remaining at Newport through the spring and summer of 1778, and their fleet having command of the waters in the neighbourhood, the people of Massachusetts, especially in the southern parts of it, bordering on the State of Rhode Island, were kept in continual alarm; and the General Court had a great duty to perform in furnishing men for the protection of that part of the country. There were but few continental troops on that station, and the militia were in service there, in greater or less numbers, for the whole of this, as they had been most of the preceding year. The enemy landed about 600 men, in the month of May, at the town of Warren in that State, and burnt vessels, dwelling houses, and public buildings, insulted and abused the inhabitants, and took away much personal property. Colonel Barton, of that State, was ordered by General Sullivan, then in command at Providence, to meet them. Before he reached the place, the British were retreating; but he pursued them, and did them much injury before they reached their boats. A considerable number of the enemy were killed and wounded in this affair. During the same month, they landed at the southerly part of Freetown, at a place called Fall river, and burnt a mill, and some other buildings; but the militia soon collected, and obliged them to take to their boats, and retire.

General Bourgoyne had left Prospect hill, and major general Phillips was the first officer of the British troops then prisoners of war, quartered at that place. He was represented as a conceited and irritable character, and seemed to suppose that he and his troops, though captives, might commit any irregularities with impunity.* One of his officers, returning from Boston, in the month of

* The moment general Phillips heard of this unfortunate event, he wrote general Heath the following note—

CAMBRIDGE, JUNE 17, 1778.

"Murder and death have at length taken place; an officer riding out from the barracks on Prospect hill, has been shot by an American sentinel. I leave the horrors of that bloody disposition, which has joined itself to rebellion in these colonies, to the feelings of all Europe. I do not ask for justice; for I believe *every principle of it has fled from* this province. I *demand* liberty to send an officer to general sir Henry Clinton, by way of the head quarters of general Washington.

WM. PHILLIPS, major general."

General Heath had previously written to general Phillips, on hearing the unhappy affair; but Phillips had not received it, when he wrote his note. If he had, perhaps he would have used different language. Heath's letter is here given—

HEAD QUARTERS, BOSTON, JUNE 17, 1778, 8 o'clock P. M.

"Sir,—I am this moment informed that an officer of the convention has been shot by one of our sentries. I have ordered the man into close confinement, and have directed the town major to desire the coroner of the county of Middlesex to summon a jury of inquest to sit on the body; and I desire that it may not be moved until that step be taken. I can only say, that you may be assured, I will take every measure in my power, which honour and justice require.

I am, Sir, &c.

W. HEATH."

General Heath answered the note of Phillips in a very spirited manner, and ordered him to be kept within very narrow limits.

June, to the British barracks, in company with two females, was hailed by the sentinel; and refusing to answer, though the call was repeated, was shot dead on the spot. Phillips and his officers were greatly enraged; and pretended it was barbarous conduct, and not less criminal than murder. He *demanded* of general Heath, who had command of the continental troops employed as guards of the British prisoners, that the sentinel be immediately punished as a murderer. He also *demanded* a messenger to convey a note of complaint on the subject to general Clinton at New York. But neither of his demands was granted. And the proud British officer had to submit to this neglect of his requests; and to resign himself to a decision, which the impartial considered fully justified by the circumstances of the case.

In the month of August, the plan was renewed of preparing a powerful force against the enemy at Newport; and if possible, to dispossess them of that place, where they were giving constant alarm to all the New England states. General Sullivan, with a considerable number of continental troops, was now on that station; but it was believed that the aid of the militia, to a large amount, was necessary to give any hope of success to the undertaking. There were already some of the militia of Massachusetts doing service in that quarter. But others were ordered out, and several volunteer companies marched there, at this period, from Boston, Salem, Beverly, Gloucester, Newburyport, and some from towns in the province of Maine. The whole constituted a respectable force. But the British were equally numerous, being estimated at 7 or 8000; and they were strongly fortified in the town of Newport. A large French fleet, then recently arrived on the American coast at the south, directed their course for Rhode Island. The plan was for the Americans to attack the British at Newport, whenever the French fleet should arrive to co-operate with them. The Americans passed over to the island, and advanced by degrees, to a short distance from Newport, and began to throw up fortifications for defence. In this situation they remained several days, waiting the return of the French fleet, which had gone out to look after a large squadron of the enemy, then recently sailed from New York, with the intention of relieving the detachment at Newport. The French fleet encountered a severe storm, at a little distance from Newport, in which they received much damage; and a part of them had a short engagement with the fleet of the enemy.*

The British made an assault upon the American troops, who were posted at their entrenchments, then lately thrown up in the neighbourhood of Newport; and were received with great spirit and bravery. They were engaged the most of the day; and many men were lost on each side. The Americans maintained their ground, but had little reason to boast. A few days after, the enemy received reinforcements from New York; and general Sullivan, by advice of a council of war, concluded to leave the island. The retreat was conducted with great order, and without any loss on the part of the American troops. This was just matter of satisfaction, as the British forces

---

* When it was known that the French would not aid in this expedition, most of the volunteers, and a part of the militia, left the island.

were then greatly superior, and they also had a large fleet in the harbour and vicinity of Newport. And yet the issue was not such as had been, at one period, confidently anticipated. Great hope had been indulged from the assistance of the French. The want of success in this expedition was the more mortifying, as it was the third attempt made, within eighteen months, to drive the British from this part of New England.

The Massachusetts militia were commanded on this occasion by major general Hancock, who happened to be on a visit to Boston, during a recess of Congress. He readily undertook this expedition, which engaged the particular attention of the General Court, and of the individual citizens of all classes. General Greene and the Marquis de la Fayette also joined this expedition as volunteers, a short time before the Americans returned from Rhode Island; and rendered great service in conducting the retreat of the troops under general Sullivan. General Lovell, who had the immediate command of the militia from Massachusetts in the action, and his officers and men behaved with great intrepidity. Colonel H. Jackson commanded a regiment of infantry, and colonel Crane of artillery, both of Massachusetts; and received the particular approbation of general Sullivan for their activity and courage. About two hundred men were killed and wounded in this engagement; among the latter was one field officer; and of the former, two lieutenants belonging to Boston and in Jackson's regiment.

The French fleet repaired to the harbour of Boston, after the disasters of the storm, where they remained some time to refit and to obtain

provisions. They sailed for the West Indies in the
month of November. La Fayette visited the capital of Massachusetts, for the purpose of confer-
ring with the French admiral.* He had then been
in America about eighteen months; and the zeal,
which he manifested, at the first moment he declared himself friendly to the cause of American
liberty, had not abated. Having for some months
served as a volunteer and without any commission,
he was afterwards appointed a major general by
Congress; and enjoyed in a peculiar degree the
confidence and esteem of Washington. He was
extremely anxious that the French admiral should
afford all possible aid to the Americans; and his
short visit to Boston, at this time, was to prevail on
count D'Estaing, to return to Newport immediately, and to remain on the coasts of the United States
for the purpose of co-operating with the army
under general Washington against the British; and
not to depart to the West Indies, where he meditated passing the winter. It was also believed
that the marquis had great influence in persuading
the French court to form a treaty with the United
States, and to send out a formidable fleet for their
assistance. Soon after this period, the marquis
again visited Boston and took passage for France.
"Congress had given him leave to visit his family,"
as he was pleased to call it: for though he could
have visited France at his own pleasure, he chose
to ask the consent of Congress and of Washington,

* He was in Boston but a single day, at this time; he hastened back to Rhode Island with the greatest speed, and arrived in season to assist in conducting the retreat of the American troops.

and to obtain a furlough for the purpose, being desirous of retaining his commission and rank in the American army.*

The French fleet had not been in the harbour of Boston many days, before the British squadron appeared in the bay, within Cape Cod, and it was believed that they meditated an attack upon the ships under command of count D'Estaing. This caused great alarm to the people in the vicinity; and nine regiments of militia were marched into the capital. They were soon discharged, as the British fleet disappeared from the coast without making any attack upon the French. Several of the enemy's ships sailed from Newport harbour, the first of September, and landed a number of troops at Bedford village in Dartmouth. They did much injury to the town, by burning the vessels lying at the wharves, about seventy in number, and the greater part of the houses in the settlement. The troops marched up the country, near the river, four or five miles; and returning on the opposite side, embarked before the inhabitants were able to collect in sufficient force to oppose

* After a period of forty-six years, this highly distinguished person, who in his youth devoted himself, with a singular ardour and disinterestedness, to the cause of America, and who in his native country had made great exertions and sacrifices in the cause of liberty, visited the United States. In August 1824, he landed at New York, where he was received with every mark of respect and affection; thence he visited Boston and other large towns and cities through the nation; in all which he was greeted with a joy and enthusiasm, which no individual but Washington ever received in this country. Every one bid him welcome with most lively gratitude; and public functionaries united in presenting their tribute of esteem and admiration, such as the most celebrated heroes of antiquity could scarcely boast.

them. From Dartmouth the enemy proceeded to Martha's Vineyard, and made a requisition upon the inhabitants of fire arms, money, cattle and sheep; and of the latter, they took off nearly ten thousand.

In November, a party of continental troops of about two hundred and fifty, under command of colonel Alden of Massachusetts, were suddenly attacked by about seven hundred British soldiers, royalists and Indians, at Cherry Valley, seventy miles west of Albany; and the a greater number were killed or taken.* They had been stationed in that place for the protection of the inhabitants in that thinly settled country, who were exposed to incursions from the Iudians and Canadian royalists. They had erected a fort, and given it the name of their commander. Colonel Alden had some intimation of the approach of the savage enemy the evening before, and placed sentinels at the two only roads by which it was supposed they could come, to give the alarm. But they approached by an old Indian path, not generally known or travelled. The fort was surprised at an early hour in the morning. The colonel and some other officers were at their lodgings in a house, a very short distance from the fort. When the alarm was given, colonel Alden directed the others immediately to repair to the fort; he delayed only a moment to throw his clothes about him, but in following them was shot down and scalped. The fort was defended by the brave major Whiting of Dedham and adjutant Hickling of Boston, who were the chief in command, after the death of

---

* Thirty were killed, and forty taken prisoners.

their colonel and the capture of lieutenant colonel Tracey. A party of militia arrived for their support, towards the close of the day. The officers and men who were taken were treated with great indignity and cruelty. Many of the inhabitants were taken and carried off by the Indians; and those who escaped, were left destitute of shelter and of support. Their humble dwellings were burnt, and their property taken or destroyed. The settlement contained about two hundred inhabitants. Colonel Alden was an intelligent and brave officer: and commanded the 7th regular Massachusetts regiment. He was a lieutenant colonel of a regiment of minute men, raised in Plymouth county early in 1775, and marched to Roxbury, on the alarm of the 19th of April.

In the summer of 1778, three British commissioners arrived at New York, especially authorised by their government to make propositions for a suspension of hostilities, with an ultimate view to reconciliation and peace with America. They addressed Congress on the subject; but they were also instructed to treat with any individual state. It was considered an artful plan to gain time to reinforce their army, to detach the United States from all connexion with France, with whom they had then recently made a treaty; or, if possible, to distract and divide the councils of America. For they believed that some of the people in the country were wearied with the expense and trouble of war, and would be ready to return to their allegiance to the crown of England, upon a probability of pardon. Congress rejected these offers. They disapproved the terms proposed; for they had little faith in the mere promises of the ministers; and they were now determined to insist upon independence. The people and their representatives in the several states applauded the firmness of Congress. They were not disposed to give up their rights to self government, or to throw themselves upon the clemency of the king and his ministers, who would grant such favours merely as it might seem fitting to their views of government to allow.

The conduct of the British ministers, in sending commissioners to America with such propositions as they were directed to make, was not less censured by many statesmen in England, when they learned what terms had been proposed, than they were by Congress. A noble lord in the House of peers, speaking of the proclamation issued by the commissioners, when they found their proposals were rejected, which threatened future vengeance to the Americans, said, "it was a proclamation contrary to humanity, to christianity and to every idea of virtuous policy." A reverend bishop observed, "he saw in the account of extraordinaries, that charges were made for the *tomahawk* and *scalping knife;* and that he supposed, from the proclamation, such expense would be continued. It is our duty," he added, "to soften the horrors of war and to act as christians." Lord Camden said "the proclamation held forth a war of revenge, such as Moloch in Pandemonium advised; that it would fix an inveterate hatred in the people of America against the very name of Englishmen, which would be left as a legacy from father to son to the latest posterity." He said "they should consider that they were christians, and that their enemies were the same." In the House of

Commons, Mr. Burke asked—" against whom are these dreadful menaces pronounced? Not against the guilty; but against those, who, conscious of rectitude, have acted to the best of their ability in a good cause, and stood up to fight for freedom and their country."

Major general Gates arrived at Boston in November 1778, to take command on that station. There was great reason to apprehend an attack from the enemy, at the time, upon some part of the state. He remained at Boston and Providence through the winter; and when he left Massachusetts in April 1779, he publicly expressed his approbation of the conduct of the people and of the legislature; and particularly eulogised the battalion of state troops, at one time commanded by colonel Crafts, but then under command of lieutenant colonel Revere.

CHAPTER VIII.

At the session of the General Court in October, 1778, an act was passed, forbidding certain individuals, formerly citizens of the state, who had left the state and joined the enemy, to return; and requiring them, if they came into the state, immediately to depart out of the country; and making it a capital crime, if they should presume, a second time, to come within their jurisdiction, unless special permission was first obtained. There were nearly three hundred persons named in this prohibitory statute. There were, however, some among them, who had never taken an active part against the country; and were not, therefore, really deserving the severe punishment which others justly merited. Some of those named in the act had leave afterwards to return into the state, and to remain. But the greater part never discovered a disposition to return; and they had proved themselves too decidedly hostile to the liberties of the country, to be indulged with the privilege, had they desired it.

In January 1779, Congress called upon the several states to raise $15,000,000. The sum apportioned to Massachusetts was $2,000,000; and the amount was to be passed to the credit of the United States, to be accounted for on an adjustment between the state and the continent at a future day. The sum required of Massachusetts was to be expended by the state, but for the purposes of general concern and utility.

The complaints of the people in most of the states had become so loud and so general, on account of the prevalence of extortion and monopoly, that in January 1779, Congress was led to inquire, whether it were not practicable to provide a preventive. They were of opinion that *regulating* statutes were necessary; and divided the thirteen states into two districts; advising that a convention in each be holden, to fix and regulate the prices of the common articles of living.* A convention of delegates from the northern district was held at New Haven, who formed a plan for regulating prices, and preventing extortion. The plan was adopted and carried into effect by most of the states composing the district. It was approved also by the legislature of Massachusetts, and a law passed on the subject; but there were many of her citizens, who considered it their interest to disregard the law; and there was remissness

* Some gentlemen in Congress, however, were of opinion that trade should be left to regulate itself. Many citizens of Massachusetts entertained similar sentiments.

in the officers, whose duty it was to see it observed, which favoured the violations of a salutary law with impunity.* The General Assembly, however, were very desirous to prevent the evil, and to save the poorer classes of people from oppression. They directed the law to be published, and to be read at the annual town meetings.

Another subject engaged the attention of the General Assembly at their session in January, which related to the support and comfort of the people. The preceding season had been uncommonly dry; which, together with a severe blight of the grain, cut off nearly one half of the usual crops. A great number of men, usually employed in cultivating the soil, was engaged in the military service through the spring and summer. This, also, had served to lessen the customary fruits of harvest : and several thousand prisoners, taken with Bourgoyne had been kept in the state. The scarcity was such as to give great alarm. Added to all other difficulties, there was an embargo laid on all vessels bound from one state to another. The General Court addressed letters to Connecticut, New Jersey, and New York, requesting flour and grain for the inhabitants. They voted $200,000,† and appointed a committee to visit those states to procure provisions. They also requested Congress to grant permission for trans-

* Nothing but a strict regard to facts could make it necessary to notice the above. As a state, Massachusetts was most patriotic, and made great exertions for the public welfare. But there were some, who sought their own without regard to the general interest. " The *Recusants* prevented the execution of the law."

† The paper had then greatly depreciated.

porting flour and corn from the southern states. The towns, particularly those on the sea coast, which suffered most severely for the want of grain, were furnished from the public stock purchased by the state, and in such proportions as their several necessities demanded.

Such was still the situation of the state and of the country, that great exertions were requisite on the part of the General Court to provide for the protection of the one, and to furnish its proportion of aid for the defence of the other. In February, a resolve was passed, as in the two preceding years, providing for men to be stationed at the towns on the sea coasts, liable to be approached by the enemy's ships; with the addition of Falmouth in the county of Barnstable, which had suffered from their depredations. Clothing was furnished for the soldiers composing the seventeen regiments of the Massachusetts line. Their families were provided for, by the selectmen of towns in which they resided, by virtue of particular orders of the legislature. To the officers on the continental establishment, large sums were also paid, or advanced on the credit of the United States; 300*l.* to the field officers; and to captains and others, 200*l.* The treasury of the state did not indeed permit of the immediate payment of the whole sum: and a part was to be paid in three and six months. The assembly wrote to their delegates in Congress, and also to the president, to be laid before that body, informing them of their proceedings to quiet the minds of the soldiers, and praying them to provide some remedy for the evils of depreciation on the public paper, and to do justice to those who were engaged in the military service of the country. The soldiers received wages from the continent; but the bills in which they were paid were so greatly depreciated below the nominal value, that they received not, in fact, one tenth or one twentieth of the amount promised; and the state of Massachusetts had engaged to them a *bonafide* compensation. The state omitted no possible means of doing justice to the officers and soldiers in the regiments it had raised; but still these brave men and their families suffered extremely, by devoting a long period to the public service. The wants of their families obliged them to part with their notes from the continent and from the state, for the tenth part of the amount due them; and individuals, who were never exposed to danger or losses, eventually received the fruit of their toils.

In February, the legislature was requested by general Gates, then commanding, on the Boston station, to call out the militia to assist in fortifying the harbour, and to collect stores and provisions. As a reason for his request, general Gates stated that he feared an attack from the British. The legislature addressed Congress on the subject, desiring their advice, and soliciting aid from the continental army, if the enemy should invade the state. They had then but recently raised 400 of the militia to serve as a guard at Boston and neighbourhood, in addition to the state battalion which had been sometime in service; and had required a detachment from Plymouth and Bristol counties to be ready to march for the defence of Rhode Island, at the shortest notice from the commanding officer in that state.

The General Court adjourned for a few weeks.

the last of February, after giving authority to the council to call out the militia and provide military stores, if the public welfare should require it; and assembled again the first of April, when they had a request from general Washington to furnish an additional number of men to reinforce the continental army. His inquiry at this time was how many they could enlist for the campaign, instead of requesting a particular number, as he had usually done. It was voted, after some discussion, that 2,000 could be raised in the state, if the public service should require it, in addition to those already in the continental army, those at Rhode Island, and those at Boston and other towns on the sea coasts. Soon after, it was ordered, that 1500 be raised, for nine months, to fill up the Massachusetts regiments, which at that time were not complete. These were enlisted, in June and July, by calling upon the several towns through the state to furnish their respective quotas* and by offering a large sum as a bounty.† Shortly after, 500 militia were ordered to Rhode Island; and a regiment of light infantry was raised for one year to serve in Massachusetts or in any state in New England. A large quantity of military stores was conveyed from Boston and vicinity to Springfield, in April; to be deposited in the arsenal which had then been just established in that place; and one hundred teams were employed in transporting them.

* Those towns which furnished the number required by the first of June, were allowed £120.

† By a law of Congress, these men have received the same pension, for several years, as those who engaged at an earlier day for the whole term of the war, and had no bounty.

In February 1779, the General Court again proposed to the people to form a constitution of civil government, by recommending to them to express their opinion on the subject and to make return to the legislature in June following. The proposition was, that, if the majority of the votes given in and returned to the court in June was in favour of the measure, precepts were to be issued for the people to choose delegates for the convention, to meet in September then next : and such persons were to vote on the subject as were entitled to elect representatives. By the returns made in June, it appeared that a majority of votes given were in favour of having a convention; but there was nearly one third of the towns in the state that did not vote or which neglected to return them. Precepts were accordingly issued by the General Court in June, to all the towns for the choice of delegates to meet at Cambridge in September. They met at the day appointed, and chose Hon. James Bowdoin for their president. A large committee was appointed to prepare a draft for a constitution; and after a session of several weeks, the convention was adjourned, to meet again in January 1780.

In June, the legislature called out 800 of the militia for six months, for the defence of Rhode Island, agreeably to an agreement made sometime before at Springfield, with committees from the other New England states. The British still had a considerable force at Newport; and at this particular time. there was again an apprehension of their intending to invade the neighbouring country.

Congress resolved to raise forty-five millions of dollars; to be paid, however, in bills which they had previously emitted, and which had become greatly depreciated below the nominal value: and of this Massachusetts was to pay six millions. The General Court soon after requested and obtained a loan of Congress, for 800,000*l.*, on condition of repaying 500,000 into the continental loan office, then established in Boston, within three months. But so great were the demands upon the treasury of the state during the summer, partly owing to the expense of the expedition to Penobscot, that the sum of 300,000 was retained beyond that time. A few weeks after this, the assembly of Massachusetts made a request to Congress, that they might retain the six millions, which they had been required to raise, for their own use; but the calls upon Congress were so pressing, that the request was not granted, although that body acknowledged "the great zeal and exertions of the state of Massachusetts in the common cause." At this period, Massachusetts had made advances of money for public purposes, it was supposed, much beyond its just proportion. The taxes were very great, though there had been several emissions of paper money, and large sums had been received from the sales of refugees' estates.

An expedition was prepared, in July 1779, by the state, though with the knowledge of Congress, against the British troops at Penobscot, which had not long before fallen into their hands. The force of the enemy was not very great, supposed to be about 1000: and it was concluded, that no additional troops could be sent there from New York or Newport. This was a popular undertaking;

and there was a sanguine hope of success. Some of the first merchants in Newburyport were in favour of the plan; and offered to provide several vessels to the state. Fifteen hundred men were ordered to be raised for the purpose, in addition to those on board of the public ships: but only about nine hundred* engaged in the expedition. The whole fleet consisted of ten ships, several of them sloops of war, from 16 to 28 guns, one of 32 guns, seven armed brigs, and twenty-four other vessels which served as transports. Some of the militia marched from the lower counties of Maine. Commodore Saltonstal was appointed commander of the fleet; and generals Lovell and Wadsworth had command of the land forces. The expedition was too much hastened; and when the troops arrived in the vicinity of Penobscot, there was not a perfect agreement between the naval commander and general Lovell, in taking measures for the attack. It was determined, however, to make an assault, upon the fort occupied by the enemy, at every hazard. The American troops landed, and had to climb up a cliff almost perpendicular, and of great height; this they effected, amidst a heavy fire from the British, who had every advantage of position; and drove the advanced troops of the enemy into their entrenchment. They lost many men in this onset; and not being reinforced by marines from the fleet, as was expected, they were obliged to retire to a distance from the fort. In the mean time, a large naval reinforcement was received by the British, which rendered further at-

---

* And some of these were *pressed* into the service.

tempts against the place altogether desperate.* The Americans destroyed many of their own vessels, and others fell into the hands of the enemy. They endured great sufferings, in returning through a large tract of unsettled country : and the affair reflected no honour upon the state, or the individuals who planned and conducted it. A committee of the General Court was appointed to examine into the causes of its failure; who reported that much blame attached to the naval commander, for want of decision and energy; but that Lovell and Wadsworth had shown great activity, intrepidity and courage.

The people continued to complain of the evils arising from depreciation of paper money, the common circulating medium of business, and the practice of monopolizing which still prevailed. A convention was held at Concord in July, attended by deputies from more than three fourths of the towns in the state, except Maine and the county of Berkshire. It was a very respectable assembly. Certain prices were fixed for all the products of the country, and a recommendation published for a general effort to prevent the greater depreciation of the public paper. It was also voted to request the citizens in Boston and other sea-ports, who had articles of foreign growth or manufacture to dispose of, to have reasonable prices stated for all such commodities. A meeting was soon after held in Boston, and regulations were adopted conformably to the advice of the convention. In the

* A regiment of continental troops under colonel H. Jackson, embarked from Boston to aid general Lovell; but they had intelligence of his defeat and returned.

month of October following, on the suggestion of the legislature of Massachusetts, there was a convention at Hartford in Connecticut, attended by delegates from the New England states, to devise a general plan of checking the mischiefs of extortion and speculation. Some partial and temporary relief was afforded to the people, by these repeated efforts of the patriotic citizens, who were desirous of alleviating the public distresses. But no permanent or general good was effected. The respective legislatures of the states and Congress were obliged to allow greater sums to the soldiers and to others engaged in the public service; and those still suffered; for when they received their wages or their salaries, the paper had become much less valuable, than when their services commenced. The clergy, also, suffered exceedingly, on this account for several years. But in several towns, the people discovered a generous disposition towards their ministers, and provided for their relief. Congress, afterwards, negotiated foreign loans and received specie, which was put in circulation; and the legislature of Massachusetts concluded rather to raise money by taxes, than to issue more bills, which only increased the depreciation. Some of the paper, at this time, was of so little value, as that thirty and even forty dollars were exchanged for one in specie.

The enemy at New York made no attempts to penetrate the country in that quarter, as the Americans were ready to oppose them with a powerful force. Reports were often circulated, that they intended to attack the capital of Massachusetts. It was necessary, therefore, to guard the coast at several points, and to keep a number of troops stationed in Boston. From the spring of 1776, when the British left that place, there had constantly been a regular state regiment, and one or more continental battalions, (besides detachments of militia for short periods) except when called away, as already stated, on some sudden emergency. In September, though there was then the usual number employed in guarding the metropolis, 400 of the militia were ordered out, to repair and man the forts; and the regiment, commanded by colonel H. Jackson, who had lately been detached to assist in the expedition at Penobscot, was placed at Castle Island in the harbour of Boston. The board of war was directed to purchase provisions and military stores, as well as some large ships, to be armed for the service of the state, to supply the place of those destroyed at Penobscot. They were allowed 600,000*l.* for these objects : but this was in the paper currency of the state, at its depreciated value. Massachusetts sustained a great immediate loss in that undertaking. Besides the destruction of several valuable armed ships, it was obliged to pay for a number of vessels, which were the property of individuals.

In the course of this year, taxes were laid by the legislature of Massachusetts to the amount of two millions, in addition to the sums raised agreeably to the requisitions of Congress. The payment of their part of the continental army, of the militia called out for the defence of Rhode Island, for Boston and other towns on the sea-coast within the state, and the appropriations necessary for military stores of various kinds and in large quantities, and for clothing the men employed in the public service ; all these required immense sums, which the treasury, with many old demands upon it, was not adequate to meet. Nor was this the whole of the expense, to which the state was necessarily subjected. The term for which those soldiers engaged, who had enlisted for three years, would soon expire. And a great portion in the Massachusetts' regiments were engaged for that period ; only a few had enlisted to serve till the close of the war. It was necessary therefore to provide for their reinlistment, or to engage others in their place. The former was desired, as they were accustomed to martial discipline, and the commander in chief was anxious that the most of them should be retained in the service. A committee was sent on by the General Court, to visit the army, and to prevail with the soldiers to enlist for a further time. They were furnished with $200,000 to enable them to fulfil the object of their mission : and $300 were to be allowed as a bounty to each man who would again enlist. Shortly after, 500,000 dollars were remitted to general Heath, for a similar purpose. The same sum was also promised to the officers, as had been offered in February preceding; and the several towns in the state were again required to furnish clothing for the army, according to their respective wealth and population.

While efforts were making for the accomplishment of these objects, Congress, at the instance of general Washington, called upon Massachusetts for 2,000 men to reinforce the continental army, until others could be engaged for a longer period. An order was issued to raise them in the counties of Suffolk, Essex, Middlesex, Worcester, Hampshire and Berkshire. The General Court engaged to pay a sum in addition to that promised by Congress; and the towns were required to advance 30*l.* to every man who should enlist. The board of war was voted 200,000*l.* besides the sum appropriated to that department, a short time before; to be taken from the receipts on sales of the estates of refugees.

The General Court had an adjournment in October; having been in session more than six months from the first of January, and having given authority to the Council to call the assembly together whenever the public service should render it proper; and to order out the militia, not exceeding 4000, if any exigency should occur to require it. They also appointed a public fast, which was unusual at that season of the year. This was evidence of the great distresses of the people, and of the apprehension of public calamities. In such circumstances, the pious rulers of Massachusetts had always appointed a day for humiliation and prayer; and the people were ready to acknowledge the overruling providence of God, and to unite in seeking his guidance and blessing.

The southern part of the United States was the principal scene of hostilities at this period. Major general Lincoln of Massachusetts had been sent to take the command in South Carolina and Georgia. The enemy had a powerful force in that vicinity, while the continental troops were but few. Lincoln was obliged to depend much upon the aid of the militia and volunteers. The French fleet arrived from the West Indies, and landed a considerable number of men, to cooperate with the Americans. They besieged the city of Savannah without success. The French commander would not consent to remain a sufficient time for carrying on the siege in a regular manner. In an unsuccessful assault upon the place, the Americans were repulsed, with considerable loss. Among the slain, was the brave Count Polaski, a Polish nobleman. Count d'Estaing also was wounded in this unfortunate affair. If he was deficient in judgment, in urging the attack, unprepared as they were, he discovered great personal courage; and was justly esteemed as an ardent friend to America. General Lincoln retired from before Savannah, and marched to Charleston, in South Carolina. The enemy in that quarter were soon after reinforced by a large number of troops from New York, and set down before that city. After a siege of nearly five months, Lincoln was obliged to capitulate. His force was comparatively small, and he was unable longer to hold out against a powerful enemy, distant as he was from all succour that could be afforded by general Washington. He was anxious, also, to save, as far as possible, the lives and property of the citizens of Charleston.* Lincoln was an intelligent and brave officer; but his love of glory never overcame his feelings of humanity.

The convention for forming a constitution met again in January, 1780, when they agreed upon one; and in March, ordered it published and sent to the several towns in the State. The votes of the people on this subject were directed to be returned in June following; when it appeared that more than two thirds of the votes given, were in

---

* The inhabitants of that city repeatedly and earnestly requested general Lincoln to surrender the place to the British, before he was induced to do it.

favour of adopting it. The convention had assembled, at that time, to receive and examine the votes of the people. The vote in Boston was in favour of the constitution as submitted; but they expressed a desire for several alterations, and instructed their delegates accordingly. They proposed an alteration in the third article of the bill of rights, which provides for religious instruction. They were satisfied of the importance of religious teachers to the welfare of society and the morals of the people; but they wished also for perfect toleration, and for no degree of compulsion in religious sentiments or worship. They apprehended that liberty of conscience might be infringed; and they suggested that all should be required to pay; but that the amount assessed upon such as attended no place of worship should be appropriated to the poor, or to some other useful public purpose. They wished the provision respecting the privilege of habeas corpus to be more accurately defined, and more liberally granted, so that the citizens should not be subject to confinement on suspicion. And they were in favour of a power in the governor, without leave of the legislature, to order the militia to an adjoining State, in time of danger. But their acceptance of the Constitution did not depend upon the adoption of these amendments. Nor was it in the power of the Convention to incorporate them into the instrument, without another appeal to the people, which would not have been judicious.

There were also objections made by writers in the public papers, to some parts of the constitution; chiefly to the third article, which required all classes of people to contribute to the support of religious teachers. It was intended by the framers of the constitution, that every citizen should enjoy perfect liberty of conscience; and it was believed that all really religious persons would acquiesce in that article: for every one was to worship according to such form or mode as his conscience should dictate, and to pay to such teacher as he might attend. It was also provided that no one should be molested on account of his religious opinions; and that no denomination of Christians should have any exclusive or peculiar privileges. The Baptists were the most inclined to complain, for the teachers of religion were generally of the Congregational order; and although every one had the liberty, as was his right, to worship with the Baptists, and to join their societies, yet those who had belonged to other churches, and were desirous of becoming members of these, were subjected to the inconveniences (which they considered oppressive, and inconsistent with their rights) of applying for license so to do. By impartial men, in other States and countries, that part of the Constitution was, however, generally acknowledged to be wise and liberal. Some writers insisted that the instrument should provide absolutely for a convention, in fifteen years, to revise the Constitution, instead of barely allowing for such a revision at the end of that period. But this objection had little weight; for if a general desire should be manifested to have a convention to alter the constitution, it would certainly be called; and, without such desire or conviction, it would be very unwise to make such a meeting necessary. In 1795, when the question was submitted to the people, they declared against calling a convention. Notice was officially given to the General Court, that the Constitution was accepted by the people, and that the convention had fixed, as authorised by the people in their returns of votes, on the last Wednesday of October, for the organization of the government, agreeably to its provisions. The election of governor, lieutenant-governor, and senators, took place on the first of September; and the representatives were chosen in the month of October, and ten days previously to the last Wednesday.

In pursuance of a plan of Congress to prevent the depreciation of paper money, and to remedy the evils and sufferings it produced, that body, early in the year 1780, resolved, that 15,000,000 dollars should be called in monthly, for the term of one year; and the several states were required to provide for collecting their respective quotas. The whole amount of paper which Congress had issued was about 160,000,000 dollars. The portion to Massachusetts of the 15,000,000, to be paid or called in monthly, was 2,000,000. But the bills had become so much depreciated, that, at the rate of exchange of paper for specie, which was now one for forty, the sum was really but 50,000 per month. This even was a large amount, and the state was not able to raise it. A part of the plan of Congress, therefore, was that each state should either become debtors to those who brought in the old continental paper, and become answerable to pay them at a future period, or periods, and charge the same to the continent; or should have a new emission of bills, amounting to one twentieth of the sum called in from circulation and destroyed. The new bills were to be considered equal to specie; and to keep up their value, Congress also engaged to be responsible for their payment, and to pledge the faith and credit of the continent; and advised the several states to provide for their redemption and payment, by annual instalments, within the period of six years. A great quantity of depreciated paper was thus taken out of circulation; and a new emission substituted, of far less amount indeed, but which retained its nominal value only a short period. This was a necessary consequence of the heavy debt, which the state was then owing, and of an apprehension that it would not be able to redeem the bills at the nominal value, or within the time promised. It was attempted also to borrow specie; but for the reasons here suggested, the attempt was attended with very little success.

The debt of Massachusetts, exclusive of the amount which the state had to provide, as its quota of continental arrears, at this time, was nominally two hundred millions of dollars; though, (on the calculation before mentioned, of forty for one,) the difference between the bills to be paid and specie, or the new bills to be issued, was so great, that the debt was really but five millions.* And it is also to be considered, that if the state was liable for this amount, it had large claims on Congress; as much of the expenses incurred for several years, were for continental purposes, and a reimbursement would be required. The amount, for which the state would be solely and eventually

---

* The valuation returns at this time gave but 11 millions as the property of the state; but it was supposed to be double that amount.

liable, therefore, would be less than the debt standing against it.

In March and April of 1780, two tax bills were voted, amounting in the whole to nearly a million of dollars, in specie value, or if paid in the new bills then ordered to be issued; by which 36 millions of depreciated paper, which were then forty for one, would be called in. And these were ordered to be defaced or destroyed, and bills of the new emission to be put in circulation. One third of the amount of the new emission was ordered to be retained for the use of the state, and the residue appropriated to purposes of the continent, as Congress might direct. It was also resolved by the legislature, that an annual tax of 240,000 dollars should be laid for seven years, to enable the state to fulfil its promises to the public creditors, including the officers and soldiers of the army. And it was provided, that if the Court should not pass a tax bill to that amount in any of these years, the treasurer should issue his warrants for it.

The heavy debt of the state was the occasion of much complaint among the people; and the General Court was charged with inattention and want of economy. But the expenses were great beyond all former times; and it is rather wonderful, that the credit of the state was not wholly lost, when it is recollected what public services were performed, and what numbers of men were employed in the army at different times. Most public purchases were made under disadvantages, and it was well known by those who served the state, or furnished articles at the request of its agents, that the day of payment was far distant. Perhaps, in no country, under such pressing circumstances, were there ever fewer defaulters, or less loss to the public interests. The expenses of the British government for supporting troops in America for five years, then past were 37 1-2 millions sterling.

Large sums were put into the hands of the board of war, who had the care of furnishing military stores for various places, and of supplying the officers and soldiers with necessary clothing. Those who continued in the army were provided with clothes out of the treasury of the state, in addition to their regular wages, or by way of bounty: and such as enlisted for the first time, to fill up the regiments of the state, on the continental establishment, received large bounties, as well as many articles for the comfort of their families. Most of the clothing for the army was furnished from the cargoes of prizes taken from the enemy. But these were not at all times sufficient: and during this year, (1780) an agent was employed by Massachusetts to procure goods in Europe, on the credit of the state; or by loans taken up on its behalf.

Though the public mind was chiefly engaged in political concerns, the interests of science were not wholly neglected. The academy of arts and sciences was this year formed, consisting of about fifty members, who were distinguished for their literary researches and attainments. James Bowdoin was its first president; a gentleman celebrated as well for his patriotism and virtue as for his philosophic pursuits.*

* An academy was also established at Andover in 1780, for the instruction of youth in the higher branches of litera-

A singular phenomena occurred on the 19*th*
day of May, this year, which was the occasion of
great alarm to the common people, and of much
speculation among the learned. The morning was
cloudy, and in some places a little rain fell. By
the middle of the day there was an unusual darkness; which increased till two or three o'clock, so
that it was as necessary to have artificial lights, as
at one hour after the setting of the sun. The
birds and beasts repaired to their places of
nightly rest. The darkness did not extend beyond Connecticut, nor very far at sea. It was attributed to a thick smoke, (united with the
heavy clouds,) which had been accumulating for
several days, occasioned by extensive fires which
then raged in the northern parts of New Hampshire, where the people were making new settlements.

The inhabitants in the eastern parts of Maine
were exposed to depredations from the enemy at
Penobscot, and from their armed ships which
were hovering on the coast. Besides the two
companies at Machias, one of infantry and one of
artillery, for the protection of that place and
vicinity, it was ordered that 750 men should be
stationed on the western shores of Penobscot bay
to check the incursions of the enemy from that
place. These were raised chiefly in that part of
the state ; and were put under command of general Wadsworth, who had been second in command
in the expedition to Penobscot, the preceding
year. The state of New Hampshire was also re-

ture than were attended to in common schools. It has proved a nursery of useful learning.

quested to furnish a number of men for that station; and a French frigate, in company with a sloop of war belonging to Massachusetts, cruised sometime on that coast, for the security of the inhabitants.

CHAPTER IX.

State of the country ... More militia ordered ... Treachery of Arnold ...
General Court under new constitution ... Governor's speech ... Burdens and complaints of people ... Loans ... Militia at northward ...
Recruits for army ... Large bounties ... Committee to revise laws ...
Further discontents ... Great taxes ... New calls of Congress ... Excise acts ... And impost proposed ... Militia marched to Rhode Island,
and to New York ... Capture of Cornwallis ... renewed military preparations ... Complaints ... Riot in Hampshire.

It was now five years since the war commenced : and general Washington seemed to be desirous of more efficient and decisive operations against
the enemy. The British forces indeed were formidable ; and recruits were necessary to act merely on the defensive, with the hope of affording
protection to the country. The enemy had a
great number of regular troops in the southern
states, and were committing depredations without
much check. General Gates, who commanded in
that quarter after the capture of Lincoln in
Charleston, was not fortunate in his efforts
against the British. They were victorious in all
places, till general Greene was sent into that department : and though his numbers were comparatively small, and insufficient wholly to arrest
their progress, he was able, by great efforts and
skill, to put some limits to their destructive march.
The enemy at and near New York, under general

Clinton, were also very numerous; and, at times, meditated an attack upon the American lines. His navy was of great advantage to his plans and movements in that quarter. But Washington was not satisfied with preparations to receive an attack from the British commander; though this, perhaps, required all his vigilance and all the force he could calculate upon with certainty. French troops were expected this season; and he was desirous, on their arrival, to strike a decisive blow; and if possible, to induce the enemy to quit the country. The marquis de Lafayette had then recently arrived from France, where he had been for about a year on a visit to his family, and to prevail upon the king to take a more active part in favour of the United States. The intelligence by the marquis was, that another fleet and several thousand troops were destined for America, to act in concert with the army under general Washington. He had represented to the French court, that the Americans would make a great effort the ensuing campaign; and, with the assistance of some troops from France, would probably be able to conquer the enemy within a short period. On his arrival, he made this statement to Washington, to Congress and to some leading men in Massachusetts;* and urged them to raise an additional number of men to be able to act with effect, when the French troops should arrive. General Washington had already made an urgent request upon the state for 4000 men for six months, to reinforce the continental army; a great part of which were

---

* Particularly to Hon. S. Adams, then both a member of Congress and of the legislature of Massachusetts.

needed to fill up the regular regiments belonging to the Massachusetts line. The General Court immediately issued orders to the several towns in the state to enlist or draft their respective portions of the number required; and great exertions were made to induce the men to engage. Within a month after the former requisition, there was a call for 4,700 of the militia, for three months, to be marched to Head quarters, with all possible dispatch. The towns were also required to raise these men in a similar manner. By request of general Washington, a few weeks subsequently, one thousand horses were furnished the army from Massachusetts; and two thousand head of cattle for beef.

In consequence of the difficulty of raising men for the continental army, when required, and of the complaints of the people against the General Court, as if it might have prevented in some measure the great embarrassments which existed, it was proposed by Massachusetts to some of the other states, to invest Congress with greater power, so that it might provide all necessary supplies for the army, without calling upon the states in their separate capacity. Several of the states favoured the plan; but it was never matured. The difficulty which was complained of, did not arise from the want of authority in each individual State, but from the circumstances of the times, which under any government would have imposed a heavy burden upon the people. About the same time there was a second meeting, at Hartford in Connecticut, of committees from the New England states, to consult on some uniform mode of raising troops for the next year.

In September of this year (1780,) general Arnold, who commanded the continental post at West Point, on Hudson's river, a very strong fortress, and the key to that part of the country, treacherously concerted with the enemy to deliver that place into their hands. Had he not been discovered and defeated in this most iniquitous plan, the British, in possession of that fortress and with a large fleet in the river, would have cut off all communication between the New England states and the more southern parts of the continent. And such an event might have been most disastrous. General Washington was at Hartford, at this time, where he had gone to meet the commander of French troops then lately arrived at Newport. The plot was seasonably discovered, but the traitor escaped. Arnold had many troops from Massachusetts and the other eastern states under his command: but not one of his officers or men was implicated in the nefarious design. This man had been a brave and active officer in the American army for five years: and at one period enjoyed the confidence of the commander in chief, and of his companions in the army. Some time before this affair, however, he had discovered a most avaricious spirit; and was charged with very dishonourable and iniquitous conduct, in appropriating the public monies to his own private use.

On the last Wednesday of October, (1780) the civil government of Massachusetts was organized, under the constitution then recently adopted by the people of the state. John Hancock was elected governor; but no person was chosen lieutenant governor by the votes of the people. The General Court elected James Bowdoin to that office;

but he declined it. James Warren was then chosen, and he also declined the trust. Afterwards, Thomas Cushing was chosen, who accepted the appointment. Jeremiah Powell was elected President of the Senate; and Caleb Davis, speaker of the House of Representatives. The House consisted of two hundred members. In his public speech, a few days after his election was declared, the governor recommended to the legislature to provide for completing the state's quota of men for the continental army, and for the payment of wages to the officers and soldiers. He urged them to cause the men to enlist for the time the war should continue, as it was the particular desire of general Washington, that they should so engage. He also entreated them to make every effort to maintain the credit of the state; to see that the taxes assessed were collected with greater punctuality; to cherish the interests of education; to consider the sufferings of the clergy; and to patronize sabbatical institutions, which in the time of war were apt to be disregarded.

At this period, there were loud complaints among all classes of people, as well those who remained at their homes as those who were in the army. The former were subject to almost constant calls to enlist men for the military service, and to pay their portion of the heavy and repeated taxes, which were assessed. Of this class too, many were creditors to the state; but were unable to obtain payment; the others had suffered exceedingly by the depreciation of money, in which they received their wages; and the state was greatly in debt to them, which it could not discharge for many years. Many also of those who had loaned money, or furnished goods to the public, had been subjected to loss by receiving depreciated paper. The officers and soldiers were importunate for their wages; the public creditors were anxious for their dues; those who had articles to supply the wants of the state were unwilling to dispose of them; and all who had taxes to pay complained of their inability to contribute so largely as required.

But the patriotic efforts of the legislature were in some measure proportionate to the difficulties they had to encounter; and with all the complaints and wants of the people, they generally had confidence in the integrity and ability of their rulers. A great part of the depreciated paper had been taken out of circulation, and new bills substituted, which for some time retained nearly their nominal value. Much specie was also circulated; for large quantities had been brought into the country by the French, and by the prizes taken in the West Indies by the American armed vessels.

The legislature determined to raise by direct taxes all that was practicable, to force the sales of Refugees' estates, and to collect such sums as public spirited individuals would loan to the commonwealth.* The state had already borrowed large sums, which it had not been able to pay, as promised; and it had also, within six months, attempted to raise more by loans, but without much success. But necessity urged them once more to

---

* At this time, the General Court ordered the sale of the manufacturing house in Boston and the valuable lot of land adjoining to it.

make the effort. Committees were chosen by the General Court, of the most patriotic and respectable citizens,* in each county, and in the large and populous towns, to solicit loans. The sum of 400,-000*l.* was voted to be raised; but there is no evidence that the whole was obtained; though considerable sums were collected by the committees appointed for that purpose.

In an address to the people, at this time, with particular reference to the great amount of taxes, of which many complained, the General Court said—" We conjure you by all the ties of honour and patriotism, to give up every consideration of *private* advantage; and that, without delay, you assist in supplying the treasury, as it is impossible to support an army, if the people withhold their taxes. Let it be evident, on the contrary, that the people of Massachusetts are animated with the same principles which inspired them in the early stages of the contest, and that the salvation of the country absorbs every other object. Thus shall we dash the last hope of the enemy, founded as it is upon the inattention and *avarice* of *any* part of the community."

The Canadians and Indians gave an alarm to the inhabitants of the northern parts of the State of New York, in the Autumn of 1780, and invaded some of the frontier settlements. As there was no large regular force in that quarter, they had been emboldened to attack several towns, and threatened to commit more extensive depredations.

* In Boston, W. Phillips, E. Payne, S. Higginson, J. Rowe: In Beverly G. Cabot: In Salem E. H. Derby and J. Ashton: In Marblehead, E. Gerry, J. Glover: In Newburyport, J. Jackson and N. Tracy.

The militia of Berkshire were ordered out, in considerable numbers, under general Fellows, and marched to north river and the lakes, to prevent the further incursions of the enemy.

A large number of the soldiers in the continental army, belonging to Massachusetts, had now completed their time of enlistment, and were resolved to return to their homes. It was necessary to engage them for a longer period, or to enlist others in their room. As an inducement to them to re-enlist, a bounty of sixty dollars in specie was offered to each man. £60,000 were appropriated for this object, and a great part sent on to the army, by agents employed to engage the soldiers to remain in the service. To those who had wages for a long time due, both officers and soldiers, and were still belonging to the army, several months' pay was also forwarded in specie, or the new emission of paper. The payment of wages was then chiefly in specie, so far as it was made at all. The officers had still large demands upon the State or Continent for compensation.

In the course of this year, (1780) a new arrangement of the army took place. The regiments were reduced to 29 of infantry, 4 of artillery, and 4 of cavalry. Massachusetts was required to have only ten regiments of infantry, and one of artillery; which, however, was nearly one third of the whole establishment. The oldest officers had the choice of retiring from immediate service, on half pay; liable to be called out at any future time, and entitled to all bounties of land, and other gratuities, promised to those who served during the war.

The number of men required of Massachusetts,

to complete its proportion of the continental army, calculating that all the soldiers would retire whose term of service was about to expire, was 4200. Under the circumstances of the times, it was very difficult to engage such a number. Some, however, were induced to enlist again; for the terms offered by the General Court were more favourable than had been proposed at any former period. Several towns in the Commonwealth were still delinquent, though they had been often required to furnish a certain number of soldiers. These were now enjoined immediately to enlist the number which had been allotted them; and authorized to give a bounty of fifty dollars, which should be allowed on the settlement of their taxes. All who would enlist were to be excused from a tax on their polls and personal estate. General Washington was urgent in his request, that this number of men should be furnished early in the ensuing year, (1781); and he was equally desirous they should be engaged for the time the war should continue; for he had suffered for want of regular troops, who were accustomed to military discipline; and the militia, besides, were not always furnished at the time required.

The General Court was adjourned, in the month of December, after an active and useful session, to meet again in January; having appointed a committee* " to revise the laws in use in the Commonwealth, to select, abridge, alter, and digest them,

* This committee consisted of the Judges of the Superior Court, the Attorney General, James Bowdoin, and John Pickering. This committee was also requested to prepare bills for the due observation of the Sabbath, and for the prevention of drunkenness and profanity.

so as they should be accommodated to the present government."

In the winter of 1781, a spirit of discontent and complaint prevailed, as much as in the preceding year; particularly in the western counties of the Commonwealth. This was owing, principally, to the heavy taxes, and to objections to the new form of government. There was some evidence that persons inimical to American independence were the authors of this uneasiness; for there were then a few secret enemies of liberty remaining in the country, whose object it was to render the people dissatisfied with their government. It is always easy for artful men to poison the minds of the common people, and to misrepresent the conduct and designs of rulers. A committee of the General Court was appointed to institute enquiries; and if there should be evidence of insidious attempts to interrupt the regular course of government, to take the authors of them into custody, for trial.

To quiet the minds of their constituents, the General Court published an address, in which they stated the debt of the Commonwealth, the amount of taxes necessary to be assessed, and the means for paying the expences of the State. They reminded the people that the arduous contest in which the country was engaged, necessarily demanded great efforts and sacrifices; and intreated them to consider, that the blessings of freedom were too valuable and precious to be hazarded by any want of pecuniary contributions. They declared, also, that all possible economy should be practised, which was consistent with a due regard to the public welfare. The sums necessary during the year, they stated, would be 950,000*l.* Some of the items were these : for the civil list, 30,000*l.* ; interest on public notes, and on wages due officers, 213,000*l.* ; for Congress, 86,000*l.* ; instalment of public debt to be paid, 500,000*l.*; clothing for the army, two years, 50,000*l.*; with others of a less amount. This was to be discharged by the tax to be collected, of 320,000*l.* ; by loans of 400,000*l.* ; by a specie tax then due, and assessed some time previously, of 72,000*l.*; from sales of absentees' estates, 40,000*l.*; &c. By the measures adopted, and exertions made this year, the debt was lessened, without increasing the taxes beyond the amount required the preceding year. Loans, however, were resorted to ; and considerable sums were raised in this manner, by the solicitations of the agents of the State, and the friends of government. It was found, that it would be utterly impracticable to raise sufficient by direct taxes, to meet all the extraordinary demands of the State, and of Congress, to pay old debts, and defray the necessary expences which would arise in the year. And it was considered just, that those who would enjoy the great benefits expected from the revolutionary war, should be liable to pay a part of the price at which they were purchased.

The disposition of the House of Representatives to maintain its peculiar rights and power, was manifested, at this session, in a manner which shewed that they would contend for their authority in an unimportant and doubtful case. The Senate chose a committee to enquire, whether the late returns of valuation were correct from all the towns. The House objected to the Senate in having originated the enquiry ; and contended that it was a subject relating to money, and, according to the constitution, therefore, must originate in the House. The dispute was referred to the Judges of the Superior Court, who decided that it would be proper to have a joint committee on the subject, and that it could be of no importance in which branch of the legislature the enquiry or the appointment of a committee originated. In compliance with a recommendation of Congress, a tax of eleven millions of dollars was laid by Massachusetts this year, (1781) for the purpose of calling in the old bills, then greatly depreciated; the real value of which was estimated at 275,000 dollars. That part of the debt of the State which was for monies loaned, amounted to a million of dollars; and to pay the interest, 60,000 in specie were appropriated. This year, the bills of the new emission of paper, which in 1780, had by statute been made a tender in all payments, would not pass at the nominal value, and the law was repealed.

In the course of this year, Congress proposed to the states to lay an impost duty; but Massachusetts objected to the plan, because it was supposed it would operate unequally. They had much more commerce than any other state, and their products from the soil were less. They said, that by such a tax they should be liable to pay much more than their portion of the public revenue. And they suggested, that if an impost act should pass, they ought to reserve for the use of the state a certain part of the monies thus raised. This reasoning was more specious or more selfish than correct. But it might have had some influence; for the plan of raising money by impost was not then adopted by all the states as proposed by Congress. In the following year (1782) however, the legislature of Massachusetts passed a law for raising money by an impost, which was to be wholly appropriated to the use of Congress, for the purpose of discharging the public debt; or to be expended in the state, but for meeting the expenses incurred by order of Congress for the welfare of the continent. There were conditions annexed to the statute; one of which was, that all the other states should adopt a similar law; and the other, that Congress should annually state the amount of the public expenses and the sum collected from the impost act. Some of the states neglected to pass such a law, and nothing was collected in this way till 1783. Massachusetts then enacted another law in favour of the measure. An excise act was passed by the legislature laying a duty on wine and several other articles of luxury sold in the state; and upon carriages which were used solely for pleasure.* A tax was also laid on auctions, at the rate of one per cent. on all goods sold.

In the month of February 1781, twelve hundred of the militia were ordered for Rhode Island, for forty days, under command of general Lincoln. They were called out by the particular desire of the French general, who was then apprehensive of an attack from the British at New York. These men were marched from the southern parts of the state; and the rest of the militia were directed to be in readiness to proceed to that place at the shortest notice.

The General Court had a recess of a few weeks

* The monies thus collected were particularly designed to pay interest on the debt of the state.

in March, and met again in April. But during this time, they gave power to the Executive to order out the militia, if there should be a requisition for them ; and to furnish such military stores to general Washington as he might request, if they could be procured in the state. The board of war had then been discontinued ; and the service formerly allotted to them now devolved upon the governor and council ; and the quarter-master or commissary general, under their directions. Soon after this, general Washington called for men, both militia and others to fill up the regular regiments of the permanent army. For with all the exertions which had been made, the state was still deficient in enlisting the full number of soldiers for the term of the war, which had been required. The General Court repeated its call upon those towns, which were delinquent ; and while it held out great encouragement to the men to enlist, it imposed a heavy penalty upon the towns that should not forthwith procure the number of soldiers, which it was their duty before that time to have furnished. And in consequence of a requisition from general Washington the state procured again this season, for the use of the continental army, large quantities of clothing and provisions.* This was an expensive method of providing for the army ; but it was not in the power of Congress to make provisions otherwise than by calling upon the respective states.

At no period of the war, was there greater effort necessary to maintain an army sufficient for

* Two thousand head of cattle, 4,000 blankets and 8,000 pair of shoes and hose.

any decisive purposes, which the commander in chief might have in view; or a greater demand upon the resources of the country. Washington was resolved to attack the enemy in New York, or to bring all his forces against those, who were committing depredations in the southern states. General Greene was in that quarter; but his force was not sufficient to enable him to make a successful stand against the British. General La Fayette had been sent on with the light troops* of the American army to oppose lord Cornwallis in Virginia; general Wayne was also ordered to reinforce the latter, with some continental troops and the militia of Pennsylvania. Still Washington kept up a formidable force in the vicinity of New York: and probably, at one time, seriously intended to make an attack upon the island, then in possession of the British. He called for large portions of the militia from the New England states. Massachusetts was required to furnish 6,000 for three months. But 500 which had just before been marched to Newport were to constitute a part of the number. An additional quantity of provisions was furnished by Massachusetts, at this time, and some ordnance and a supply of powder was sent on to head-quarters, at the urgent desire of general Washington. He collected a large army near New York, and the enemy expected an assault. This had the effect intended. No reinforcements were sent by the British general in New York to Cornwallis; and Washington, by forced marches, proceeded with a part of his army to assist in an attack upon the enemy at the south. The French

* Many of these were from Massachusetts.

naval and land forces assisted in the capture of the British army in Virginia. Several thousand French troops under count Rochambeau joined the Americans in that quarter, in the month of September; and the fleet was so formidable as to deter the British admiral from approaching the coast. Indeed, it was not until it was too late for the British commander at New York to afford succour to Cornwallis, that he was fully sensible of the object of general Washington. The British troops in Virginia under Cornwallis surrendered to the allied army under general Washington, on the 19th of October 1781. The French troops were of great importance in this affair; and both officers and men behaved with singular bravery. Count Viomenel, as well as Rochambeau, was distinguished by the approbation of general Washington; and among the American general officers who received his particular commendation, were Lincoln,* La Fayette,† Knox, and Wayne. Colonel Scammel of Massachusetts received a mortal wound during the siege, which he survived but a few days. His death was greatly regretted. He was a brave and judicious officer; and possessed in a high degree the esteem and regard of the whole army. For some time, he acted as adjutant general, and shared largely in the confidence of the commander in chief. He took an early and active part in the revolution.

* General Lincoln was soon after appointed secretary at war, by Congress.

† The marquis La Fayette was a major general in the American line (not in the French) and had command of the light infantry.

This successful event induced the British court to think of peace with the United States. But they were not then even, prepared to offer such terms as America could consistently accept. Congress had determined not to negotiate, without an acknowledgment of the independence of the United States; and the assent also, on the part of France, to the conditions of peace. The British ministry discovered no disposition to propose or to agree to such terms. They had publicly declared their intention to prosecute the war, notwithstanding their recent heavy loss, in the surrender of Cornwallis; and it was known in the course of the winter 1782, that great preparations were making in England for another campaign. It became necessary, therefore, for Congress, desirous as they sincerely were for peace, to adopt measures for the defence of the country. As a great portion of the troops employed, during the year 1781, were militia, and had been discharged at the close of the year, they called upon the several states to enlist men to complete the permanent regiments, or to furnish militia again to reinforce the continental army. They negotiated loans in France again to a large amount; and in the course of this year, the American envoy in Holland obtained loans; but a great part of these sums was appropriated to discharge debts previously incurred in France for goods and military stores, which had been taken up there on the credit of the United States. The requisitions upon the states were still great. Massachusetts was required to furnish the sum of 1,300,000 dollars, as her portion of 8,000,000, the whole amount to be raised by all the states. Fifteen hundred men were also ordered to be raised to complete the regiments in the continental line.*

Under all these requisitions, the burdens of the people must have been exceedingly heavy. The voice of complaint was heard through the state: but it was loudest in the country towns. A part of the old taxes was still unpaid; and within a short period 1,650,000 dollars were required in addition. Depreciated paper was no longer current; and it was necessary to collect a part of the taxes in specie or in bills of the new emission, so called, which were not easily procured, as this emission was comparatively small. The farmers had little of surplus produce to spare, and they had no other resources. Besides, the taxes had been high for six years; and the bounties they had given to induce men to serve in the army amounted to large sums. Some designing and selfish individuals took advantage of these difficulties, and inflamed the minds of the people to such a degree, that, in the western part of the state, a number collected to prevent the regular course of justice. They endeavoured to interrupt the business of the Supreme Court in the county of Hampshire. One Ely who had been an ordained clergyman in the state of Connecticut, and who, perhaps, was as deficient in judgment as in principle, was the chief agent in producing this alarming excitement. He was taken into custody; but the people, thinking he was the sincere advocate of their rights, attempted to rescue him. They were soon induced,

* The towns were classed, and each class was to furnish a man, or to pay the sum necessary to engage one for the military service.

however, to give up their favourite, and to retire quietly to their several homes. A committee of the General Court was sent into that county, who satisfied the citizens, that their rulers were ready to afford all possible relief to them, and that the great amount of taxes was entirely owing to the expenses of the war.* The greater number of the inhabitants in that part of the state, however, were the firm supporters of government, and condemned the proceedings of the deluded or designing men who were the authors of the riot. The legislature, soon after, ordered the treasurer of the Commonwealth to suspend executions against collectors for taxes, for several months ; a proof of the great distress which prevailed through the state.

* In the fall of 1780, 400,000*l.* ; in 1781, 675,000*l.*, and in 1782, 400,000*l.* ; but these taxes were payable in part in depreciated paper.

CHAPTER X.

In the early part of 1782, the war with America becoming more unpopular in England, on account of the great expenses and the misfortunes which had attended it, the ministers were obliged to resign their places ; and others, more favourable to peace with the United States, were called to advise his Majesty. In anticipation of such an event, Congress had already given authority to their ambassadors in France and Holland, for forming a treaty of peace. Some general instructions had been forwarded them, to guide their negotiations. The acknowledgment of INDEPENDENCE, was the only absolute ultimatum, upon which they were to insist : except that they were not to make a treaty, without the king of France was a party to it. They were, indeed, further instructed to contend strenuously for certain boundaries of the United States, which were such as the treaty afterwards made, recognized: and for the common use of the fishing grounds, to which the inhabitants formerly had access.

The legislature of Massachusetts, in which the people were more generally engaged in the fisheries than in any other state, knowing that Congress were considering the terms of peace, and giving directions to their envoys in Europe on the subject, wrote their delegates to that body, and expressed their sense of the importance of securing these ancient privileges. This letter, which was written in October 1781, was referred to a committee of Congress, who did not report on the subject until January 1782. In the report, they did not confine themselves, however, to the subject of the letter from the Massachusetts' legislature; but gave an opinion as to the *general* instructions, which would be proper to forward to the ambassadors in Europe, who were authorized to negotiate a treaty of peace. This was, in substance, such as had been given them the year before. No treaty should be made, they reported, which did not, in the very outset, recognize the INDEPENDENCE of America, and in which the French government was not included: for the treaty of alliance between France and the United States provided, that neither power would make a separate peace with Great Britain. The report indeed, went farther, and recommended, that no other terms, than such as the court of France might approve, should be required by the American envoy; and that the king of France be requested to secure for the United States the most favourable conditions he could obtain: thus acknowledging, in effect, the foundation for a future claim upon their gratitude.

As to the boundaries of the United States, they were to contend, though not as an *ultimatum*, for those by which they had been known when colonies of Great Britain. The ambassadors were also to be instructed, according to this report, " to contend for a right to the fisheries on the banks of Newfoundland, and in the North American seas." But this was not to be insisted on as an *ultimatum*. Nor did the report even propose, that a right should be claimed to fish on the coast of the British territory, or within three leagues, the distance, to which all nations claimed the exclusive jurisdiction, according to international law. It went into the enquiry, what that distance was, as recognized by the general consent of the civilized nations of Europe : by which it appeared, that in some cases it was considered to be three leagues, and in others, fourteen miles : and that it depended upon particular provisions of a treaty, if any greater privilege was allowed. This report was also committed, and in August 1782, it was offered again and accepted, with some verbal alterations.

By the statement made and the reasoning used in this report, it does not appear, that Congress considered the claim to the fisheries, even on the high seas, of so indisputable and rightful a character, as that of *Independence.*⁺ The arguments used, however, and the usage of nations, as to a common right on the ocean, justified them in contending most strenuously for it ; and in instructing their ambassadors not to consent to an abandonment of such right or claim, except that peace could not otherwise be obtained. There was, probably, no necessity for such particular instructions respecting a right to fish " on the banks of Newfoundland and in the North American seas." For the British, monopolizing and exclusive as their spirit was, did not, from any thing which appeared, ever meditate to exclude the people of the United States from fishing, any more than sailing, upon the high seas. This claim, or this right, then, was secured by our envoys, without much difficulty. But the privilege of taking and curing fish near and on some of the British coasts, which they obtained by the treaty of 1783, was an important one, especially to Massachusetts; and was proof of great ability and of devotion to the interests of the country, in the American ambassadors.

In May 1781, Congress authorised the establishment of a national bank at Philadelphia, agreeably to a plan proposed by Mr. Morris, who was then superintendant of finance. The legislature of Massachusetts passed a law in March 1782, for the purpose of giving currency to the bills issued by that bank within the state, authorizing the treasurer and others to receive them for payment of the debt of the state, and subjecting those to severe punishment who should counterfeit them. The first bank in Massachusetts was established in 1784. The charter had no limitation, as to the period of its continuance. For several years it was the only banking company in the state; and the profits which it yielded to the proprietors were very great.

The constitution of Massachusetts adopted in October 1780, provided that the highest judicial tribunal in the state should be denominated the

Supreme Judicial Court. In July 1782, a court with this title was established by law. The legislature had sometime before enacted, that the judges of the superior court of judicature, the name formerly given to the highest judicial court in the Commonwealth, should exercise the powers given by the constitution to the supreme judicial court.*

From a disposition hostile to the Independence of America, or, more probably, from the hope of gain, many citizens of the United States engaged in illicit trade to the territories of the enemy. Those whose ruling passion was the love of gain were tempted to this intercourse, as the profits were then very great, on account of the scarcity of British goods in the country. Congress considered this conduct highly unjustifiable, in the existing state of the two countries; and they objected to it, also, because it drained the United States of specie, which was the only article given in exchange for English goods. The legislatures of the several states were desired to prohibit all such intercourse. The general assembly of Massachusetts readily co-operated in this object, by passing a law to prevent all trade to the British colonies or with British subjects: and the citizens of Boston entered into an agreement to prosecute all who should be discovered engaged in such illicit intercourse. The General Court, also, responding to the public declaration of Congress, expressed its disapprobation of the insidious designs of the British ministry, in its attempts to negotiate with

* The judges, at this time, were Cushing, Sargeant, Sullivan, Sewall: and R. T. Payne was attorney-general.

the United States separately from France : and gave a decided opinion, that peace should not be made, desirous as they were of such an event, without a recognition of American Independence, and on such terms as should be acceptable also to the court of France. Propositions had then recently been made to Congress for peace, by sir Guy Carleton, the British commander at New York, in which no notice was taken of the existing treaty between France and America. This was justly considered as inadmissible by Congress and by the people of the United States. And it appeared afterwards, that an attempt was made by the British to form a separate treaty with the French government.

Though Massachusetts was not again required to furnish men for the army, it had a great debt to discharge, and many of the soldiers were returning to their families and their homes, wholly destitute of the means of subsistence, for whom the state was bound, both by justice and gratitude, to provide. The amount owing to the officers and men belonging to Massachusetts was such as would require many years to discharge. The greatest efforts were made by the legislature to pay them a small part of their wages. For the greater part, they were paid in notes, which, on account of the immense debt of the state, soon became so depreciated as to be sold for an eighth of the nominal value. The war worn soldier, who had devoted many years to the cause of liberty and independence, was obliged to part with his reward, which should have cheered the residue of his years, for immediate support. But it was believed, that the defenders of the country would never be neglected by a grateful and generous people.

In the beginning of 1783, when peace was announced, and the army was about to be disbanded, an alarming spirit of discontent was manifested, which, for a short time, threatened both the tranquillity and liberty of the nation. There appeared an indisposition in some members of Congress to fulfil all the promises which had been made to the officers and soldiers, to the full extent, to which the latter were ready to interpret them. The half pay for life, which, at one period, was promised, was afterwards declined by Congress, because some of the states objected to such a compensation.* This difficulty was finally adjusted, by engaging to pay them the amount of full wages for five years. The officers assented to the alteration; for they had learned that the establishment of half pay for life was very obnoxious to a great portion of their fellow citizens. And they were too patriotic to insist even on a just claim, at the hazard of the public tranquillity.

Congress was able to pay only a very small part of the wages due, which were so much needed; and the officers and soldiers were expecting to be dismissed from the service of the country, entirely destitute; and to be thrown upon the justice or pity, as some of them said, of the several legislatures; the measure of which they also were to decide. All professed to be desirous of having

---

* Many in Massachusetts even opposed both to the half pay and to five years full pay to the officers. They said it would render the officers rich and insolent; that the taxes were already very oppressive, and that the people were generally dissatisfied with it.

justice done, or guaranteed them by Congress; but many were aware of the present inability of government, and considered it a solemn duty to acquiesce in its decisions. Others were less considerate, or more selfish; and endeavoured to prevail with their companions to adopt a resolution, not to separate or lay down their arms, until their demands and wishes were fully complied with. A combination was projected, of a very dangerous character, which threatened to subject the country to a military despotism. The principal authors of this nefarious project were unknown; but they were justly obnoxious to the censure and indignation of a virtuous people. General Washington, and other officers of high rank,* expressed strong disapprobation of this daring plan; and gave themselves no rest until it was wholly abandoned. But the spirit had taken such deep hold of the army, that it required all their influence and exertions to suppress the combination.

In the course of the year, (1783) the troops were disbanded, and retired quietly to their respective homes. General Washington previously addressed them in a solemn and affectionate manner ; and while he acknowledged their past services, he exhorted them to demean themselves as obedient and useful citizens. When he took his final leave of the officers, he was much affected ; and they also were deeply penetrated by mingled sentiments of regret and esteem ; which rendered the parting interview most pathetic and interesting.

* General Knox, and colonel Brooks of Massachusetts were among those who exerted themselves to suppress this dangerous conspiracy.

The taxes had been so great for several years, and the public demands so urgent, that many individual debts had been neglected. Great indulgence had been generally granted; but creditors at length began to call in earnest for their dues. Where small sums were to be collected, the costs amounted almost to the original debt. This became a subject of great complaint among the common people : and a law was made for the purpose of affording them relief, by authorizing justices of the peace to take acknowledgment of debts; and if the same were not paid within a stated period, to compel payment by execution. The usual costs of Court were thus avoided; but in some instances there was cause of complaint on the part of the creditor, that too much indulgence was granted by the magistrates, or that he suffered through their ignorance of the common forms and principles of law.

A tax of 200,000*l.* was laid early in the year (1782) but the collection was long delayed, and the wants of the army being very pressing, the legislature was obliged to borrow large sums, and to pledge the tax for the payment. In addition to the pay of the militia who were employed during the preceding year, and the interest due to those who had loaned their money to the public, the General Court had to provide for paying balances, to a large amount, to the continental soldiers belonging to the State. It was bound to pay them the real value of their wages; and for two or three years, the depreciation of continental paper, in which they were paid, was very great : for the whole of their wages also, at one period, the State had to provide; though the sum thus advanced was to be passed to its credit, in a final adjustment with the continent. For 1783, the public tax was the same as the preceding year; and new loans were obtained, by prevailing on those public creditors who were entitled to a part of the principal due them by the State, to receive new paper instead of specie. Had the creditors of the Commonwealth insisted upon payment when it was due, it would have been possible to comply with their demands, only by resorting to new loans to a great amount. Even the soldiers, destitute as they were, could only obtain a small part of their wages in cash; and notes were given them, payable at different periods. Those who retained their certificates for several years, were fully paid; but many were necessitated to throw them into the market, by which they suffered extremely. During this year, the act was passed for raising money by impost, and it afforded great facility in discharging the demands upon the public treasury. The amount collected through the United States was little short of a million annually, for several years. In compliance with a requisition of Congress, in the month of May, the General Court caused large sums to be remitted to the continental Financier, to enable him to pay the officers and soldiers then about to be disbanded, a part of their wages, which had been expressly promised them.

Some of those native Americans, who had joined the enemy when the war began, or afterwards, when the British army was most successful, proposed to return to the State at this time. The return of such characters was prohibited by a law of the General Court in 1778. There appeared a disposition to disregard or to evade the law of the State; and some individuals of this description, perhaps, might have been permitted to return and reside in the United States, without any danger to the public tranquillity. But it was found difficult to discriminate. At a subsequent period, however, some of those who had not been active against America were granted liberty to come into the State; and were justly esteemed as honest and useful citizens. The families of even those who were justly obnoxious to the patriots of Massachusetts, if they remained in the country, were treated with great indulgence, and allowed a reasonable part of the estate which belonged to their absent head.

It was stated by Congress, that the necessary expenses for 1783, including interest and instalments on the public debt, would amount to six millions of dollars; four of which were to be borrowed in Europe, and two to be raised by the States. The proportion required of Massachusetts was 320,000. This sum was to be paid quarterly, and charged to the account of the United States. In the course of this year, Congress also recommended to the several States, to provide for raising their respective quotas of a million and half of dollars annually, for twenty-five years; the part assigned for Massachusetts, amounted to 224,000.

Mr. Hancock was elected governor, and Mr. Cushing lieutenant-governor, (1783) for the fourth time, with great unanimity. Mr. S. Adams was again chosen president of the Senate, and Mr. T. Dalton, speaker of the House of Representatives. The delegates in Congress from Massachusetts, were Mr. Gerry, Holten, Partridge, Higginson.

Gorham, and Osgood. Two of the ministers of the United States at foreign courts, at this period, were citizens of Massachusetts. John Adams had been five years in that capacity; and with Franklin, Jay, and Laurens, was specially empowered to make peace with Great Britain, agreeably to instructions given by Congress. Francis Dana was appointed minister to Russia in 1779, and returned to America towards the close of 1783. The next year, he was chosen one of the delegates to Congress, with Messrs. Gerry, Partridge, and Osgood; and in 1785, appointed a Judge of the Supreme Judicial Court.

The intelligence of peace was received with the greatest joy by all classes of people. The preliminaries were agreed to early in 1783; but the definitive treaty was not signed till the 3d of September. It secured to the United States the rich blessings of liberty and independence, for which they had maintained an arduous struggle during eight years. A great debt, indeed, was accumulated by the war; but, by the truly patriotic citizens, this was considered a price for civil freedom, which they were most willing to pay. The short-sighted complained, because of the immediate sacrifices it required of them: but the more intelligent were satisfied of the abundant resources of the country, and perceived the high destiny which awaited it. The great majority of people, even in the United States, where the means of education are provided for all, are generally governed by their feelings rather than by reason; and are influenced in their opinions, by immediate calamity or prosperity, more than by the prospect of great but distant good. The burden of taxes was too heavy to be endured without complaint, except by the virtuous and considerate part of the community : and envy had some influence in adding to the general discontent. It was pretended, that the officers of the army, especially if they should receive half pay for life, or full wages for five years, after they had left the public service, would have a greater allowance than they could justly claim ; and that they would therefore probably consider themselves of a higher grade in society than their fellow citizens. It was also said, that if the officers of the army had ably served the country and suffered much in its defence, the people who remained at home had been obliged to make great efforts to procure and pay men at various periods of the war. The argument was more specious than solid. For most of the officers had left their regular occupations in life ; and it was difficult to resume them. And they, more than any other class of people, suffered by the depreciation of the public paper.

The governor, in his public address to the General Court, in October, the first session after the peace, felicitated the members on the auspicious event, and reminded them of the great obligations the country was under to provide for a just and full compensation to those who had been engaged in the war of the revolution. Their meritorious services, he said, should never be forgotten. He also advised to immediate and effectual measures to maintain the public credit and to satisfy the demands upon the state. A tax of 140,000*l.* was soon after assessed upon the inhabitants of Massachusetts, for the sole purpose of paying that part of the notes formerly given to the officers and soldiers of the revolutionary army,* which were then due.

The legislature, at a succeeding session instructed their delegates to obtain a resolve of Congress for settling the accounts of the state, for expenses incurred during the war. It was confidently believed, that Massachusetts had made greater advances towards the general expenses than its just share : and, at a later day, when an adjustment was made, it appeared that the opinion was not unfounded. The General Court of Massachusetts also proposed, that Congress should have power granted to it by the several states, to make laws for the general regulation of foreign commerce. Some of the states still omitted to pass a law for raising a revenue by duties on goods imported into the country as recommended. This led to an evasion of the laws for that purpose, in the states adjoining. During this political year a resolution was adopted by the legislature expressing an opinion of the impropriety of the appointment by Congress, of any of its members to lucrative offices ; several instances had occured, and was considered contrary to the principles of a republican government.

A judgment of the Supreme Judicial Court in the course of this year, given in the county of Worcester, was a final decision unfavourable to the existence of slavery in Massachusetts. The case originated some time before, and was occasioned by a citizen beating and imprisoning his negro servant, whom he considered a slave. Public opinion had, indeed, been long decidedly against the prac-

---

* The pay of the representatives for *five* sessions amounted only to 11,000*l*.

tice of holding any human being in involuntary slavery. The odious and highly criminal traffic of human beings was never allowed in Massachusetts. A few years after the first settlement of New England, the court ordered two Africans brought into the colony by the captain of a vessel, with the intention of being sold for slaves, and supposed to have been kidnapped on the coast of Africa, to be sent back to their own country. Many however were holden in bondage within the province, till the revolution. The inconsistency of such a practice with the theory and the claims of the Americans was very apparent; and generally those negroes who wished for freedom were granted the indulgence by their masters. The first article in the declaration of rights, which is a part of the constitution of the state, adopted in 1780, acknowledges "that all men are born free and equal." This was inserted, no doubt, as a general axiom. But it was also said, at the time, that there was a reference to the condition of the Africans, which had been held in slavery in Massachusetts, and was still advocated in some other parts of the country, by the plea of necessity. The man who claimed to own the slave and pleaded a right to beat and imprison him, was adjudged guilty of an assault, and sentenced to pay a fine of forty shillings.

In the spring of 1784, the General court ordered that the number of people should be ascertained; and the return gave only 358,000. When a census was taken eight years before, it appeared there were 349,000. But there was a great objection to the measure at the latter period, and many omissions in the returns at the former: an opinion prevailed that the number was much greater at both periods.* The small increase for these eight years may be accounted for by the fact, that some removed from the state during that period, to Vermont and New York; and that great numbers perished in the field, in camp and in prisons. Eight or nine thousand were lost to the state in these different ways. A great portion of these died in confinement when prisoners of war. The charge was repeatedly made, and probably with some truth, that the American soldiers and seamen, when taken by the British, were not treated with that attention and humanity, which might have been expected from a civilized and christian nation. In the prison ships at New York, great numbers died through gross inattention.

In April 1784, Congress called upon the states to furnish five millions and an half of dollars, to meet demands against the continent, and necessary to be discharged in the course of the year: but a great part of this sum would be furnished by payment of the arrears of three preceding years. Its requisitions for the three years were twelve millions of dollars; and the amount required of Massachusetts was 1,800,000. The state was still in arrears for this sum, 730,500 dollars. No additional direct tax for the continent, therefore, was required this year; but the amount of what was already due, besides the impost† and an appropriation by the state for the payment of a part of the wages, which had been before promised the soldiers, constituted a large sum, which it was exceedingly diffi-

---

* It was supposed the whole number was at least 400,000.

† The imposts collected for Suffolk for the year 1784, was $27,000 : for the whole state $57,000.

cult to raise. Many of the soldiers, discharged the preceding year, received notes payable in a few months, as there were no funds to pay them at the time, which now become due; Congress was unable to obtain any new loans in Europe, this year, (indeed, the French minister informed Dr. Franklin that the interest and a part of the principal of the debt due to his nation would be expected) and a new requisition was *confidentially* made to the several states for the sum of 636,000 dollars to satisfy immediate demands, the share of which for Massachusetts to furnish was 95,000. There was an unwillingness to have the great necessities of the country publicly known.

The General Court appointed a committee to state the accounts of the Commonwealth for expenses incurred in defence of the country during the war, and to prepare for a settlement with agents to be chosen by Congress. An application was made to that body for such an adjustment. They requested an allowance also for the expenses attending the expedition against the British at Penobscot; which, though projected by Massachusetts, was designed for the general welfare, and was undertaken with the knowledge of Congress. At the same time, the delegates were instructed to have provision made for an allowance to the state, on account of the bounties it had given men to enlist in the continental army; and for an indemnification to those citizens of Massachusetts who held the depreciated paper of the continent, and by which they must suffer, except Congress should allow them some compensation. When a recommendation was made to the states two years before, to call in their respective quotas of the bills of the old emission, Massachusetts collected its full portion. It could not receive any more, but at its own loss, as there was no resolve of Congress to redeem them. Those individuals, therefore, who were in possession of such bills, were believed to have a fair claim upon the continental government.

At a subsequent session of this political year, while Congress were considering the subject of a permanent military* establishment, the two houses ordered letters to be written to their delegates, to oppose any plan which should provide for maintaining a large force. They were opposed, from principle, to a standing army in time of peace; and the consideration of the expense furnished a powerful objection. But Congress did not consider it proper to disband all the troops; for the British had not given up the posts on the northern and western frontiers; and the Indians in some places, still discovered a hostile disposition.

The legislature likewise passed a resolve, in which they expressed an opinion, that interest ought not to be recovered on British debts, the validity of which the treaty had acknowledged, during the period of the war. They considered it unreasonable that interest should be required while the two countries were engaged in hostilities: and their feelings, probably, had some influence in the opinion they formed on the subject, as many demands were made by those who had deserted the country, when their aid and their services were necessary for its welfare. The property of

* The number proposed was four regiments of infantry, one of artillery, and one of engineers.

such persons had been declared forfeited to the
state; and their credits were justly liable to the
same disposition. There was less objection to
paying the debts due to British merchants, contracted before the revolution; but it was contended that these even should not receive the usual
interest during the time, when all connexion was
suspended between the two countries.

The treaty of peace with Great Britain provided, " that there should be no further confiscation
of the estates of those Americans who adhered to
the English government in the revolution :—that
creditors on both sides should recover their bona
fide debts—and that Congress recommend to the
respective states to restore the property of all
British subjects, living in the other provinces of
Britain, or who had not borne arms against the
United States. The legislature of Massachusetts
did not immediately comply with all these propositions. A law was passed in 1784, in which,
assuming and declaring its rights as a sovereign
state, and consequently its authority to forbid the
residence of aliens, and to decide what conduct
would be proper for the state to pursue towards
all such, it was enacted that those who had fled
to the British for protection in the revolution
were to be considered and treated as aliens, and
not intitled to claim and receive any estate or property left within the state; that no property
confiscated would be restored; that the credits,
as well as the real estate of the absentees, belonged to the Commonwealth; and that they would
not be permitted to return to the country. They
also provided by law for the judicial court to suspend judgment on actions brought by any British

subjects until further directions from the legislature, as they were of opinion the interest during the time of the war ought not to be recovered. This, perhaps, was an improper interference, on the part of the legislature, with the powers and duty of the judiciary. Congress afterwards declared, that the treaty ratified by that body, was binding in all its parts upon the several states, and enjoined a repeal of any laws repugnant to its stipulations. Massachusetts soon after passed a bill repealing all laws of the state which were contrary to, and inconsistent with, the articles of the treaty with England. The legislature had before ordered, that no further confiscations should be made, and allowed absentees of a certain description, and who had not actually aided the British in the war, to return and reside for a limited time, with the particular consent of the supreme executive of the state.

The General Court also passed a law in 1784, to excuse a debtor from paying interest on money, of which he had tendered payment before the first of January 1777. Many persons refused to receive the paper in circulation, at an early day, even before it had depreciated; and it was deemed just by the legislature, that they should lose the interest afterwards. But many supposed the law was not sanctioned by the constitution.

Towards the close of this year, a representation was made to the governor, that the British were making encroachments on the eastern part of the state adjoining to Nova Scotia. This might have been done without a design to trespass upon the American territory; for it was a question, which was the true river St. Croix, intended in the treaty, as the boundary between the British territory, and the United States, there being two, to which that name had been formerly applied. A committee was appointed to enquire as to the facts, both of the encroachments and of the true boundary; and application was made to Congress for their advice 'on the subject. The next year, a report was made by the committee stating the uncertainty of the boundary line, and the probability that the encroachments were not made from a hostile disposition. Commissioners were soon after appointed by Congress, and the bounds were amicably fixed.

During the winter session of the legislature in 1785, governor Hancock resigned the office of chief magistrate, giving as the reason the very infirm state of his health. His constitution was never apparently very firm; and ten years of unremitting public service, under circumstances of great anxiety and responsibility, had rendered him extremely feeble. He needed repose from political duties and cares, and there were some of his fellow citizens who complained of his administration. It was a period of great discontent among the people of Massachusetts, on account of the extreme burden of the public taxes. Many were of opinion, the evil might have been lessened by more efficient measures for collecting the taxes within the year in which they were laid. But they had been suffered to accumulate for several years; and the successor of Mr. Hancock was subjected to more than ordinary difficulties in his administration on this account.

The patriotism of Mr. Hancock was never doubted; nor were his talents or fidelity even called in question: but he was deficient, perhaps, in that uniformity and firmness, which are highly important in a chief magistrate. In a public officer, however, popularity is no certain proof of ability or honesty of purpose : and opposition is sometimes made to the most upright administration. In their address to Mr. Hancock, in reply to his communication resigning his office, the General Court regretted both the event and the occasion of it; and expressed a high sense of his patriotic and useful services to the country.* Lieutenant governor Cushing filled the chair the residue of the political year.

At this session, an additional excise act was passed, "on paper, parchment and vellum," on which a fee was required for deeds, writs, policies of insurance, &c. to be paid over to a public officer for the use of the Commonwealth. A great quantity of British goods was imported this year into the state, and was the occasion of much uneasiness among the people. For the manufactures of the country were thereby checked, and the amount of specie in circulation was rapidly diminishing. The intelligent patriots lamented this eager desire for articles of foreign production; and were anxious to restrain it by regulations on foreign commerce and on the importation of goods from other countries. But they believed Congress could more effectually provide against the evil by negotiation with foreign nations. The common people com-

* Mr. Hancock was chosen a representative for Boston in May following. The legislature appointed him a delegate to Congress the same year; when he was again chosen to preside over the deliberations of that body.

plained more loudly.* They saw British merchants and British agents crowding their goods into the state, many of which they considered as mere luxuries, for which nothing but gold and silver was given in exchange: and yet many, who perceived and complained of the detriment which was afflicting the country, gave their sanction to these speculations, by purchasing the articles imported. But it is more common to detect and to censure a mischievous policy, than to practise that self denial which would prevent its deleterious effects.

* Some of the importers of English goods were insulted by the populace.

CHAPTER XI.

AT the election in 1785, Mr. Bowdoin was chosen
governor, by the Senate and House of Representatives, the people not having given him a majority of votes. By those who were ignorant of his
true character, or who had selfish purposes to
promote in opposing him, he was represented as
unduly attached to the British government; so
early was this accusation made against some of
the purest patriots of the country. There was
not in truth, any foundation for such a charge.
He had early and uniformly opposed the oppressive measures of the British ministry. He was
repeatedly debarred from a seat in the council, by
Hutchinson, when elected to that body by the
patriotic assembly of Massachusetts. He was one
of the first delegates to the Continental Congress
in 1774; and president of the Supreme Executive Council in 1775 and '76 : and his conduct had
been that of a decided, consistent advocate of

the liberties of America.* But he was less ardent in his disposition, and less desirous of conforming to merely popular sentiments than many others; who became, therefore, the greater favourites of the common people. He was distinguished for correctness of judgment and for great moderation in action; but was possessed also of that firmness and decision of character which procure respectability, and qualify a man for the duties of a public station. The favour and applause of the people were not his chief object; he sought rather their true and permanent welfare, by reminding them of their obligations, and giving them an example of all the social and moral virtues.†

Mr. Bowdoin came into the chair at a critical period. There was a very great debt standing against the State, and the public credit was not yet placed upon such a foundation as to satisfy those who had demands upon it. Many were in immediate necessity for their dues, and others had not entire confidence in the disposition of the legislature to do them perfect justice. The people were still complaining of the allowance of five years' wages to the officers of the late army, and of the high salaries given to some public officers. Some were dissatisfied with the impost, and some with the excise. The commercial intercourse

* One of Mr. Bowdoin's sons in law was an English gentleman. But he was a man of most excellent character, and a friend of America. This circumstance served as a pretext for the charge of British partiality.

† Messrs. Gerry, Holten, Partridge, and King were delegates to Congress for 1785, and Mr. Hancock part of the year.

with other nations was not beneficial to America, nor was there any practical reciprocity in the trade of the United States and foreign countries. Many of those who adhered to the British government during the revolution, were now returning to the State; and if a great portion of the people were opposed to their residence in the country, others were of opinion that a discrimination might justly be made, by which some of that description should be allowed to return, with the expectation of their demeaning themselves as good citizens.

In such circumstances, it would have been impossible for the governor to relieve all the wants, and remove all the complaints of the people; or even to avoid the censures of some particular class or party of citizens. It was too great a task for any individual, or any legislative body to perform at once. Nothing but the resolute efforts of the whole community could remedy the distress and evils which prevailed. The citizens, generally, were so well principled, that they would have endured any privations for the liberty of the country, as they had often done in the period of the war; but it was their unhappiness to have lost a just confidence in some of the most upright statesmen, and to have imbibed mistaken views of the course and the means necessary to the permanent welfare of the country.

Mr. Bowdoin had a deep sense of the responsibility of his station, and of the necessity of great exertions, both in the legislature and the people, to provide a remedy for the difficulties which existed. The following extracts from his speech, when the General Court informed him they were ready to proceed upon the public business, will shew his views on commerce and public credit. After declaring his determination to make the constitution his guide, he observed :—

"The state of our foreign trade, which has given such general uneasiness, and the operation of which, through the extravagant importations, and use of foreign manufactures, has occasioned a large balance against us, demands serious consideration. To satisfy that balance, our money is exported, which, with all the remittances now in our power, falls far short of a sufficiency. Those means, which have been greatly lessened by the war, are gradually enlarging; but they cannot increase to their former amplitude, so long as Great Britain and other nations continue the commercial systems they have lately adopted. They have an undoubted right to regulate their trade with us, and to admit into their ports, on their own terms, the vessels and cargoes which go from the United States, or to refuse an admittance; their own interest, or their sense of it, being the only principle to dictate those regulations, when no treaty of commerce is subsisting. The United States have the same right, and ought to regulate their foreign trade on the same principle. And it is a misfortune that Congress has not yet been authorized for that purpose by all the States. If there be any thing wanting on the part of this State to complete that authority, it lies with you, gentlemen, to mature it; and until Congress shall ordain the necessary regulations, you will please to consider what further is needful to be done on our part, to remedy the evils, of which the merchant, tradesman, and manufacturer, and indeed all other description of persons among us, so justly complain.

"These evils, so far as they arise from the contracted system adopted by Great Britain, will be felt by herself; for it not only abridges the means of paying the great balance due to her, but must lessen the future demand for her manufactures; in consequence of which, it may be expected that her merchants and manufacturers, when they experience those effects, of which they are already sensible, will petition their parliament to take off the duties and restraints to which the new regulations have subjected the American trade.

"Though we feel a present inconvenience from these regulations, they will eventually produce a happy effect, by lessening our use of British commodities, most of which are superfluous and unnecessary; and by compelling us to adopt a plan of frugality and economy, the want of which is the principal source of our difficulties.

"Lately emerged from a bloody and expensive war, a heavy debt upon us in consequence of it, our finances deranged, and our credit to reestablish, it will require time to remove those difficulties; and this must be effected by the same means a prudent individual, in like circumstances, would adopt; by retrenching unnecessary expenses, practising strict economy, providing ways for lessening his debts, duly paying the interest, and manifesting to his creditors and to the world, that in all his transactions he is guided by principles of honour and strict honesty. In this way, and in this way only, can public credit be maintained or restored; and when government, by an undeviating adherence to these principles, shall have firmly established it, they will have the satisfaction to see that they can obtain loans, in preference to any other borrowers whatever. If I am not mistaken, a fund may be established for the regular payment of a great part of the interest of the public debt.*

"It is of great importance that Congress should be vested with all the powers necessary to preserve the Union; to manage the general concerns of it, and secure and promote its common interest. That interest, so far as it depends on a commercial intercourse with foreign nations, the Confederation does not sufficiently provide for; and this, and the other States are now experiencing the wants of such a provision.

"This deficiency of power may be the result of a first principle, a caution to preserve to each State all the powers not necessary to be delegated; with respect to which, as there was room for a variety of opinions, they could not all be certainly known at the time of forming the confederation. Experience, however, has shown the necessity of delegating to Congress farther powers; which, on the same principle of caution, may be limited to a certain time; and afterwards continued or altered, at the pleasure of the States. This matter merits your particular attention; and if you think that Congress should be vested with more ample powers, and that special delegates should be convened

---

* The plan of the governor, to which he here referred, was a large manufactory or manufactories for pot and pearl ashes; great quantities of which were then made in the interior towns, where the people were clearing new fields. The governor supposed, if encouraged and well managed, they would yield a large public revenue, or enable the people to discharge the taxes due the government.

to settle and define them, you will take the necessary measures for obtaining such a convention, or Congress, whose agreement, when confirmed by the States, would ascertain those powers."

The two houses united in reply to the speech of the governor, in which they expressed the highest respect for his character; and said—

"It shall be our earnest endeavour, at all times, to contribute to the establishment of the federal government of these States on a firm basis, and on such principles as may best tend to procure a just distribution of power, perfect the Union, preserve and secure the rights and liberties of individuals, and promote public, private, and social happiness." They also declared their resolution to provide for the support of the public credit, and the payment of the debts of the State.*

The General Court passed the following resolves, on the subject of the inefficiency of the powers of Congress, and of the expediency of having a convention to revise the articles of Confederation.

"As the prosperity and happiness of a nation cannot be secured without a due proportion of power in the rulers of the State, the present embarrassed situation of our public affairs must lead the mind of the most inattentive observer to realize the necessity of a revision of the powers vested in Congress by the articles of confederation; and as we conceive it to be equally the duty and privilege of every State in the Union freely

* The merchants and tradesmen of Boston presented an address to the governor, congratulating him on his election, and declaring their confidence in his integrity and patriotism.

to communicate their sentiments to the rest, on every subject relating to their common interest, and to solicit their concurrence in such measures as the exigency of their public affairs may require, therefore, *Resolved*, that, in the opinion of this Court, the present powers of Congress, as contained in the articles of confederation, are not fully adequate to the great purposes they were originally designed to effect.

Resolved, that, in the opinion of this Court, it is highly expedient, if not indispensably necessary, that there should be a convention of delegates, from all the States in the Union, at some convenient place, as soon as may be, for the sole purpose of revising the Confederation, and reporting to Congress how far it may be necessary to alter or enlarge the same.

Resolved, that Congress be requested to recommend a convention of delegates from all the States, at such time and place as they may think convenient, to revise the Confederation, and report to Congress how far it may be necessary, in their opinion, to alter or enlarge the same, in order to secure and perpetuate the primary objects of the Union."

A letter was written to the President of Congress, by desire of the legislature, and signed by the governor, requesting that these resolutions might be laid before that body; and the delegates from Massachusetts were instructed to the subject.

A few days after he took the chair, the governor issued a proclamation, exhorting the people of the State to cherish the interests of learning, and to provide for the education of youth; and urging the importance of industry, frugality, and sobriety.

By request of the General Court, the governor wrote also to the executives of the other States, proposing to them to pass laws regulating commerce and navigation, for the purpose of preventing the contracted and monopolizing policy of England; and suggesting the propriety of giving more power to Congress on the subject, by which a uniformity of proceedings, in relation to commerce with foreign countries, might take place; the result of which, it was believed, would be beneficial to the United States, and induce Great Britain to a more liberal conduct in the concerns of trade. Such a law was passed by the legislature of Massachusetts, in June, (1785), by which British vessels were forbidden to carry the products of the United States; they were also prohibited entering and unloading their cargoes, if brought from ports and places from which American vessels were excluded; and confined to Boston, Falmouth, (Maine), and Dartmouth, as ports of entry. The object of the acts, then recently passed by the British government, was to prevent vessels of the United States transporting their own produce, or importing such goods as they wanted for their own consumption; and to engross the whole business of navigation, especially the carrying trade to themselves, which was a very serious and alarming evil to the people in the New-England States. The impost law was also revised, and higher duties charged to all articles imported, which were considered superfluous, or which might interfere with the manufactures of the country, which it was then the policy of the government to encourage. This was a wise provision; for the people indulged in much extravagance in the use of foreign goods, and the country was greatly impoverished.

The plan of government for raising a revenue to the state by the manufacture of pot and pearl ashes was not carried into effect. The design was that the people should be encouraged to manufacture and deposit it with some public agent, and that it be sold for the state, the individual to be credited on his tax to the amount for which it sold, and thus prevent the purchase of foreign and superfluous goods, which was usually taken in exchange for ashes. Such a plan would have put some limits to extravagance and increased a valuable manufacture. A law was made, however, for the survey and inspection of ashes, which had a salutary effect. The article exported from Massachusetts has always been considered more pure, and has commanded a higher price than from any other state. The governor also advised to the manufacture of gun powder, and to the raising of sheep, for the purpose of gradually lessening the amount of imposts, and exciting people to provide more generally the necessary articles of life. The importation of common woollen cloths were very great at this period.

The legislature, at this session, authorised their delegates in Congress to agree to an alteration of the eighth article of the confederation of the thirteen states. As it originally was, it provided that the quota of each state's tax to the continent should be fixed according to the value of lands and buildings. The amendment provided, that it should thenceforth be according to the number of white and other free citizens, and of three-fifths of all other persons. As an inducement to the people to pay their taxes, at an early day after they were assessed, the governor proposed that a premium should be offered for prompt payment, and the interest be required of such as did not pay at the time fixed by the statute.

Soon after governor Bowdoin came into office, his firmness was subjected to a severe trial by the insolent behaviour of a British naval officer, whose ship was then lying in the harbour of Boston. In consequence of the monopolizing policy of the British government, relative to trade and commerce, and of the arbitrary conduct, both of its individual subjects and public agents in several instances, the prejudices of the people were very strong, at this period, against all British officers ; and in this particular case, some insults were offered to the captain and a party belonging to the English frigate. The captain, exaggerating the affair and pretending to be in fear of further insult, applied to the governor, who assured him, that he should be protected. It afterwards appeared, that the captain claimed a certain man as his servant, who was formerly in his service, and attempted to seize and convey him on board his ship by force ; and that he had received the insult, of which he complained, on account of his own violent and illegal conduct. When, therefore, he complained a second time, the governor informed him, that the laws afforded protection to strangers as well as to native citizens. But the officer was offended, that the governor did not adopt some special measures to gratify his pride, and accused Mr. Bowdoin of prevarication; still claiming of him particular interference in his behalf. The governor repelled the insolent suggestions in the captain's letters with great dignity and firmness. Finding his situation unpleasant, and probably sensible of the impropriety of his conduct, which was universally condemned, he soon left the harbour. As this behaviour was an insult to the country, as well as to the governor of Massachusetts, Mr. Bowdoin gave information of the affair to Congress; and a resolution was passed to represent the affair, through the American envoy, to the British government. The conduct of the officer was justly censured in his own country.

The governor gave particular attention to the finances of the state; and in October, at the second session of the General Court, he made a full statement of the debt of the Commonwealth, and suggested the means of providing for the payment, in such manner as he believed would be satisfactory to the public creditors. The amount of the debt was 5,000,000 dollars.* The receipts on excise and imposts for the year past was 190,000, and on auctions 3,600. An additional sum was expected to accrue from the revised impost act; which, with 100,000l. tax for fifteen years, would discharge the whole debt, both principal and interest.

A great part of the debt consisted of army notes, and consolidated notes† so called; but these, it was proposed to renew, as many of the public creditors would be willing to wait a longer time, on assurance, of receiving their interest with punctuality. There were, besides, large sums still to be collected, on account of taxes laid for some years before, both for the

* This was the state debt; the proportion of the continental debt was estimated at nearly the same amount.

† Those were so denominated, which had been given to the public creditors, when the state was unable to pay their demands, and paper money was called in.

state and continent. But, though this would lessen
the amount of a new tax, to be assessed for the
current year, it would, in fact, afford no relief to
the people, who, by being called upon for all arrears, were required to pay large sums into the
public treasury. For want of prompt and uniform
measures through the states to regulate commerce,
and to put a stop to large importations of foreign
goods, and that in foreign vessels, with little in return but specie, the embarrassments of the country continued, the people of all classes complained,
and it was extremely difficult, in many cases impossible, for them to pay the taxes which were assessed upon them. The governor was very urgent with the General Court, to provide for the
debt of the Commonwealth, and for the payment
of the sums required of the state by Congress.
He acknowledged that the burden of taxes was
very great : but he reminded them also, that it
was the price of their independence; and that extraordinary efforts were necessary to maintain the
public credit, and to save the country from ruin.
His advice and recommendations were considered
most judicious and seasonable, by all intelligent citizens : and had the legislature pursued the course
he pointed out, with unwavering steps, it would
probably have saved the state from the disgrace
and expense of an insurrection, which took place
at the close of the following year. But many of
the General Court were wanting in sufficient resolution to lay the taxes, or to order the collection
of them, which the exigency required. There
was, indeed, some apology for their remissness,
arising from the sacrifices, which it would be necessary for the people to make, in order to pay

the amount of taxes, in addition to those before assessed and unpaid, which the full support of public credit required. But the public burdens should have been timely met by corresponding exertions. Delay served only to increase the difficulty, without affording any real satisfaction to the people. If the General Court had firmly supported the views of the governor, the creditors of the state would have had confidence in the government, and willingly renewed their loans to the Commonwealth; while, so long as the state was supposed to be unable, or was unwilling, to pay its just debts, its creditors would be earnest in their demands for immediate payment. It was well known, that the distresses of the people were great, and there was a sincere disposition to relieve them: but it was also seen, that the only remedy was in extraordinary efforts, and in frugality and economy.

The governor referred, in his speech to the legislature, in October, to a convention then recently held in Portland for the purpose of forming the district of Maine into a separate state. There were several persons, in that part of the Commonwealth, desirous of a separation; and they had prevailed with others, from various parts of that district, to convene, and consider the expediency of such a measure. The proceedings, as those believed, who assembled, were very regular, and consistent with good order; for it was their intention to ascertain the opinion of the people generally, and if agreeable to them, to petition the General Court for a separation. But the governor spoke of their conduct, as " of bad tendency ;" and there were many in Massachusetts who believed it was not the proper and regular mode of proceeding to hold conventions in the manner that was called; but to obtain the consent of the General Court to refer the subject, in the first place, to the people for their opinion. Before the General Court was prorogued, a joint address was presented to the governor from the senate and representatives, thanking him for his attention and fidelity in the concerns of the state,* admitting the importance of providing for the support of public credit, and promising to attend particularly to the subject, at the next session. One excuse for declining to vote a tax, at that time was, that a valuation had been ordered to be taken of the property of the Commonwealth, which, when received would enable them to apportion it more equitably upon the respective towns.

The governor had other reasons, besides his own conviction of the propriety and rectitude of the measure, to urge the General Court to take immediate order for collecting the taxes already assessed, and to make provision for still further sums, with all possible despatch. In the course of three or four months, he had received several letters from the continental commissioners of finance, requesting immediate remittance of a part of the arrears, which had been long due from Massachusetts, and stating the necessity of receiving the remainder within a short period. They also gave information, that a new requisition would be made on several states for a large sum, which would

* They referred, especially, to his statement of the public debt, and the plan for reducing it; and expressed an earnest desire, "that he would continue to give his attention to the important subject."

be expected to be paid early in the year 1786. Before the legislature assembled again, which was in January, the governor had additional communications from Congress, pressing the payment of the former quotas, and requiring the further sum of 448,000 dollars to be provided at an early period, as their faith was pledged for a large amount. All these papers were laid before the two houses, by the governor, who again expressed his deep sense of the necessity of their *immediate* attention to the requisitions of Congress and his anxiety at the embarrassed condition of the Commonwealth. The whole sum called for by Congress, being the amount of arrears and new apportionment, wás 981,000 dollars; only one third of this however, was to be paid in specie, the other two-thirds might be provided for by new loans, at the option of the state. A continental loan office in the capital of the state facilitated such a measure, so long as the credit of the Commonwealth was maintained, by paying the demands of those who held notes payable at the office, or by a prompt payment of interest, and a renewal of such loans as the creditor was willing to grant. The whole amount to be collected by direct tax, on account of the state, was 333,000 dollars: and the sum of 300,000 was calculated would be raised by the impost and excise laws.

A law was enacted in 1785 for the confinement of certain convicts to hard labour on Castle island. Public opinion was opposed to corporal punishments; and it was believed, that imprisonment, united to laborious service, would be likely to reform the criminal. The laws already required confinement to houses of correction in the different counties for some offences; but there were few such buildings erected in the state; and it was only for the lesser crimes, that such punishment was provided. It was now ordered by the General Court, that a large workshop should be erected on the island, and the barracks fitted for the reception of those sentenced to hard labour and confinement for a longer term than a year. Afterward, when that island was ceded to the United States, a building was provided at Charlestown, for the reception and employment of convicts, with the view of effecting their reformation, as well as of preventing the further commission of crimes. The great benefit expected in reforming those confined has not been fully realized. But it is difficult to decide, whether this be owing to a defect in the system, as there is no real solitary confinement, or to its insufficiency to reform the very depraved persons who are the subjects of its discipline.

The General Court of Massachusetts early perceived the advantages which would attend a uniform system of commercial regulation, and had, by a particular resolve, given power to their delegates to Congress to agree to such a plan: but it was on condition, that all the other states should conform to the system. They were also desirous of having the revenue, thence arising, collected by their own officers, and of retaining a part of the amount received for the payment of the debts of the state. The system, which Congress would approve, required the collectors to be by continental officers, and the whole revenue to be at the disposal of that body, to discharge the debts of the United States. The sums collected by the impost duty were, indeed, greatly wanted by Massachusetts, to pay its own particular debts: and it was also confidently believed by many intelligent citizens, that the state was paying, from year to year, much more than its proportion of the continental debt, as on a settlement, it would be found that she had advanced more than her share of the expences of the war. Congress urged Massachusetts and the other states, which had not then given such power, to authorise their delegates to consent to it. The governor also in October 1785, and January 1786, endeavoured to prevail on the legislature to pass a new act giving complete and unconditional power to Congress to regulate foreign commerce. Before this was decided by the court, a proposal was made, by the assembly of Virginia, for a convention at Annapolis, in September following, to consist of committees from all the states, to take into consideration the commerce and trade of the continent; and to agree upon some general plan, or to delegate power to Congress to legislate on the subject. A committee was accordingly appointed by the General Court, consisting of Caleb Davis, B. Goodhue, T. Dalton and J. C. Jones : several of these gentlmen declined, and F. Dana, S. Higginson, G. Cabot and E. Gerry were appointed. Only five states were represented in this meeting, and therefore no plan was adopted for the general regulation of the commerce of the country. But it was recommended by the meeting, that there should be a convention at Philadelphia in May 1786, to be composed of delegates from all the states, for the purpose of revising the articles of the confederation, and giving power to Congress sufficient for adopting and enforcing all such regulations, " as should be necessary for the credit, respectability and prosperity of the country."

The finances of the continent at this time were in a very unsettled and embarrassed condition. Its debt in Europe was very great, and the Congress was owing a large amount, exclusive and independent of what the respective states individually were bound to pay for the common benefit. Had the states collected and paid over to the continental government the sums demanded for several years, the debt would have been much lessened. But all the states were greatly in arrears to Congress, each having debts of its own to provide for. The governor was desirous to comply with the requisition of Congress, by giving to that body the whole power over the imposts, or to appropriate the revenue arising from it, to such purposes as was required. But it was not till the federal government was organized under the new constitution, that Congress had the full power to regulate commerce, and to command the revenue arising therefrom.

Mr. Bowdoin was chosen governor, in 1786, by the people, having received about three fourths of the votes of the whole state. Mr. Cushing was again elected lieutenant governor; Samuel Phillips, Junr. President of the Senate, and Artemas Ward, Speaker of the House of Representatives. The House of Representatives consisted of two hundred members; many of whom were not of the house the former year. The counsellers were, Spooner, Holton, Gill, Cushing, Greenleaf, Cutts, Fuller, Phillips and Ellis; the delegates to Congress, Goreham, Sedgwick, King and Dane.

The governor particularly urged upon the attention of the legislature the interests of Harvard College. He alluded to the article in the constitution, which required the General Court to provide for its support and prosperity, and proposed that all former grants of lands be secured, and a portion in the new township reserved for its use. He reminded them, that it was always an object dear to their fathers; that even the British government had extended to the institution its fostering care; and he expressed his confidence, that a republican legislature could not neglect the interests of science. But a great part of his elaborate speech had reference to the finances of the state. As he had done at the two former sessions, he expressed great concern on account of the pecuniary embarrassments of the Commonwealth, and declared again his solemn opinion, that some more prompt and efficient measures had become indispensably necessary. A large amount was due on army notes and other public securities; a great part of the former taxes remained uncollected; and the portion required of the state, by Congress, for the arrears of three past years, with the additional sum for the present year (1786;) making in the whole almost a million and a half of dollars. This indeed, was a heavy tax. The exhibit was alarming and discouraging to the people. It was impossible perhaps to collect it in one year. But the evil might have been avoided in a great degree by an earlier attention on the part of the General Court. The governor had discharged his high duty, by giving early information, urging some provision, and warning the General Court of the disastrous consequence of inattention and delay. He did not indeed insist, either at this time, or at the two preceding sessions, when he referred to the subject, that the whole tax of the state and the sums required by Congress should be raised, at once. But he did most earnestly urge upon them, the necessity of paying the interest; of furnishing the third of the amount desired by Congress, in specie; and of opening new loans, connected with such a plan for paying promptly future interest and annual instalments on the principle, as should satisfy public creditors of the disposition of the assembly to do them ample justice, and to give them confidence in the promises of the government. But many of the General Court were actuated by mistaken views of the public welfare, and were unwilling to press the people to such payments as the condition of the state imperiously demanded. More energy during the years 1783 and 1784, and a full statement to the people of the public debt, might have afforded seasonable relief, and prevented, in some measure, the embarrassment, with which the Commonwealth was now struggling.

In 1781, when the officers and soldiers of the army were urgent for their wages, and when it was extremely difficult to prevail with them to continue in the public service, the legislature engaged punctual payment of interest, and payment of the principal in six successive years; and passed a law authorising the treasurer to issue warrants even if no tax bill should be voted by the legislature, for assessing and collecting the sums necessary for the purpose. The governor reminded the General Court of this law, and stated that it would be the duty of the treasurer to issue warrants in July, unless they should expressly direct him to suspend them. He suggested, that if a part now due, with the interest, was provided for, the residue might be met by giving new notes to the creditors : but that seven hundred thousand dollars appeared to be necessary, to be collected, the greater part, by a direct tax, to discharge demands upon the state ; and 224,000 dollars, to comply with the requisitions of Congress. And yet the legislature directed the treasurer to suspend his warrants for the sums necessary to pay off the public securities, for which such taxes had been previously promised.

The conduct of the legislature was represented by some as wavering and inconsistent. Perhaps, as it regarded the majority, there was little foundation for such a charge. The situation of the Commonwealth was very critical; and the immediate representatives of the people were desirous of affording all possible relief to their fellow citizens ; yet, at the same time, they discovered a disposition to support public credit and to comply with the demands of Congress. They granted a large sum at the request of that body, to satisfy demands before made, by a tax on the polls and estates of the people. When a proposition was made to issue paper bills, to order them to be received in payment of public debts and even to be made a tender in all cases, and also to allow the payment of common debts by specific articles of produce, it received the negative of five sixths of the representatives.

The General Court was prorogued, early in July, to the month of January ; but, on account of the prevailing complaints among the people, which, in August, were followed by county conventions and open opposition to government, in stopping the courts of justice, and threatening the entire prostration of law and order, the governor called a special session in September. The council unanimously advised to this measure. The principal complaints of the people were the following. The excise law, and the application of the revenue arising from that and from the impost law to the payment of continental taxes, and notes due at the loan office and to the officers and soldiers of the late army, instead of being put into the treasury to discharge the common expences of government.—The usual mode of apportioning direct taxes; the poorer classes alleging that the poll tax was too high, and the farmers that land was valued too highly, and commercial property not enough: the compensation allowed the officers of the army was considered a *grievance* by some, and objections were made to paying them, "at the expence of the sufferings of their fellow citizens," as was pretended. This was, indeed, a singular complaint; for they had the notes of government, which it was not in the power of the legislature to cancel; and a great portion were too just, as well as too grateful, to wish to deprive them of their due. Another source of discontent was the great amount of private debts, which had long been suffered to accumulate.—The costs in civil suits, and in the collection of debts gave occasion for complaint also: and it was pretended that lawyers had an undue influence and were growing rich, at the expence of the common people. Some even objected to the courts of common pleas as an unnecessary burden. Objections were made to the constitution of the state; and the senate declared to be superfluous, or worse. Some desired a new emission of paper, in the hope that a remedy would thereby be provided for their pecuniary embarrassments. Some proposed the payment of the debt of the state by paying only the sum for which public paper was purchased, when at its greatest depreciation.

The single fact, that the taxes were extremely high and burdensome, is sufficient perhaps, to account for all the uneasiness, which prevailed. But, to the well informed and reflecting citizens, the disposition both of the governor and of the General Court to grant all the indulgence and forbearance consistent with the public credit, was sufficiently apparent; and must have induced them, most willingly, to submit to the requisitions, which were made upon them. But many of the lower class of people had imbibed improper notions of government, in consequence of the revolution, and of the opposition formerly made to the arbitrary acts of the British parliament. And a few artful and unprincipled men took advantage of their mistakes and sufferings, and persuaded them, that they had a right, in irregular conventions and by force, to rid themselves of the restraints of law and government. The riots which took place, however, were rather the effect of excitement under their heavy burdens, than of any settled belief with many, that they might justly oppose the laws of the state. A vast majority of the citizens were too intelligent and too well disposed, to resolve, deliberately, to disobey the authority of government. There was, indeed, at one time, much cause for alarm, when even a comparatively small portion of the people were so infatuated as to take up arms to oppose the government of their own creation, or to refuse to pay the price of their civil privileges; and it required the vigilance, the wisdom, and firmness of the friends of good order to quell the spirit of misrule.

CHAPTER XII.

In the early part of August a convention was holden at Hatfield, composed of delegates from about fifty towns in the county of Hampshire, being five sixths of the whole number. They assembled openly, and declared their object to be, " to consider and provide a remedy for the grievances they suffered." They professed to disapprove of all mobs and riots; and probably a majority of them were sincere in the declaration and did not meditate any forcible opposition to government. The error, in the well disposed, was to assemble in such a manner; as it only served to inflame the minds of the more ignorant, and gave opportunity to the more artful to exert an influence extremely dangerous. The regular mode of seeking a redress of their grievances and sufferings would have been an application to the legislature, through their representatives, who would have afforded all suitable indulgence and all possible relief. For the legislature, composed of citizens of the state, whose interests, whose prosperity, whose rights and whose destiny, were the same as those of all the people, would be as ready to provide for the comfort and the rights of their constituents, as for the authority of government.

This convention continued in session three days. Their first vote was, "that the convention was constitutional." They then proceeded to consider the causes of complaint among the people; which they believed to be the following.—The senate in the legislature, which they alleged was not a representative body of the citizens, and was a restraint upon their immediate deputies or agents. The rule of representation was objected against as unequal ; all salaries, they insisted, ought to be granted annually, and all civil officers appointed by the General Court.—Fees for judges and others, they believed were too great.—The courts of Common Pleas and of sessions were unnecessary.—The *whole* appropriation of the impost and excise duties to pay the public debt, especially army notes, was condemned; and a suggestion made that a part of it ought to be applied to the annual support of the government.—Some salaries of public officers were too high.—The existing rule of laying taxes was objected to, in assessing so much on polls and on lands; expence of law suits ; want of circulating medium ; General Court sitting in Boston; neglect in settling with Congress, as it was believed the state was called upon for more than its portion; and the haste with which collectors were required to collect the taxes, many of which were due.

The convention proposed that paper bills should be issued, that they should be made a tender, and be received in payment of public securities and other notes due the officers of the army or those who had loaned money to the Commonwealth. They also declared an opinion for having the constitution revised and altered. And they passed a vote, that the governor should be required to call the General Court together immediately to act upon these various subjects. Their votes and proceedings were ordered to be published, and copies to be forwarded to Worcester and Berkshire, where conventions were already proposed to be holden : and the chairman was authorised to call another meeting, if application should be made to him for the purpose.

It was evident, that many of their complaints were unreasonable, and that some of their proposals were inconsistent with the dignity of government and the honour and good faith of the states. No one denied that the public burdens were difficult to be borne ; nor were there any who did not lament the condition of the people, and desire to provide some relief. But the convention, even supposing a majority of its members to have been averse from open opposition to the laws, was considered an improper means for redress. When one was proposed in the county of Suffolk, in 1784, with a view to prevent the payment of the commutation promised to the officers of the army, the citizens of Boston, Roxbury and some other towns severely condemned the measure ; choosing rather to submit to the opinion of the General Court on the subject, which was the only competent body, indeed, to decide upon it.

In three weeks after the convention at Hatfield, notwithstanding its censure upon all mobs and riots, 1500 men, chiefly armed, assembled at Northampton, the shire of the county, and prevented the sitting of the court of Common Pleas. They were determined there should be a suspension of the regular processes of law: But probably they had no settled plan, as yet, to dispense with all judicial courts. On a representation of this alarming outrage, the governor issued a proclamation, forbidding all assemblies of the people for unlawful purposes, and calling upon the officers of the government and the good citizens of the Commonwealth, to aid in suppressing such dangerous combinations. The council were not in session at the time; and he consulted the attorney general and senators and representatives, the judges of the court, who were in the vicinity. The prudent proclamation of the governor had little effect. The evil increased; the discontented became bold and forward in their censures upon the conduct of the General Court, and of the executive. The spirit of misrule and insurrection spread extensively and rapidly. In Worcester, Middlesex, Bristol, and Berkshire, it threatened similar acts of disorder as had been committed in Hampshire.

The first of September, the Court of Common Pleas for Worcester county was not suffered to be opened. About 300 armed men assembled, took possession of the Court House, and would not permit the judges to enter: and, soon after, when the Supreme Court held a regular term at Springfield, the insurgents collected in large numbers, to prevent them. The governor was early informed that they would probably interrupt the sitting of this court, and he ordered major general Shepard, commanding the division of militia in that county, to take possession of the Court House, if there was just reason to apprehend any violent proceedings, on the part of the malcontents. General Shepard collected 600 of the militia, and prepared to obey the order of the Supreme Executive. Many of the officers and men who joined him, were very respectable for property and information. The insurgents, however, assembled, on the morning of the day fixed for the sitting of the Court, and in greater numbers than it had been supposed they could collect. The principal and most active leader of the party was captain Daniel Shays, who had been sometime an officer in the continental army. They appeared much disappointed and enraged to find the Court House already in possession of those, who resolved to support the authority of government. The Justices of the Court exhibited great firmness on the occasion; refusing to receive any message from the rioters, who had requested that no indictments might be sustained against any of their party. But the alarm and anxiety of the citizens was so great, that it was concluded to adjourn the court on the third day of the session.

The conduct of the insurgents was very insolent; and in some cases they threatened those who would not join them. There was a serious apprehension, at one period, that they would have attacked the militia under general Shepard. But they were probably convinced of his resolution and bravery, and prudently avoided a contest. His conduct was highly applauded for moderation and coolness. Indeed, his object and his orders were to act on the defensive, and to support the civil authority. On the fourth day after they had assembled, the insurgents dispersed, much to the relief and comfort of the good people of Springfield and vicinity.

The Justices of the Supreme Court did not consider it prudent to go into the county of Berkshire, at this time; believing that it might irritate the discontented part of the people, and that probably no business could be regularly accomplished. The insurgents expected the Judges would come into the county to hold the Court, although it had been otherwise reported; and a considerable number of them collected, many of them armed, in the shire of the county, with an intention to prevent the sitting of the Court. Their behaviour was very reprehensible; the people were greatly alarmed, and some were threatened with personal injury.

Major general Cobb, of Bristol county, who was also the chief justice of the court of common pleas, was apprehensive of violent proceedings by the discontented in that quarter; and although he had received an intimation from the governor,* that the militia would not probably be needed on the occasion, he had ordered several companies to appear at Taunton, the shire of the county, on the morning the Court was to meet. This was a

---

* In the absence of the Council, the governor consulted some civil and military officers, on the expediency of ordering out the militia, both in Middlesex and Bristol, to support the courts, which, it was apprehended, would be interrupted. It was hoped there would be no opposition, and therefore the governor gave directions merely to call out the militia in case of necessity.

seasonable and judicious measure. The malcontents appeared in greater numbers than the militia, who had been ordered for protection of the Court. But the firm and spirited conduct of general Cobb* convinced them of the extreme danger of their enterprise; and they separated, without any attempt to prevent the sitting of the Court. It was decided, however, by the Court, that the great alarm and uneasiness which prevailed, rendered it proper to adjourn to a future day.

In Middlesex, the malcontents succeeded in obstructing the Court. It was believed, by many respectable citizens of the county, that the proclamation of the governor, together with the influence of the friends of order, would deter them from resorting to force, and prevail on them to seek relief from the legislature. But they were mistaken in the favourable opinion they had formed of the discontented part of the community. The insurgents assembled, and forbid the justices to transact the ordinary business of the Court. They were not so numerous in Middlesex as in Worcester or Hampshire; but expecting they would not appear in forcible opposition to the Court, the governor had not ordered out the militia for its protection. A convention had then been lately holden in the county, but it was not attended by delegates from a majority of the towns; nor did it complain of all the measures of government, which had been censured at similar meetings, in other parts of the Commonwealth.

* He approached the insurgents, and declared to them, " that he would sit as a judge, or die as a general." They knew his character too well to think of intimidating him.

But there were some persons in Middlesex who openly avowed the most disorganizing sentiments, and whom nothing but fear could deter from violent proceedings.

The General Court met the last of September, in obedience to a special summons from the governor, to consult on measures for allaying the discontents of the people, and maintaining the dignity of the laws. The governor gave a full and faithful statement of the recent proceedings of the malcontents in different parts of the Commonwealth, and of the measures which he had pursued in relation to them. He gave a decided opinion in favour of some efficient measures to restore tranquillity, and to support the authority of government; while, at the same time, he expressed a desire that all suitable forbearance and relief should be extended to the people, under their heavy burdens. He expressly condemned the conduct of the insurgents, in the manner they were seeking redress, whatever might be their sufferings, by forcible opposition to constitutional authority; and pointed out the regular mode for obtaining relief by application to the legislature. All that was proper in the executive, he had done, with great promptness and decision; and he was aware of the propriety, in a free government, of having the immediate representatives of the people devise means for preserving order in the Commonwealth, and furnishing such redress as the exigency required, or the condition of the state would admit.

The General Court censured the irregular and violent conduct of the insurgents; and the majority were disposed to make all suitable provisions for giving due strength to the arm of government. They passed a law against all riots and unlawful assemblies; and, after some discussion and some opposition, suspended the privilege of the writ of *habeas corpus* for eight months. While they were in session, on a report that the discontented would probably attempt to obstruct the sitting of the Supreme Judicial Court in the county of Bristol, they made a particular request to the governor and council, to give orders to the major general of that division to be in readiness, with the militia, to protect the judges in their official duty.*

This was a great relief to the governor; for there was a disposition manifested by a portion of the citizens, to represent his firmness as severity, and to charge him with a want of feeling for the distresses of the people. But proof was thus afforded, that all branches of the legislature were alarmed at the violent proceedings of the insurgents, and were united in support of the constituted authorities of the state.

The discontented, who were opposed to the sitting of the Supreme Court in the county of Bristol, again assembled, and most of them with fire arms; but the promptitude and resolution of the major general, as on a former occasion, when the Court of Common Pleas convened, obliged them to disperse. It was proof of great lenity in government, as this was a second design, by force, to interrupt the regular course of justice, that the leaders were not immediately seized and punished; or confined,

* This request was made by a joint committee of the General Court, consisting of S. Adams, J. Brooks, D. Davis and T. Dalton, who personally waited on the executive for the purpose.

as an inducement to others to cease their opposition.

Several acts were passed, at this session, for the immediate relief of the people; some of which could not have been considered proper, except in the existing state of the country, which required all possible indulgence. Indeed, if every thing was not done for the alleviation of the burdens of the people, which they expected or desired, it was because a supreme regard to justice, to order, and to constitutional principles, forbid. The legislature could not annihilate the debt of the Commonwealth, nor dispense entirely with the collection of the taxes laid to discharge it. They could only provide for deferring a part to a future day; and allow the people to pay in such articles as their farms and their occupation would command.

They accordingly passed acts for lessening the expenses of suits at law; for allowing the debtor to discharge executions by real or personal estate. Provision was also made for paying a part of the state tax in specific articles, instead of specie. A part of the revenue arising from excise and imposts, though formerly pledged for the payment of interest on the debt of the state to officers of the late army, and to those who had loaned their money to the Commonwealth, was appropriated to the support of government; by which the necessity for collecting the direct tax would be less urgent. And all who would appear before some magistrate of the county in which they resided, acknowledging the impropriety of all forcible opposition to government, and taking an oath of allegiance to the Commonwealth, and an oath to support the constitution and the laws, were to receive a full pardon and restored to the rights of citizenship.

An address to the people was likewise prepared and published by the two houses of assembly, in which a statement was made of the public debt, of the particular object and appropriation of the taxes, and of the requisitions of Congress. The people were solemnly urged to consider the fatal consequences of a repetition of such irregular proceedings, as had taken place in several counties; and to make an effort, by great frugality and economy, to lessen the amount both of public and private debts. They were assured, that the legislature was fully disposed to afford all relief and indulgence, consistent with good faith and with a just regard to constitutional principles; but that those who continued to oppose the wholesome laws of the state and the regular course of justice would be treated as rebels against the Commonwealth.

An agreement was made, at this period, by a number of the most respectable characters in the state, to discourage the use and importation of foreign goods; to wear domestic cloths; and in other ways, to encourage economy and industry. The governor, lieutenant governor, several members of the council and senate, and many other persons of wealth and influence joined the association. Much of the distress of the times was owing to an extravagant use of foreign articles, which commanded a great price, and by means of which, the specie, which should have been applied to the payment of taxes and common debts, was sent out of the state.

While the legislature was in session, and in the early part of November, it was apprehended, from the movements of some malcontents in the northern parts of the county of Middlesex, that they

would attempt to interrupt the usual sitting of the
Supreme Court in Cambridge. As in the case of
Bristol county, a short time before, the senate and
house made a particular application to the governor to issue orders to the major general of the militia of the third division, to be prepared with a
sufficient force to afford such protection to the
Court as might be necessary. Orders were accordingly given to major general Brooks, commanding officer of the militia in Middlesex, to make his
arrangements for calling out several regiments on
the occasion. Two regiments were also detached,
from Essex and the same number from Suffolk, to
be in readiness for marching to Cambridge, if they
should be required.

The insurgents were too prudent to appear at
Cambridge, at the meeting of the court, when they
learned how powerful and resolute the friends of
government were in that vicinity. The whole
number of militia, to be called out on this occasion
were to be under the immediate command of general Brooks, in whose great prudence and firmness, the governor and legislature had the most
perfect confidence. The distant troops, which had
been detached, were not ordered out, as it was believed a few regiments would be sufficient to protect the court. Such was the abhorrence of the
conduct of the insurgents, and such the disposition
to support the government, among the citizens of
Suffolk, Essex, and a great part of Middlesex, that
the whole of the militia, which had been detached, were prepared to march to Cambridge ; but
only three regiments and four artillery companies
in Middlesex ; two independent companies and

two companies of artillery from Boston were required to appear.

The militia, which was assembled, made a fine appearance, under their excellent commander; and were reviewed by the governor, who was attended by the council and many members of the legislature. The commander in chief made an animated address to them, on the occasion, in which he applauded them for the zeal they had manifested in the support of government. A favourable effect was produced by this promptness and alacrity in the militia; and the friends of order felt a confidence, that, whatever might be the designs or the conduct of a few deluded or desperate characters, the great body of the people had a just regard for the constitution and the laws.

The General Court was prorogued early in November, after a session of six weeks faithfully and assiduously devoted to consultations and the adoption of measures for the welfare of the state: and when they separated, it was with a strong belief, that the people would not again appear in opposition to the lawful authority of the government. But there was a large portion of the citizens so infatuated and so much under the influence of a few desperate, unprincipled characters, that, soon after the legislature had closed its session, they held meetings in some of the western counties;* at which they censured the measures recently adopted by their own representatives, and resolved to prevent the regular execution of the laws of the state. A daring spirit was manifested, threatening

* One was holden at Hadley in Hampshire county, and one at Worcester in the former part of the month of November.

forcible opposition to government; and the people were publicly addressed by unauthorised individuals, with the design to inflame and mislead them, and to induce them to arm themselves against the lawful authority of the Commonwealth. It is hardly possible they could have promised themselves success in their rebellious projects; and yet they sometimes discovered a boldness and a confidence, which usually inspire those who are engaged in a righteous cause. There were very few men of respectability or property, however, who countenanced these irregular proceedings; and many who attended the conventions were seeking relief, in their own opinions, only in a reasonable manner, without intending any forcible resistance to the civil authority.

On the day appointed for holding the Court of General Sessions of the peace, for the county of Worcester, towards the close of November, a number of the discontented citizens appeared, and prevented the justices from transacting the usual business of the court. This was not a very large body; and had any opposition to the sitting of the court, at this time, been expected, it might have been easily suppressed by the militia in the vicinity. The malcontents complained that the legislature had not complied with all their requests; and some of them appeared actuated by the belief, that they owed no other obedience to government, but in so far as they might approve of its measures, and that they might dispense with any laws, which were obnoxious to them, at their pleasure. Very few, probably, would have openly avowed such dangerous opinions.

Such was the conduct of the insurgents at Worcester, and some other parts of the state, particularly in the counties of Hampshire and Middlesex, at this time, that the governor considered it his indispensible duty to adopt some decisive measures; and to show to that deluded portion of the people, who seemed still determined to obstruct the regular course of the laws, that the legal guardians of the public welfare would not be silent spectators of such outrages. He issued a general order, as commander in chief of the militia of the Commonwealth, calling upon the several major generals through the state, to see that the men belonging to their respective divisions were equipped, and ready to obey any sudden call for the public service.

The discontented still complained loudly against the conduct of the legislature, and accused them "of being oppressive, or insensible to the distresses of their constituents;" and declared their intention " to seek redress of their grievances in any way which was practicable." The governor was convinced that the period had arrived, when it was to be decided, whether the just authority of government was to be maintained; or whether a lawless force was to be suffered to prevail over all order, justice, and the constitution. And with the wisdom and firmness, for which he was always distinguished, he immediately resolved to make use of all the legal and just authority, with which he was clothed, to crush this daring and alarming insurrection.

But the malcontents were not deterred, by this prompt and decided step in the governor, from continuing their open and forcible opposition to the regular authority of the state. Their leaders probably now expected a severe punishment; and there was no doubt of a secret correspondence be-

tween them, by which they encouraged one another
to pursue the course they had begun. They were,
probably, deceived as to the numbers who would
eventually join them in their opposition to government. They hoped to become sufficiently powerful,
to secure their own pardon from the civil authority,
and to dictate to the General Court such favourable measures as would afford relief, without a total
prostration of law and order, though this was the
issue to which their conduct directly tended. Many
who complained, and who attended the first conventions, were afterwards convinced of their errors, and had no further intercourse with the insurgents.

A regular term of the Court of Common Pleas
was to be holden at Cambridge, for the county of
Middlesex, early in December; and it was proposed by the governor, to call out the militia for its
protection. Several regiments were ordered to
be in preparation to march to that place, if required. But some individuals in Middlesex undertook
to promise the discontented, that, if they were
quiet, the militia would not be ordered to march.
The governor received intelligence of this promise, and believing that no attempts would be
made to obstruct the court, did not call out the
militia; for he was unwilling to cause any unnecessary expense to the state, or to give needless
irritation to the discontented.

But a number of the malcontents collected at
Concord, with a hope of meeting others from
Bristol, Worcester, and Hampshire, and with a
plan to proceed to Cambridge to prevent the sitting of the court. There was evidence, that an
effort had been made, notwithstanding the agree-

ment before mentioned, to assemble a large body of the citizens from distant places, to dictate measures to the executive, and to suspend, for some time at least, the usual process of law. But in the county of Bristol, the opposition had, in some measure, ceased, in consequence of the late acts of the General Court, designed for the relief of the people. In the more western parts of the state, also, some who had censured the measures of government, were hesitating as to the propriety or prudence of further opposition. From the county of Worcester, some of the malcontents resolved to join those in Middlesex, as invited, and proceeded a part of the distance; but from some cause, did not prosecute the undertaking.

This renewed act of insurrection, even after the lenient measures of the legislature, and the forbearance of the governor, justly exposed the leaders to the displeasure of the executive; and warrants were accordingly issued against several persons in Middlesex, who were the most active in preventing the sitting of the court, and in exciting the people to oppose the authority of government. Their conduct was most dangerous to the welfare of the state; and by virtue of a late law, suspending the writ of *habeas corpus*, the executive ordered them to be apprehended, and to be committed to prison, to take their trial before the Supreme Judicial Court. The sheriff of Middlesex, a man of great resolution and firmness, was charged with the execution of this unpleasant duty. But he was assisted by several gentlemen of the county, and a company of cavalry from Boston, who volunteered their services on this occasion, in support of the government. A party of the citizens of Groton, in that county, also, readily joined the sheriff in this expedition. Three of the principal insurgents, belonging to the county of Middlesex, were apprehended by the sheriff and his party; one of them, however, and that the most obnoxious to government, was not taken, till after a long pursuit, and a personal rencontre with one of the cavalry, in which the former was badly wounded. The persons who were apprehended on the warrants of the governor, were conveyed to Boston, and lodged in Suffolk jail.

A party of horse, from the town of Roxbury, consisting of about forty, were sent into the county of Worcester, at the same time the sheriff of Middlesex and his party went in pursuit of the insurgents in this latter county. They were not furnished with warrants, nor authorized to apprehend any individuals; but were instructed to visit the shire of the county, and some other towns, to obtain information as to the plans and movements of the insurgents. Soon after the return of this party, the governor was informed that the insurgents were still collected in a large body, in that county, and would probably attempt to obstruct the sitting of the Court of Common Pleas; a regular term of which was then soon to be holden. A number of the malcontents, as was apprehended, assembled in Worcester, on the first day of the court; but the militia and other citizens of that town, amounting to about two hundred, appeared under arms, near the Court House, on the side of government; and no attempt was made by the rioters to obstruct the court. The judges, however, did not proceed to business, having received advice from the governor to adjourn to a future day. This

was in pursuance of a plan to postpone the courts
for a few months, with a view to remove even
the pretended causes of complaint, and to decide
on a system of conduct, proper to be pursued
with efficiency, for the support of government,
and the entire suppression of such a daring insurrection.

In the meantime, the insurgents collected from
different parts of the county of Worcester, and
some from the more western parts of the state ;
and the day after the adjournment of the court,
although the weather was uncommonly severe,
and the travelling much impeded by a heavy fall
of snow, they were estimated at one thousand.
They placed guards at the houses where the
judges resided, who still remained in the town ;
and they billeted themselves upon the inhabitants ;
and yet, in other respects, their conduct was not
marked by any peculiar degree of injury or inso-
lence towards the citizens.

In the county of Hampshire, also, a number of
the malcontents were embodied under arms, and
manifested a disposition to seek redress by force,
for their pretended grievances. An address to
th people assembled in this hostile manner, and
one purporting to be from their leaders, to the
pub. c, appeared in the newspaper printed in that
county ; from which it was evident, that their
great dissatisfaction with the late measures of the
General Court still continued, and that they were
so much under the influence of prejudice and
error, as to expect to obtain the object of their
wishes by a change of government, or by compelling the legislature to a compliance with all their
requests. The lenity of government served only

to embolden some of them in the prosecution of their dangerous plans. They unjustly accused it of severity, in its declarations of a purpose to punish such as continued their opposition; and, at the same time, by a strange perversion, construed its past forbearance and lenity into weakness or fear. They had neglected seasonably to avail themselves of the clemency of the supreme authority of the state; and they seemed now to set its power at open defiance. This, indeed, was the case with only a part of the malcontents; for many lamented the part they had taken, and were desirous of withdrawing from the conspiracy against the public peace, could they have done it without subjecting themselves to the vengeance of their more daring and inconsiderate companions.

The forbearance of the executive was justly to be attributed to a hope that reflexion would induce the malcontents to desist from their disorganizing plans, and to a strong desire that the mild measures already pursued, would effect what otherwise must be attempted by a military force. But such a hope was weakened by the lapse of every succeeding week and day, which brought new proofs of the dangerous views and intentions of the insurgents, and served to convince the friends of government that a resort must speedily be had to the strong arm of power, to prevent the final triumph of anarchy and misrule. So bold and so infatuated were some of the insurgents, that they proposed to collect all their force, and march to the capital, to liberate those who had been there lately confined. What other objects they contemplated, were not disclosed;

but it was necessary to place the militia in a state of preparation, to prevent such a desperate undertaking. Whether the majority of the malcontents ever deliberately agreed upon such a plan, is difficult to decide; for they generally acted with little concert or system; and if they had formed any plans, they were such as their situation or their fears induced them to adopt, without much previous consideration.

There was, however, so much anxiety and alarm, that the executive directed major general Lincoln, commanding the militia of the first division, to issue orders for the protection of the capital, and to provide for obtaining early information, as to the movements of the insurgents. Major general Brooks was also instructed to have the militia of Middlesex in a condition to march at the shortest notice, to meet them on their approach to the metropolis, should they attempt it.

General Lincoln immediately issued orders for the militia of Boston, and some other parts of Suffolk, to be in readiness to defend it; assigned several military corps their respective stations; and gave directions for an alarm to be given, by the firing of cannon on Fort hill in Boston, if the insurgents should be hardy enough to approach that place.

No attempt, however, was made to march to Boston, for the rescue of the prisoners; and the insurgents left the town of Worcester after a few days, finding it difficult to obtain the means of subsistence. A small portion of them returned to their houses; but not, generally, with any just conviction of the great criminality of their conduct, or with a full determination to forbear all further opposition to government. A considerable number of them, with Shays, their leader, repaired to Rutland, a distance of about twelve miles, and took shelter in some old barracks, which had been erected during the war of the revolution. They suffered exceedingly from the severity of the weather, it being about the middle of December, as well as from the want of provisions: and it was reported, that at that period, several even of the most active among them, lamented the part they had acted. But it was now too late to claim the pardon, which the General Court had offered two months before, as the insurgents had continued in arms against the government, instead of submitting to its authority and taking the oath of allegiance to the state, the conditions, on which forgiveness had been promised to them. There was, indeed, reason to believe, that Shays made informal intimations to the executive, that he would abandon his plans and his companions, on the assurance of pardon. All that the governor and council could promise was an act of clemency, on his surrendering himself, should he be convicted by the Supreme Court. But there is no evidence, that the promise, if made, was ever communicated to him. Little reliance could be placed in an engagement of the insurgent chief, thus informally made. Many of the party had discovered no intention to adhere to their promises, further than their immediate interest was concerned. It would have been easy for Shays, afterwards, to declare that he had authorised no such engagement; nor would it have been proper in the executive, except in a case of most direct and explicit offer on the part of the insurgents, to give assurances of an act of oblivion for such dangerous conduct. The executive was disposed, no doubt, to exercise all the lenity towards individuals, which was consistent with the authority of government and the welfare of society; and they might have been satisfied, that, by detaching the leaders, the rest of the citizens, who had appeared in arms, would soon and peaceably retire to their respective homes. It is certain, however, that in a government like ours, the executive could not justly give an absolute assurance of pardon : and it is also to be considered, that if the leaders of the insurrection were sincerely resolved to refrain from all further opposition, it was their duty quietly to disperse, and to trust to the mercy of government, of whose clemency they had the strongest proofs.

But many of the insurgents, it is probable, from their conduct, still had hope of prevailing on government, by threats and by force, to grant their demands; and concluded likewise, that they had already proceeded too far to expect full indemnity for their crimes, and that their only prospect of personal safety was in the success of their opposition. They continued to complain of the legislature, to threaten the officers of government, and to oppose the regular administration of the laws. The court in Hampshire county when they met at Springfield two months before, had adjourned to the latter part of December. Shays and his party proceeded to that place, the day preceding that appointed for the sitting of the court; where others joined his standard, to the number of three hundred. The governor had provided no military support for the court, either hoping that the malcontents would not again appear in arms, or waiting for such movements on their part, as fully to justify more decisive and energetic measures. The court-house was illegally and forcibly occupied by the insurgents. They presented a paper to the judges, which purported to be a petition, but in which they clearly expressed their intention that the court should not transact any business. The judges were without protection, and concluded not to open the court.

The dispute which had long existed between the Commonwealth and the state of New York, with regard to the claim of Massachusetts to a part of the territory west of Hudson river, was this year brought to an amicable termination. The settlement, however, was not completed without long discussion and much difficulty. New York, at first, denied entirely the right of Massachusetts to any lands west of that river; and claimed the territory as far west as the United States extended, till it interfered with the British possessions : while Massachusetts laid claim to all that tract of land, beyond a certain distance west of the Hudson, and clearly within the early patent of New York, and lying between the southern and northern limits of the patent of Massachusetts bay; which extended in a western direction to the extreme part of the United States, as settled by the treaty of 1783.

The subject was referred to Congress in 1784, by agents from the states of Massachusetts and New York, who were particularly authorised for the purpose. Congress appointed commissioners to hear the respective claims and to settle the controversy. They had several meetings, by the name of a "federal court;" but their deliberations resulted in no opinion satisfactory to the parties. The agents of the two states met at Hartford in

Connecticut, December, 1786; and finally agreed, that Massachusetts should have the preemptive right to two large tracts of land, within the bounds it claimed, being in the whole about five millions of acres; two hundred and thirty thousand of which were situated near the centre of the state of New York, and the other, a larger tract, in the more western part of the state, bordering on lake Erie; the jurisdiction over the whole, however, to be in New York. And all the residue claimed by Massachusetts was ceded and relinquished to New York forever; excepting the most western part of the original claim of Massachusetts, west of the lake and within the southern and northern boundaries before mentioned, which had been previously granted and ceded to Congress, and formed a part of the northern and western territory of the United States, bordering on the British possessions. These lands in New York were sold in 1787, and brought into the public treasury of the state one million of dollars. About this time, Congress sold a great part of the public land within the northwestern territory which had been ceded by several states, which enabled them to pay off a large part of the continental debt.

The following year (1787) the dispute, which had long existed between Massachusetts and New York, respecting the boundary line between the two states, was also finally adjusted. This line had never been precisely fixed; and contests were frequently occuring between the citizens of these states, living on and near the supposed bounds. There had been various attempts to ascertain the line before the revolution. In 1773, commissioners from both those provinces had agreed to the principles, on which the bounds should be settled, and it was actually run to the satisfaction of both governments. But the war took place before the agreement received the necessary sanction of the king; and on the return of peace, the subject was again agitated with great interest. Skilful mathematicians and the geographer of the United States, with the consent of Congress, were employed to ascertain and fix the line between the two states, which had become more difficult to settle, on account of the new settlements made and interfering claims set up by individuals in each government. The controversy was finally adjusted conformably, in a great measure, to the agreement made, fourteen years before.

CHAPTER XIII.

WHEN the governor received intelligence of the conduct of the insurgents, in again obstructing the court in Hampshire by force, and that there was a meditated plan to interrupt it in the county of Worcester, where it was to be holden in a few weeks, he was satisfied of the necessity of calling upon the militia to suppress the rebellion, as it might now be justly called; and to apprehend the leaders of this dangerous opposition, as the only means of safety to the Commonwealth. He consulted the council on this important subject, and they advised to the course, which he suggested. The constitution, indeed, gave power to the governor to provide for the peace and welfare of the state against all hostile attacks and dangerous combinations; and the General Court, at its late extra session, had expressed an opinion, that the militia should be called out, whenever the public exigencies might require such a measure. But it was both still the duty and the wish of the governor to have the opinion of the council in a situation so novel and responsible.

It was certainly most fortunate for the state, that the executive was then intelligent, firm and decided. Any wavering policy or weak timidity, from a regard to popularity, would have proved fatal to the peace of society and the existence of government. Further forbearance towards the insurgents would have jeopardized the welfare of the whole Commonwealth; and any proposition to negotiate with them would only have given them confidence and dishonoured the government. The governor was aware that the crisis demanded promptitude and decision, and he took his measures accordingly. The majority of the council were also decidedly of opinion, that the strong arm of government must be raised in defence of law and order. Other public officers and intelligent citizens were of opinion, also, that the insurrection should be quelled, before it extended any further, or became more formidable. It was not apprehended, indeed, that the majority of the people of Massachusetts would ever become advocates for such conduct as had been exhibited by a few infatuated men. But it was considered the imperious duty of the government to suppress a rebellion, which was at once injurious and disgraceful to the state.

The executive would have failed in its duty to the people and to the state, had it neglected to adopt measures fully adequate to suppress this dangerous insurrection, with all possible promptitude. To have relied solely upon the sheriff of any county, where the insurgents were collected, with all the aid he could obtain, would have been unwise. For though in most counties of the state, there was a majority, and in all, a very large and respectable number, in favour of government, a portion of them were too timid to act openly against those who were collected under arms. Besides, while the authority of the sheriff was confined to his own particular county, the malcontents were from several counties, and marched from place to place, as their safety or their plans dictated. The only alternative, therefore, was to call out the militia; and, early in January, (1787) orders were issued for raising 4400. Suffolk, Essex and Middlesex were to furnish 2000; Worcester and Hampshire 2400.

This requisition shews the confidence which the executive had in the good people, generally, in the two last named counties, notwithstanding the greater part of the insurgents belonged to those sections of the Commonwealth. Four companies of artillery were also detached from the counties of Suffolk and Middlesex. Thirty days was to be the term of their service; and major general Lincoln was designated as the commander of this patriotic band, on whom was imposed the irksome duty of marching, in hostile array, against a portion of their fellow citizens. But the obligation was indispensable: and they cheerfully rallied, in defence of a free government and of constitutional liberty, at the call of the chief magistrate, whom they esteemed for his patriotism and wisdom, and under the immediate command of a military character, in whom were united the mildest virtues, with great firmness and resolution.

For the support of this detachment of militia

in defence of government, a loan of 20,000 dollars was effected, from a number of patriotic citizens; as the public treasury was destitute of funds, to meet the charge of the expedition. The creditors of the state were so numerous, at this period, that they were frequently obliged to wait many months for their dues; even such as was promised and had not been reloaned; and generally, the treasurer was able to satisfy them only by issuing orders on the collectors of the taxes through the state, and thus anticipate the monies which had been assessed for the public service.

In the mean time, the governor, with his usual prudence and under the influence of a disposition, by which he was uniformly actuated, to omit no efforts for the information and welfare of the people, prepared and circulated an address to them; in which he referred to the unjustifiable and dangerous proceedings of the insurgents, to his own late conduct and that of the General Court, by which every reasonable indulgence, and every possible remedy, consistent with justice, order, and the support of the civil authority, had been extended to them: and of the late measure of calling out the militia to protect the courts of law; which, though reluctantly adopted, was rendered necessary by their violent and highly criminal proceedings. "Such opposition to government and the laws," he said, "could not be longer endured; and that their actions, whatever might be their real or pretended motives, tended directly to confusion and anarchy in the state." He also appealed to the good sense, virtue and patriotism of the people, on the absolute necessity of uniting with the officers of government, in opposing the insurgents, and rallying round the standard of the constitution.

While the militia, who had been detached, were assembling at the places of rendezvous required, one of which was at Boston, and the other at Springfield, the insurgents became alarmed by the decisive conduct of government; and they forwarded a petition to the Supreme Executive, requesting the discharge of the prisoners in Boston, a general pardon to all who had hitherto opposed the government, and a suspension of the courts of Common Pleas, until after a new choice of representatives, who, they probably supposed, would be more ready to grant all their wishes. But the style of the application was not such as men in their condition might properly address to the lawful authority of the State. They had, also, on former occasions, violated their express engagements, made in a like situation of embarrassment and fear; and more than all, they had continued in arms, and in opposition to the regular authority of the government, long after the period when a pardon had been graciously tendered them. The memorial was considered, by the Executive, as an improper address, highly reprehensible in itself, and requiring an indulgence or an assurance, which the governor and council were not authorized to grant, after the recent decision of the legislature. No promise could have been correctly made by the Executive, that the conditions required by the insurgents, on which their engagement to be obedient and peaceable depended, would be fulfilled by the General Court; for they proposed in their memorial, that some of the judicial courts should be abolished: and besides all these objections to their application, it purported to be from citizens, some of whose names were not subscribed, and who were not present at the meeting when it was prepared.

In this situation, hopeless as it must have appeared, if they had impartially considered it, the insurgents determined to persevere in open defiance of all legitimate authority; and called upon their fellow citizens to unite with them " in support of their rights," which, they said, the government had denied them. Perceiving such a criminal and dangerous spirit in these deluded people, the governor directed general Lincoln to march immediately to Worcester, and protect the court, which was to be holden on the 23d of January. Instructions were given him as to the great objects of the expedition; but much was left to his own judgment and discretion, in its prosecution. The militia, who had collected in the vicinity of Boston, marched on the 19th of January, and reached Worcester on the 22d; and the insurgents in that county were too much intimidated to attempt any opposition to the sitting of the court, when such a powerful force was prepared to support it. They continued in arms, however, in different parts of the western counties, and concerted a junction of their forces at Springfield, expecting to be able to overpower the militia, called out by the Executive at that place.

Orders had been previously given to major general Shepard, in the county of Hampshire, to take post at the military arsenal in Springfield, with a thousand men, from an early apprehension, that the insurgents would endeavour to obtain possession of it. The previous occupation of this post by general Shepard, with the militia called out by the executive, did not entirely discourage the insurgents, though many of them were justly alarmed by it. But their numbers were greater than the government troops under general Shepard; and their leaders resolved to gain possession of this important post, if possible, before the arrival of general Lincoln, with the militia from the lower counties. The whole number of the insurgents amounted to about 1800, though they were not then all collected in one body, a part of them being a few miles from Springfield, on the west side of Connecticut river. But the object of all was alike criminal, in intending to obstruct the courts, and even to attack the militia, who had assembled by the orders, and under the authority of government.

The situation of general Shepard, at this time, was very critical. General Lincoln was still at Worcester: the insurgents at and near Springfield were numerous and desperate; and they attempted to persuade Lincoln that they wished to negotiate, with a view, probably, to delay his march to that place, that they might attack Shepard before he was reinforced, and obtain possession of the public arsenal. General Lincoln was not deceived by this artifice; but before he reached Springfield, whither he hastened for the relief and support of Shepard, of whose dangerous situation he had been informed, the latter was threatened with an attack by the insurgents under Shays, then encamped within a very short distance. When general Shepard found that they were resolved to attack him, and were approaching the place where he was posted, he sent messengers to inform them, that he was acting under the authority both of the state and of Congress ;* and declared his resolution to defend the arsenal, of which he had reason to believe they intended to take possession. They were not deterred, by this declaration, from continuing to advance. His situation became extremely alarming. But his prudence and firmness did not forsake him. He sent a second message, forbidding them to approach any nearer, and repeating his purpose to defend himself and post, whatever might be the disastrous event. They still advanced towards him, and in an attitude, which convinced him of their plan to sieze the place by force. Thus threatened, and thus dangerously situated, general Shepard gave orders to fire two of his cannon; to be so aimed, however, as not to injure any of the deluded people. But this measure did not produce the effect which he had hoped. They continued to advance ; when he believed the moment had arrived that required him to act with more decision and effect : for he felt himself responsible for the events of the day, and for the issue of this affair, which would probably decide the fate of the Commonwealth. For, if the insurgents had gained possession of this military post, they would immediately have become formidable to the state. It was no time to hesitate ; and he accordingly ordered several guns to be fired directly into their ranks. Three of them were killed ; and the whole party was thrown into

* Congress had, a short time before, given directions to general Shepard to protect the arsenal at Springfield, which belonged to the United States.

disorder, and fled, with great precipitation, to one of the adjoining towns.

The leaders of the insurgents were not discouraged by this unfortunate affair. Some of the party, indeed, were induced, after this event, to desert the standard of rebellion: but Shays received a large reinforcement from Berkshire county; and, thus strengthened, he meditated a second attack upon general Shepard, with the ultimate object of gaining possession of the military stores belonging to the public. But general Lincoln arrived from Worcester, on the 27th of the month, with four regiments of infantry, a battalion of artillery, and one company of cavalry, which gave great joy to the peaceable inhabitants, and afforded efficient support to Shepard, and the government party under his command.

It was concluded to pursue the insurgents without delay; and general Lincoln, with most of the men who accompanied him from Worcester, passed the Connecticut river, on the ice, in the search of a party, which had been collecting at West Springfield for several days, and with whom, it was believed, Shays would endeavour to form a junction; while general Shepard, with the militia belonging to the county of Hampshire, marched directly up the river in pursuit of Shays, who had gone in that direction, with the force under his immediate command. The former party of the insurgents retreated to Northampton, in great confusion; and those on the eastern side of the river, under Shays, proceeded through South Hadley to Amherst.

The friends of government derived great confidence from the firmness of the executive; and from the promptitude, with which the militia had obeyed the orders of the governor, and the alacrity with which they exposed themselves to arduous service, for the welfare of the state. Several volunteer companies were in preparation to join general Lincoln, if their aid should be required; and a number of distinguished citizens,* who were legally excused from military duty, offered their personal assistance, in performing such service as the public tranquillity, or the support of government might render necessary. When general Lincoln was on his way from Worcester to Springfield, and had intelligence of the greater number of insurgents collected and collecting in the vicinity of the latter place, and of their intended plan to take possession of the public arsenal there, he dispatched a messenger to major general Brooks, to march with a portion of the militia of Middlesex. The order was promptly obeyed, and a large body of them proceeded as far as Worcester, when intelligence was received, that the public welfare would not require their further service, and they returned.

But the insurgents, although they were obliged to retire from Springfield, to elude the formidable force under generals Lincoln and Shepard, were not yet induced to disperse; nor did they manifest any disposition to submit to the authority of the government. Their leaders could now justly expect no special favour, having continued in active and open hostility to the lawful authority of the state: and it was their interest to retain as many

---

* Among these were generals Tupper and Putnam, and colonel Baldwin, late officers in the continental army.

of the people in their party as possible, with the hope of final success in their objects, or the belief, that so long as the discontented were numerous, the treatment of individuals would be less severe. They were also deceived, in their calculations of support from different parts of the Commonwealth; and they even pretended to expect aid from the people of the adjoining states.

Although the different parties of insurgents were prevented from uniting their forces, they continued in such large numbers as to require the vigilance of the governmental troops. Shays retired through Amherst towards Pelham, with the great body of the malcontents, and was pursued by the militia under general Lincoln. But when the latter reached Amherst, he found it necessary to return to Hadley, to obtain provisions and shelter for his men; who had become quite exhausted, by a long and continued march, at that inclement season of the year.* Those on the west side of the river, also, remained in considerable numbers, threatening the friends of government, and evidently seeking an opportunity of joining the party under Shays, for a more decided and formidable opposition. They met with a small party of the troops, who belonged to general Shepard's command, and detained them as prisoners. The company of volunteers from Brookfield, with a few others, were sent in pursuit of this body of insurgents, and for the rescue of their brethren, who were kept by them in duress. The insurgents, who were almost double the num-

---

* An unusual quantity of snow fell in December, and for the whole month of January, the cold was very severe.

ber of the party of volunteers, were overtaken, at the distance of about twenty miles from Northampton. Each party prepared for an attack. But by the great firmness and intrepidity of the volunteer corps,* many of the insurgents were induced to give up their arms; and the others escaped.

General Lincoln remained a few days, at Hadley, from a regard to the comfort of his troops, who had been much exposed, and suffered greatly during their late rapid march, as well as from a hope, that a little time for reflection, would induce the greater part of the insurgents to quit the criminal course they were pursuing. It appeared from his letters to the governor, that he had no doubt the most of them were deceived by a few artful men, who had grossly misinterpreted the measures and views of government, and it was his desire and purpose, if possible, to suppress the insurrection, without further bloodshed. Knowing, also, their want of system, and of all sufficient means of becoming really formidable to government, he felt no necessity of an immediate attack upon Shays and his party.

Attempts were made for holding conventions, in several counties, at this time, by a class of men, who affected to censure the conduct of the insurgents for overt acts of opposition to the government; but who pretended that the discontents of the people were so great, that such meetings were necessary to consult on measures for the public quiet. But many of those who favoured this plan, were known to have apologized for, if they had

* Tupper and Baldwin were in this party of volunteers.

not fully approved, the proceedings of the insurgents. It was also considered, by the majority, as a very irregular mode of obtaining relief, for any real or supposed grievances; and that the legislature, composed of the representatives of the people, was the only constitutional body authorised for the purpose, was then to meet in a few days. The intelligent and patriotic citizens, therefore, in all parts of the state, were found in opposition to these county meetings.

On the second day after general Lincoln arrived at Hadley, he addressed a letter to Shays, then at Pelham, about twenty miles distance, but in the same county; in which he referred explicitly to the criminal purposes and conduct of the insurgents, in assembling under arms against the government of the state; to their embarrassed situation; and to the personal consequences of their continuing in a posture of rebellion. As the lawful agent of the executive, he required Shays to communicate the letter to the deluded citizens who were assembled with him at Pelham, that they might avail of the lenity of government, and prevent a severe, but just punishment. But he gave no intimation of pardon to the leaders of the mob, or to those who had distinguished themselves by their open hostility to the officers of government, other than might be justly hoped, from the wisdom and lenity of the legislature. He added, that if they did not peaceably separate, he should immediately march his troops to Pelham; and if attacked or resisted, the leaders of the insurgents would be answerable for all the consequences which might ensue. Resolute as he was in the discharge of his duty as a public officer, he was, at the same time, desirous of sparing the lives of his fellow citizens.

In their reply to the note of general Lincoln, Shays and others, who were considered officers of the insurgent band, proposed several conditions, which it was impossible for him to approve or accept. They insisted upon an assurance of a general and unconditional pardon; intimating, that they had sought only for a redress of real grievances, which they suffered. If this could not be promised, they asked for a suspension of all hostilities, until they could present a petition to the General Court, and learn the result. To this evasive and unsatisfactory answer, general Lincoln immediately replied, that their request was inadmissible, as his instructions would not justify any delay in his operations, and that he had no authority to decide ultimately upon their fate; that he had not commenced hostilities; that he must again warn the people assembled in arms against government to disband, as they would avoid the evils which might follow from a disregard of this warning.

The time had now arrived for the meeting of the General Court, which had been prorogued from the former session, to the last of January. The governor immediately gave them full information of the proceedings of the malcontents, subsequently to the previous session; of the measures which he had adopted to suppress the disorders in the state; and of the success, which had hitherto attended the troops under general Lincoln, ordered out for the service of the Commonwealth. This conduct of the executive was highly approved by the legislature;* and they publicly and deliberate-

* As the course pursued by Mr. Bowdoin was considered

ly declared the existence of a dangerous *rebellion* in the Commonwealth. The views of the General Court cannot be so well exhibited, as by referring to their declaration *in extenso*. It was adopted by the two Houses on the fourth of February, a few days after they assembled.*

They also promptly authorized the governor, by a special resolve, to re-inforce the militia, who were in the service of government under general Lincoln, if it should be deemed necessary ; to cause the most active among the insurgents to be arrested ; but to pardon such as had probably been deceived, upon surrendering up their arms and taking the oath of allegiance to the Commonwealth. The term, for which the militia who were first enlisted, had then nearly expired ; and it was reported, at the time, that the insurgents were increasing, in some of the western counties.

The insurgents forwarded a petition to the General Court, as they had before done to the executive, from the town of Pelham, where they were principally collected, except a small party in Berkshire ; in which they acknowledged their error, in opposing the government by force ; though they insisted that they had reason to complain of grievances which ought to have been redressed—and promising to lay down their arms and to disperse, upon an assurance of pardon for all their past conduct. The legislature voted that they could not lis-

by some, probably from good motives, as unnecessarily severe, we will give, in the appendix, his speech to the General Court, at this time, and the answer of the two houses thereto. In the senate, it passed *unanimously ;* and the house concurred in it by a very large majority. See Appendix No. 2.

* See Appendix No. 3

ten to a petition from men in arms opposed to government; and that no promise of pardon would be made to the leaders who were justly chargeable with the aggravated crime of rebellion, after repeated warnings and former assurances of clemency. The measures of the General Court on this occasion, were very firm and decisive : and contributed, with the previous course of the executive, to discourage the spirit of insurrection, and to give confidence to the friends of constitutional liberty and order.

Two days after the petition was sent on to the General Court, the insurgents marched from Pelham to Petersham, a distance of about twelve miles; probably with a view to a better accommodation. General Lincoln who was still at Hadley, had early notice of this movement; and thinking, that Shays might proceed eastward and gain new adherents or annoy the inhabitants, he immediately resolved to pursue him. He left Hadley late in the evening and reached Petersham the next morning, after a circuitous march of thirty miles, during a very cold night, in a great part of which a snow storm raged with uncommon severity. The men suffered much by this movement, and several of them were badly frozen. But the object was in a great measure accomplished by this spirited and rapid expedition; and general Lincoln acknowledged the singular patience and fortitude of his troops, in this season of exposure. The insurgents had no intelligence of the approach of general Lincoln ; and were thrown into extreme surprise and alarm, as he entered the town. They fled in various directions and in great confusion, without making any opposition. One hundred and fifty of them were taken in attempting to flee ; but the leaders and the residue of them escaped the vigilance of the constitutional troops. A large number returned, separately, to their homes; and some left the state, as the only probable means of safety. It was supposed that they might have given a formidable resistance to general Lincoln, if they had opposed him with all their force ; for his men were exceedingly exhausted by their long march at that inclement season. But he was not justly chargeable with any indiscretion, by which the men under his command would be exposed to great danger. He well knew the want of decision and of mutual confidence among the insurgents; and he made the most judicious arrangement of his troops when he entered Petersham, so that had he been attacked, he felt himself fully prepared to meet them.

The intelligence of this affair spread with rapidity through the state, and gave great animation to all good citizens, especially to the friends of the executive who was responsible for the course adopted to suppress the insurrection. But there were not wanting those who secretly wished for a failure of the measures pursued in support of government. Mr. Bowdoin had political opponents ; and many of the timid and wavering citizens had been averse from the decisive steps, which he considered it his duty to take. The result was such as could not fail to satisfy all impartial men of his judgment and patriotism. And yet a portion of the people complained that the insurgents were not treated with sufficient lenity.

The conduct of general Lincoln received the particular approbation of the legislature ; and the great body of the people were ready to acknowledge both his prudence and firmness. The new recruit of men, which had been ordered, by government, before the dispersion of the insurgents at Petersham were not sent on; but the legislature authorised the raising of 1500 for four months to supply the place of those who first engaged, if their services should be so long needed. Several small parties of the malcontents were still collected in different parts of the state, and threatened further opposition to the civil authority : and many were known to be restrained only by their fears; ready to rise again, should they have reason to hope for success. In the county of Berkshire, there was still just cause of alarm to the peaceable inhabitants. The insurgents were numerous in that part of the state ; and they expected support from the discontented in New York and Vermont. About 500 of the citizens formed a voluntary association for their mutual protection and the support of government. A small party of these were met by a body of the insurgents, who fired a few guns as they first approached; but from a want of confidence in the justice of their object, or a regard for the lives of their fellow citizens, they were reluctant in obeying the orders of their leader to continue their fire ; when one of the party who had assembled for the defence of the state, with great resolution rode up to their front, and ordered them to throw down their arms. Some of them fled; but the greater number gave up their arms and were admitted to the oath of allegiance.

Another party of malcontents soon after collected in a different section of the county, and threatened vengeance on the supporters of government. Major general Patterson who commanded the militia in Berkshire, went in pursuit of them but they fled. He followed them from Adams to Williamstown where they were dispersed. But assembling again in still greater force, he sent an express to general Lincoln at Petersham, for assistance. Before the arrival of Lincoln, Patterson met the insurgents at Lee: upon their proposal to disperse, he promised his influence with government to obtain their pardon, or a trial within the county. Soon after this, another party of insurgents entered the county of Berkshire from New York, but chiefly inhabitants of Massachusetts. They proceeded to Stockbridge, where they threatened and put under guard several respectable citizens. Colonel Ashley collected some militia from Great Barrington and Sheffield, for the purpose of opposing them. As he approached them near the latter place, they fired a few guns; but he advanced, and the firing became general on both sides for a few minutes. But the insurgents soon dispersed leaving two of their number dead on the spot where the action took place; and about thirty of their party wounded. Two of the militia under colonel Ashley were also killed.

About the same time, a number of the insurgents collected at New Braintree in Worcester county, and another party at Northfield in the northern part of Hampshire, which put the inhabitants in fear, by their threatening and abusive conduct. The militia were ordered out to disperse them; but the insurgents fled immediately; not, however, without firing from their hiding places upon the people, who were sent against them, and wounding several of them. Near Northfield, a citizen,* who was in pursuit of one of the leaders of the insurgents, and who met him in a narrow pass, was shot dead. He discharged his piece, at the same moment his antagonist did, but without effect. The criminal escaped to Vermont; but was pursued and taken by a small detachment of militia under captain Buffington, who rendered important service to the state, on several occasions during the insurrection.

The insurgents having fled into the adjoining states, where they could not legally be apprehended by the authority of Massachusetts, the governor, by request of the General Court, made application to the executives of those states respectively, for causing them to be arrested. The chief magistrates of Connecticut and New Hampshire promptly adopted measures for taking up and delivering to the authority of Massachusetts, any persons who had been active in the rebellion, found within their several jurisdictions. In Rhode Island and Vermont, the aid requested was not immediately afforded; but after some delay, and some objections from a portion of the legislatures of these states, they also informed the governor, that they would not protect or harbour any of the citizens of Massachusetts, who had been in arms against the government thereof. The governor of New York, after the legislature gave their sanction to the measure, issued orders to the militia to suppress all riots, and to arrest any of the insurgents of Massachusetts, who might be found within the

* This was a Mr. Jacob Walker of Whately, a worthy and useful citizen.

state. He also proceeded to the eastern boundary of the state, to meet general Lincoln, then in Berkshire; and readily offered all proper assistance for the dispersion or capture of the insurgents.

Before the General Court was adjourned, they passed a resolution for holding special sessions of the Supreme Judicial Court in the counties of Berkshire, Hampshire, and Middlesex, for the trial of the persons who had been taken into custody, on account of the late opposition to the government. The regular term in Worcester would then be at an early day; and therefore no additional provision was made with respect to that county. But it was also particularly provided, that no person who had been engaged in, or had favoured the late rebellion, should be admitted to sit as jurors. The governor was likewise requested by the General Court, to apply to Congress for troops to guard the public arsenal at Springfield, and for authorizing general Lincoln to proceed into the other states, should circumstances render it expedient, to apprehend those persons charged with rebellion in Massachusetts.

With a view to extend all reasonable lenity to that portion of the people, who through ignorance or inconsideration had been induced to rise in opposition to the lawful authority of the state, and towards whom it would be difficult for courts of law to show that indulgence, which a thorough acquaintance with the circumstances of the case would justify, the legislature appointed three commissioners to go into the western counties, and promise indemnity to such as they might consider sincere in their professions of attachment to government, and who had not been among the leaders of the rebellion. General Lincoln, and the Hon. Samuel A. Otis, and the Hon. Samuel Phillips, jr. were selected for this delicate and responsible business. They entered upon the duties of their commission in the month of April; and about 800 persons received the favour of government, which was thus offered them.

Desirous, also, to afford every possible relief to the people, consistently with a just regard for the public welfare, and the support of government, it was agreed to lessen the number of terms of the Court of Common Pleas in several counties, and to reduce the amount of fees in various cases of public officers. A bill also passed the two houses for reducing the salary of the governor one third part. When it was laid before the governor for his signature, he objected to it as unconstitutional. He considered it improper also, so near the close of the political year, and uncertain as it was who would next be chosen to the office he held, to give his consent to such a reduction. The salary, which the governor then received, was established soon after the constitution was adopted, and by the express letter of this instrument it was provided " that it should be of a fixed and permanent value." Complaints were made against the governor for objecting to the bill; but, perhaps, he would have been more justly censured had he approved of it.

At the term of the Supreme Court holden in Berkshire, several persons were indicted for treason, six of whom were convicted; in Hampshire the same number were found guilty, and one in each of the counties of Middlesex and Worcester :

and the sentence of death was accordingly passed upon them by the court. Eight of these received the pardon of the supreme executive, and to the others a reprieve was granted. Many others were convicted of seditious practices, a few of whom were magistrates or officers of government. A representative was proved guilty of open opposition to the civil authority ; and was sentenced to sit on the gallows, and to pay a heavy fine.

The commissioners of the General Court, who went into the upper counties to tender the clemency of government to such as they should believe would prove peaceable citizens in future, had an opportunity of learning the sentiments which prevailed respecting the measures of the legislature, and of ascertaining the causes of complaint. They found that the lower classes of people had been misinformed as to the conduct and views of government; and that there was an unreasonable indulgence in the use of foreign articles, which led them to neglect manufactures, and to expend, in superfluities, what should have been appropriated to the payment of debts and taxes. Private debts had been suffered to accumulate, and the taxes, which each year were very great, had been neglected, till they amounted to such large sums as to destroy almost all hope of discharging them. The appointment of these commissioners had a happy effect, as it discovered a desire in the legislature to discriminate between the artful and unprincipled, who had been the occasion of the rebellion; and those, who, although not entirely justifiable, had been lead to improper practices by misrepresentations or threats. It was proof, likewise, of a disposition in government, to extend all reasonable indulgence towards the deluded citizens. The General Court, which was in session in May, by a particular call from the government to fill the office of treasurer,* resolved also that the taxes for the preceding year might be collected, in part, by public securities.

While the legislature were in session, in March, the subject of enlarging the powers of Congress was again agitated; and it was agreed to send delegates, to meet in convention, at Philadelphia, in the month of May following. It had been sometime considered, by those who attended to the situation of the country, and who perceived the want of uniformity in the several states, in a prompt compliance with the requisitions of Congress, and in their regulations respecting foreign commerce, that a national government was necessary for the purpose of making laws, which should be really obligatory, instead of being simply advisory; and for forming treaties with other nations, which would eventually advance the interests of navigation, and augment the public revenue. The governor and legislature of Massachusetts had suggested the expediency of vesting Congress with additional powers, for these purposes, more than a year before. The committees, which met at Annapolis in Maryland, in 1786, had expressed an opinion in favour of the plan. The House of Assembly, of Virginia, afterwards, particularly approved of a convention of delegates from all the states, for the attainment of this object. And Congress had also voted to recommend the speedy adoption of such a measure.

* Mr. Ivers, the treasurer of the state, died suddenly, and there was no provision by law (as afterwards) for an appointment by the executive.

The credit of the nation was suffering at home and abroad. A great debt was due to France and Holland, which Congress had incurred for the benefit of all the states, in a season of uncommon embarrassment; and for the greater part of the sums due to the officers and soldiers of the revolutionary army, Congress was solemnly bound to provide. When requisitions were made upon the states for their respective quotas of these sums, they delayed payment; and at the close of the year 1786, most of them were in arrears for 1784 and 1785, besides the large sum then required. Several of the states also, which passed acts for raising a revenue by impost duties, which were designed to be wholly applied to pay their proportions of the continental debt, afterwards appropriated it to the discharge of their own.

An entirely new constitution was not generally contemplated, at this period; and it was afterwards objected to the system by some, that it was such as the convention were not fully authorised to form. The delegates chosen to attend the convention, were only instructed, in most cases, to give power to Congress for enacting uniform laws, in relation to commerce and navigation; and for applying, to the discharge of the continental debts and expenses, the revenue which would arise from the duties imposed by that body.

During this session, the General Court provided for collecting 160,000*l.* of the public paper, which had been given in payment to the officers of the late army, by a land lottery. This land was situated in the eastern part of Maine; and every ticket entitled the purchaser to a prize; the only difference being in the location and quality of the lot.

CHAPTER XIV.

THE elections which took place, in April and May, (1787) of governor, senators and representatives, afforded new proof of the difference of opinion among the citizens, respecting the propriety of measures pursued towards the insurgents. Mr. Hancock was chosen governor by a large majority of votes, and the greater number of senators and representatives were new members. In many towns, indeed, it was openly avowed by the people, that they should select their rulers from those who had been opposed to the decisive measures adopted for suppressing the rebellion. It was said by some, that the burdens of the people were so great, that, if they could not be justified, they might be excused: while others believed, that the firmness and energy manifested by the executive had saved the Commonwealth from anarchy and ruin. This was the opinion of the most judicious part of the citizens; and yet there was no doubt of the sincerity of some of those who entertained a different opinion. It could not be justly said, that Mr. Hancock had ever apologized for the conduct of the insurgents; but it was a fact, that many of those who favoured his election believed he would be more indulgent to their errors than his predecessor.* But there was a desire of change, in many of the people, who were led to hope, at least, for some legislative relief. A number of the citizens had always been opposed to Mr. Bowdoin, on the supposition, though entirely unfounded, that he had an undue partiality for the British government and nation. That Mr. Bowdoin was a sincere patriot, no one presumed publicly to deny; and that the measures he adopted were necessary to check the spirit of disorder, which prevailed, was admitted by all impartial citizens. Large majorities both of the senate and representatives approved of the course he pursued; and the administration which followed did not, even by implication, censure his policy.

The insurgents were no longer really formidable to the Commonwealth; the leaders having departed from the state, and the great body of those who had been induced to join in opposition to government, being disposed to submit quietly to the civil authority. Those who had left the state, however, were very inveterate in their feelings towards the friends of law and order; especially in the western counties; and they made attempts,

* Hon. S. Adams, however, was chosen president of the senate; and he had been very decided in favour of the measures adopted by governor Bowdoin.

hopeless as was the prospect of success, to strength-
en their party, that they might be able, at least,
to alarm and annoy such as had been most active
in opposing them. They were not able to effect
their purposes to a great extent; and it was surprising that they were ever permitted to remain
in a neighbouring state, when their criminal plans
and projects were known. But they found means
to sieze two citizens belonging to towns in the
northern parts of Hampshire county, and convey
them into the state of Vermont. They intended
to detain them as hostages; and had the presump-
tion to threaten them with death, if any of those
should be executed who had been convicted of rebellion. This was a great outrage upon any civilized government; and the authority of that state
did not long connive at it; and the prisoners were
permitted to return home.

The intelligence of this affair was received in
the capital the last of May; and induced governor
Hancock to recommend the employment of the
troops then in the service of government, in the
counties of Berkshire and Hampshire, after their
former engagement should expire, which would be
in June. He expressed a decided opinion, that the
measure was necessary for the security and peace
of the citizens in that section of the Commonwealth. The General Court thereupon voted to
raise 800 men, to remain in service for six months,
if such a period should be found necessary. An
attempt was made by those who viewed the conduct of the insurgents with little abhorrence, to
connect with this resolve a general pardon and a
repeal of the disqualifying act formerly passed, but
without success. After much discussion, however,

it was agreed to extend the clemency of government to all those who had been engaged in the insurrection, with the exception of nine, upon condition of their taking the oath of allegiance within three months. The legislature resolved, likewise, that no further lenity should be extended towards such as might, thereafter, be found in arms against the government of the Commonwealth. The governor was, moreover, requested to obtain permission from the civil authority of any adjoining state, to which the insurgents had escaped, to march the militia within their limits, to arrest or subdue them. And he was accordingly authorised to raise a force to be thus employed.

A proposition was made, during this session, for inquiring into the expediency of reducing the salaries of some of the officers of government; and it was urged, that, in a season of great embarrassment, while taxes pressed heavily upon the people, such a measure would be just and proper. The compensation of the chief magistrate was particularly mentioned; and while the subject was before the house, in this incipient stage, the governor proposed to give up one third of his salary for the current year; but expressly stated, that he hoped it would not be urged as a precedent on any future occasion, and intimated that it was not a greater sum than was necessary to the dignity and expenses of the office. But though this part of the salary of the chief magistrate was relinquished for the year only, it was found difficult afterwards to obtain the consent of the General Court to raise it to the former amount. Mr. Hancock, while in the chair, and in the course of the year following, intimated an expectation of receiving the sum originally established; but the legislature made no provision for it, and passed a special law to repeal the original act on the subject.

It was proposed also by some members of the house, that there should be an emission of paper money, and that the General Court should sit in some town in the interior of the country. But neither of these motions obtained; and for the former measure there was only one third of the members present. The tender act was continued, which afforded relief, especially to the people in the interior of the state, who found it difficult to pay their debts in specie. The creditor often suffered by the operation of this law, as he was obliged to receive articles, which he did not need, and of which he could not dispose, without a loss. But the scarcity of specie and the embarrassments of the people were believed to justify the act.

In June, the persons under sentence of death for treason were again reprieved to the month of August: and again to September, when four of them received a full pardon; one was ordered to be confined to hard labour as a commutation of his former sentence, and the others escaped from prison and left the state. Two of the most active and criminal of the insurgents, who fled for safety to an adjoining state, and even to Canada, when their adherents were dispersed by general Lincoln, afterwards became sensible of their crimes, and earnestly prayed for liberty to return; but the request was not granted. In August, a part of the troops raised in June were discharged; and, in September, the tranquil situation of the Commonwealth justified the disbanding of the residue.

The friends of good government and of constitutional liberty rejoiced, that a dangerous insurrection, which at one period threatened the welfare of the whole Commonwealth, was so soon suppressed, and that so little expense and, bloodshed had attended the decisive measures of the executive. Although there was cause for alarm, at a particular time, when the insurgents found many apologists for their opposition to the authority of the state, the citizens generally derived great satisfaction in reflecting upon the firmness and wisdom of the legislature, and the success which attended the plans of the governor. It was also a flattering eulogy upon the measures of administration, that the great body of the people approved of the course pursued for suppressing the rebellion, when they had time for correct information; and that most of the insurgents themselves regretted the part they had taken in the affair, and begged to share in the favour of government. The event was deeply and justly regretted, as a stain upon the character of the people of the state; but it afforded an opportunity to show the strength of a republican government : and the union of firmness with clemency in the rulers, served to attach the citizens more strongly to the constitution, and to convince them of the necessity of a supreme civil authority in the Commonwealth.

The efforts which had been made by many of the citizens for promoting a spirit of industry and economy, were not without effect; and the opinion prevailed of the importance of encouraging various manufactures in the country. But a great change, so as to check a taste for foreign superfluities, and to make frugality both fashionable and practicable could be only gradually introduced. Commercial enterprises, however, increased, although attended with great embarrassments, which gave employment to many of the people; and products of the Commonwealth were exported in greater quantities, instead of specie. The legislature was desirous of adopting some effectual means for restoring and supporting public credit; but so great were the demands against the Commonwealth, and such the inability of the people to pay the taxes assessed, with punctuality, that the paper of government was much below the par value,* and those who were obliged to dispose of it made great sacrifices of property. It was not until the adoption of the federal constitution, and the decisive measures pursued by the general government for the payment of continental debts, that the public paper rose to the value which it nominally bore. A great part of the taxes assessed at this period, and for several preceding years, by the respective states, was for discharging debts contracted by promises and resolves of Congress, but which were apportioned among the states according to their different population and property.

The General Court met again in October, as had been usual for many years; and continued in session until the last of November. The governor informed the two houses, that an additional tax would be necessary, and advised that those which had been long due should be speedily collected. Several taxes were then, in great part, unpaid, and

---

* The consolidated notes, as they were called, and the army notes were sold, at this time, for about one sixth part in specie.

the government was frequently obliged to borrow, for the purpose of discharging those debts which could not be postponed;* and the taxes assessed, as well as the revenue arising from impost and excise, pledged for payment. The legislature directed, that executions be issued against those collectors who were delinquents for the years 1784 and 1785, and that a further time be given for collecting the two last taxes. It may appear singular, that a new tax should be ordered, when former ones were still due, and even further delay permitted for collection; but in some towns the taxes were more promptly paid; and some relief was also given to public creditors, by this measure, as the treasurer was allowed to issue orders upon the collectors in various parts of the state, by which both they and the public creditors received a present accommodation. Some idea of the heavy load of taxes, which pressed upon the people at this period, may be formed, not only from the fact, that several had been sent out through the state, and remained uncollected from a real inability, in many cases, to discharge them; but by considering that the sum of 300,000 dollars was necessary to pay the interest merely of the debt of the Commonwealth. Army notes to a large amount were also now due; and some had been due for one and two years, without renewal. The whole dependence, however, was not on the direct tax, but a considerable revenue was also raised by the excise and by imposts.

* So urgent were the demands on the treasurer, that 20,000 dollars were applied to the immediate wants of government arising from the impost, though it had been expressly engaged to pay off army notes and interest on the public debt.

That no financial system more efficient was adopted this year, was probably to be attributed to the hope of a new organization of the general government, which would be vested with power to regulate foreign commerce; by which the trade of the country would be placed in a more prosperous state, and the revenue arising from it, being much increased, would be at the disposal of that government for the payment of the continental debts.

At this session of the legislature, the governor communicated the federal constitution proposed by the convention, then recently held at Philadelphia, by delegates from each of the states. This constitution, designed to give more power to the legislature and government of the United States, than was granted by the articles of confederation, and which it was believed the prosperity and welfare of the country required, was prepared and laid before Congress, in September, (1787) with a request that it be forwarded to the legislatures of the several states.

The governor spoke of it as the result of great deliberation, and of a spirit of conciliation in some of the wisest and most patriotic citizens of the nation;* and suggested the necessity of calling a convention to whom it must be submitted. There was some opposition even to the examination of the instrument, with a view to its adoption. But the objection to a convention was overruled by a large majority in the General Court; and it was

* General Washington, Dr. Franklin, Madison, and Hamilton were among the number. The delegates from Massachusetts were judge Dana, Mr. Gerry, Mr. Gorham, Mr. Story and Mr. King.

provided that the towns should be notified to elect delegates, in the same manner representatives were chosen, who should meet in January following, and determine on the expediency of adopting it.

The convention met in Boston, January 1788, and consisted of 360 members; most of the towns having sent the full number, to which they were entitled by their population. His excellency governor Hancock was chosen president, and the honourable William Cushing, chief justice of the state, vice-president. A great portion of the convention had strong prejudices against the constitution. If a vote had been taken, soon after they assembled, it would probably have been against it. After a discussion of several weeks, and some converts were made by the able arguments and eloquent appeals of its more decided advocates, there was only a majority of nineteen, in that large assembly, for its adoption.

It was acknowledged by those who were most desirous of adopting it, that some parts of it were liable to objections. But the opposition of many, who were prepared to reject it, was evidently founded in prejudice or mistake. When the constitution was first published, it was represented as giving too much power to the general or national government, which would be established; and as lessening or interfering with the authority of the individual states, to such an extent as to leave them with scarcely the name of sovereignty. It was conceded, that a federal government was requisite for some general objects, and for regulating commerce and the intercourse with foreign nations. But it was feared, that the authority vested in a general legislature, as proposed in the constitution would produce a concentration of all political power in that body, and reduce the states to merely municipal corporations. The small number of representatives* in Congress and the privilege of the slave-holding states, to choose a greater number, than they would be entitled to, if only the free inhabitants were considered; were also believed to be great defects in the constitution. It was further objected, that the elections were not annual. This was a popular objection, as the elections in Massachusetts had always been for a year only. At the same time, it was admitted that the country was suffering by the imbecility of the confederation, and that greater power must be vested in the general government, in order to promote the welfare and prosperity of the nation. Some also objected, that the general convention had exceeded the powers given them, which were confined to an alteration of the articles of confederation: and yet they admitted, that without a total change of that system, so as that Congress should have full authority to require obedience to its laws, it would not afford a remedy for the evils to which the country was then subjected.† But in addition to some real defects in the constitution, or to objections existing in the minds of some honest men, who yet did not weigh as they ought the evils which would follow from a rejection of it, the prejudices of the less enlightened part of the people, in which

* The number of 40,000 inhabitants to a representative was reported, and once voted in the general convention, which prepared the constitution; but Washington proposed 30,000, and it was adopted.

† See Mr. Gerry's letter in the Appendix, No. 4.

may be included several of the delegates to the state convention, were excited by the sophistry or misrepresentations of a few men, who wrote against the instrument, and represented it as an abridgment of the liberties of the people, and little better than monarchy in disguise.

The friends of the proposed constitution believed it to be wisely framed, consistent with the liberties of the people, and calculated to secure the welfare and happiness of the country. They considered it the best system which could be formed by the citizens of such an extensive territory, so as to meet the approbation of all; and the only one in all probability, which would be accepted. They were confident the freedom and interests of the people would not suffer by elections for the period provided; but, on the contrary, that the nature of the government and the extent of the country required such elections. They contended that the power given to Congress was no more extensive than was necessary to accomplish the great national purposes, which all were desirous the general legislature should be authorised to accomplish, for the honour and welfare of the United States; and they argued, that there would not be the interference between the national and state governments, as many apprehended. They insisted, that the confederation was totally incompetent to all national purposes; and that general bankruptcy and anarchy must ensue on the rejection of the new constitution. They were satisfied, no other system could be formed, with so few defects; and they feared no further attempt would be made for a national or united government; the consequence of which would be frequent and violent collisions between the several states. The constitution expressly recognized the people as the fountain of power, whose liberty and prosperity it was intended to secure and promote; the election of their legislators and rulers was still with them; and whatever was not delegated to the general government was reserved to the people and to the states respectively.

Those who were originally opposed to the constitution, were not easily prevailed to accept it, nor would they acknowledge their objections were removed. It is probable they feared, that great abuses of power, or great abridgment of their liberty would be the consequence of a national government with such extensive authority; and that they did not realize the evils which would result from its rejection. Many were disappointed, however, when the opponents of the constitution finally voted against it, after the conciliatory proposition of amendments connected with it, which went to remove the objections they made to the instrument. But, happy for Massachusetts, and for the United States, a majority of votes was obtained for it; which probably decided the opinion of some other states in its favour, which had not then acted upon the subject, and in which a great portion of the people were ready to object. Many of those who gave their vote against the constitution might have been as honest as those who advocated it; but it is impossible to admit, that they had as great wisdom and foresight. There were only *nineteen* votes more for than against the constitution. The result was 187 for, and 168 against it. Those who opposed it in the convention, with much candour and patriotism, declared their

determination to support it, as it had been approved
and adopted by the majority. Those who were decided and active in its favour, and by whose influence it was accepted, ranked among the most distinguished patriots of the state.* They were persuaded of the necessity of a general government,
with much more extensive power than Congress
then possessed; and knowing the distresses and
complaints of the people, and the difficulty of
forming a federal system which would be universally approved, they concluded, that if the one
then presented were rejected, there would be no
hope of a substitute; and that anarchy must ensue. Perhaps, at no time after the struggle for
independence, had the country been in so great
danger; and to no men was it more indebted for
preservation from ruin, and for security of the
blessings of good government, than to those who
procured the acceptance of the federal constitution in Massachusetts.

No objection to the constitution was more powerful than that arising from a tendency to a consolidation of the states. " This," said Mr. Ames,
" was an effect, which all good men would depre-
cate. The state governments," he said, " were
essential parts of the system. The senators represented the sovereignty of the states; in the
other house, the whole people were represented.

---

* These were Bowdoin, Dana, Strong, Cabot, Parsons, Gorham, Ames, Dawes, Brooks, Sedgwick, Gore, King, J. C. Jones,
Jarvis, &c. Great support was also given to the constitution
by governor Hancock, and Hon. S. Adams, though they did
not entirely approve of every article. The former proposed
amendments, and the other supported them; without which
the constitution would probably have been rejected.

If the senators were chosen by the people, as the representatives were, a consolidation of the state governments would ensue; which, it is conceded, would subvert the new constitution. Too much provision cannot be made against consolidation. The state governments are the safeguards and ornament of the federal constitution—they will protract the period of our liberties; they will afford a shelter against the abuse of power, and will be the natural avengers of our violated rights." Although extensive power was vested in the general government, of which the constitution was to be the foundation, and although it was purposely designed to give authority to a federal legislature, for the welfare of the United States, that the new constitution had been formed, still it was believed by *all*, that no power was to be claimed by the national government except such as was expressly given; and that all besides was reserved to the individual states and to the people. Had it been supposed, that authority would be exercised, founded only upon construction or inference, it is probable the constitution would not have been adopted by a majority of the states.

Several of the amendments to the constitution, proposed by the convention in Massachusetts, were afterwards approved by three-fourths of the states, and accordingly became a part of the federal compact. One of these was, " that the powers not delegated to the United States, nor prohibited by it to the states, are reserved to the states respectively, or to the people." Another, that a state should not be liable to a suit from a citizen of another state, or from a foreign citizen.

Virginia and New York proposed, that another general convention should be called to act upon the amendments proposed by the several states; and the governors of those states were requested to communicate the same to Massachusetts, for its concurrence in such a measure. When governor Hancock laid those propositions before the legislature, he expressed an opinion of the inexpediency of the plan; and stated, that the proper course to pursue would be to urge it upon Congress to submit the proposed amendments to the legislatures of the several states for their approbation. The majority of the General Court approved of the governor's views on the subject. In his message he spoke of the federal constitution as necessary to render the United States really *independent*, and to promote the prosperity of the country.

The acceptance of the federal constitution, by the convention in Massachusetts afforded much satisfaction to its advocates in other states; and particularly in those, which had not then come to a decision on the subject.* The citizens of Boston expressed great joy on the occasion, which was manifested by a numerous procession, composed of all classes and trades, with their respective and appropriate badges, more extensive and imposing than had ever been witnessed in that ancient town. The mechanics had suffered for want of employment, on account of the embarrassments on commerce, and the great importation of articles of foreign manufacture. They believed that domestic manufactures would be encouraged, and that

* General Washington expressed great satisfaction, when he learned that Massachusetts had adopted it.

navigation would increase and furnish profitable occupation to a large portion of the people. They
were not disappointed in these expectations. It
was among the first acts of Congress, after the federal constitution was adopted, to regulate the commercial intercourse of all the states with foreign
places, and to secure greater privileges to the country than it had before enjoyed. An uniform system of revenue was formed, by laying duties on all
importations into the United States. The debts
of the several states, incurred for the defence of
the whole during the war, were assumed by Congress; in consequence of which those states which
had expended more than their proportion would
be benefited; one of which was Massachusetts, as
had been before believed to be the fact. The
continental debt was also funded, and the faith of
Congress pledged for payment, of which the prospect of an increasing revenue authorized the ful-
filment. The public paper, thereupon, gradually
arose in value; and the creditors of the nation
were eventually fully satisfied. This prosperous
condition of the country gave a new impulse to
business, and all classes of people found sufficient
employment. The credit of the state revived,
also, as a great part of its debt was to be provided
for by Congress; and the legislature discovered a
disposition to pay the creditors of the Commonwealth such part of their demands as was practicable, and to adopt a system by which funds would
be secured to discharge the residue with the interest at stated periods. The state debt, however,
was large; and for some time, the taxes, including
those of former years which had long been accumulating, bore heavily on the citizens and called

for great efforts and sacrifices. The tax ordered for this year (1788) was 220,000 dollars; and a great part of those for 1785, 1786 and 1787, remained to be paid by many towns.*

Congress appointed an agent to examine the accounts which Massachusetts had prepared against the United States, for expenses incurred by the Commonwealth for the general welfare, and which were not considered exclusively as the debt of the state. These, indeed, gave a great sum; as the defence of the state was not allowed to be carried to the national account. Of the former claims, two millions and an half of dollars, of specie value, were admitted, without hesitation or objection: and also eight millions of the old currency, which had greatly depreciated. Besides these sums, other accounts were offered of six millions, which were not then allowed, as the instructions of the agent did not authorize it; and which were, therefore, referred to a future settlement.† But the greater part of it was afterwards admitted.

In the course of this year, a quantity of copper was issued from the mint, which had been established by order of the legislature in 1786. It was also proposed to have silver coined; but Congress advised against the measure, upon the belief, that coining money was the prerogative of the United States collectively considered, and that uniformity would be for the greater convenience of the people in all parts of the union. Only a small

* The amount of arrears of former taxes was about a million of dollars.

† Hon. Nathan Dane, then a member of Congress, was very attentive to the claims of Massachusetts, and rendered great service to the state.

amount was coined; and the next year, on the establishment of the federal government, the mint in Massachusetts was discontinued.

The legislature discovered a disposition in favour of manufactures; and governor Hancock, as his predecessor had done a year before, recommended, that public encouragement be given to such as promised to be useful, and for which the state afforded materials. A duck manufactory was established in Boston, and a cotton manufactory in Beverly; both of which received pecuniary aid from the General Court, the former in the way of bounty upon the duck manufactured, and the other by a grant of eastern lands. But these establishments were very limited in their effects, and did not long continue in operation. The manufacture of pot and pearl ashes increased to a great extent in the interior of the state, and supplied those who traded to England with a valuable article of exportation. There were two hundred and forty establishments of this kind in the state, at this period. Nails were also manufactured, in some towns, in large quantities. The state was much benefited by this employment: for the demand was great for the article, and it saved the specie to the country, which would otherwise have been sent abroad in exchange for it.

A law was passed in the month of March 1788, forbidding all the citizens of the state from having any concern in the slave trade. Massachusetts had, indeed, always condemned the practice as unchristian, and inconsistent with the common rights of humanity. It had, also, before this period, abolished the odious custom of slavery through the state. If any of the citizens had been concerned in such inhuman traffic, it was unknown to the civil authority and to the public. The occasion of the law, at this particular time, was the seizing of three people of colour by the captain of a vessel in Boston, and taking them by force to the West Indies, with an intention to make sale of them. The person engaged, in thus forcibly taking or detaining any negro, for the purpose of transportation as a slave, was subject to a heavy penalty; the owners of the vessels were made liable in a large sum; the insurance was to be void; and the relations of the persons kidnapped, if these were sold in a distant country, were allowed to prosecute for the crime.

CHAPTER XV.

In 1788, Mr. Hancock was again elected governor of the Commonwealth by a very general vote, and without much opposition. It was not to be expected, that all would prefer him; and as he had been placed in the chair, the year preceding by the influence of those, who disapproved of the measures adopted by Mr. Bowdoin, there were many in the state who could not give him their cordial support. But his administration for the year past had not been such as to justify the fearful anticipations of his opponents. If he had not the firmness to oppose popular errors, or to act with suitable decision and energy in a time of general dissatisfaction and commotion, such as had prevailed in the time of Mr. Bowdoin, he was not disposed to compromit the dignity of government by any acts of weak indulgence towards the insurgents. Perhaps, no man in the Commonwealth had talents better fitted to maintain the tranquillity of society and the necessary authority of the government, when he took the chair, as successor to Mr

Bowdoin. General Lincoln was chosen lieutenant governor for this year, though there were several others proposed as candidates for the office, at the time of the elections. He possessed the most estimable qualities as a man, and was celebrated as a brave and judicious officer in the war of the revolution. He had also repeatedly been elected to the legislature and to the council board. His decision and prudence in conducting the militia raised by government to suppress the insurrection, had increased the public confidence in his character.

The conduct of the governor, this year, in relation to the captaincy of the castle, by which it was believed he manifested an unfriendly feeling towards general Lincoln, was a subject of public discussion; and, in a portion of the community, of severe censure. By some, indeed, the course he pursued was considered arbitrary and unconstitutional. By his particular recommendation, an establishment had been made by the legislature, for the castle, by which it was provided, that the executive should appoint a captain for that fortress. The lieutenant governor had long held that office; and received for it certain fees and perquisites, which amounted to upwards of a thousand dollars. These, Mr. Cushing, the predecessor of general Lincoln, had *always* received; and no other allowance was made for him by the legislature. General Lincoln received none of these perquisites, and no salary was annexed to the office. In the month of November, of this year, 1788, nearly six months after the election of general Lincoln, as lieutenant governor, the house inquired, why he had not been appointed to the command of the castle, having a reference chiefly

to the subject of compensation, which they believed he ought to receive. The governor sent a
message to the General Court, in which he not only
claimed the right to fill an office, at such time as
he might think proper; but explicitly declared it
his opinion, "that he might justly, as chief magistrate, refuse to carry into effect a resolve of the
General Court, if he judged it would involve the
state in an unnecessary expense;" which he said he
supposed would be the case, in having a captain of
the castle with so large a compensation as had been
then received. It was the doctrine advanced by
the governor, rather than the omission of appointing a captain to the castle, which was condemned;
though many failed not to charge him with a design also to deprive the lieutenant governor of the
stipend, which his predecessor had always received.
A committee was appointed by the General Court,
at the winter session, to consider what allowance
the lieutenant governor should have for his services; and their report gave occasion to an animated debate on the conduct of the governor. The
discussion continued several days, in the course of
which, resolutions were offered, disapproving of the
sentiments of the governor expressed in his message of November; but they were not acceptable
to the majority of the house, and were therefore
rejected. It was admitted by those who advocated the resolutions, that the governor had a right
to decide as to the proper time for making appoint-
ments; though even in this, there might be an unjustifiable delay, for which he was responsible to
his constituents and to the state; but it was contended, that he could not justly prevent the operation of a law, which the legislature had passed.

The committee reported a thousand dollars, as a compensation to the lieutenant governor; but the house reduced it to five hundred and thirty-three.

A difference of opinion was manifested between the two houses of the General Court, in adopting an answer to the governor's message communicated at the beginning of the session. It was the practice, at that time, for the two houses to unite in the address to the governor, in reply to his public speeches. But on this occasion, the senate and house could not agree in an answer; and the representatives voted to prepare a separate address. The subject of disagreement was, at this session, relative to several questions which came before them; particularly with reference to the payment of the public debt. The senate were decided for some provisions, by which the interest would be punctually paid, and for a larger tax, with this view, than the representatives thought expedient to assess.

There was also a proposal by the senate, for striking out a paragraph in the original draft adopted by the house, in which it was proposed, as the states of Virginia and New York had done, to call a new convention, for the purpose of incorporating the amendments proposed to the constitution, into the instrument, before any general government was organized under it. The senate were opposed to such a measure, as of fatal tendency; and agreed with the governor, in the opinion he expressed in his speech, that all which was proper for the legislature to do, was to present the proposed amendments to the Congress, and to instruct the representatives from the state to that body to use their efforts to have them recommended and adopted.

Until this period, the delegates to Congress had been appointed by the General Court. According to the federal constitution, they were now to be chosen immediately by the people. For the first Congress, Massachusetts was to have only eight representatives. The state was divided into that number of districts, for the purpose of electing one representstive in each. This number was determined by the new constitution; but was not perfectly agreeable to the ratio fixed by that instrument, for future years, which was one representative for 30,000 inhabitants. The population of Massachusetts, at that time, entitled her to more than the number above mentioned ; but no census had been then lately taken, and the number of inhabitants was not precisely known to the convention.[*] At the first trial, only four representatives were elected; these were Fisher Ames, George Partridge, George Leonard, and George Thatcher. Afterwards, Elbridge Gerry, Benjamin Goodhue, Jonathan Grout, and Theodore Sedgwick, were chosen. The first board of electors, in Massachusetts, of president and vice president, were Willim Cushing, William Shepard, William Sever, Walter Spooner, David Sewall, Caleb Davis, Francis Dana, Samuel Henshaw, Samuel Phillips, jr. and Moses Gill.

The mode prescribed by the legislature at this time, for the appointment of electors, was as follows—Two persons were to be voted for in each district, and the General Court to select one of the two who should receive the highest number of votes; and two others were chosen immediate-

---

[*] The number was supposed to be 370,000 or 380,000.

ly by the legislature. These met in Boston, on the first Wednesday of February, 1789, and gave in their votes for general WASHINGTON to be president, and Hon. JOHN ADAMS to be vice president, of the United States.

Soon after general Washington was inducted into the office of president of the United States, the legislature of Massachusetts forwarded him the following public address.

"Sir,—Your acceptance of your present exalted and important station, affords universal joy to the people of Massachusetts. They have long felt the most grateful sentiments for your character, and attachment to your person. And they reflect with pleasure on the ardour which your presence inspired in the alarming and novel circumstances of a war within their country and against their civil security, so soon restored by the discipline and success of the army under your command.

"The unanimity of the suffrages of these states in your election, is no less a testimony of your merit, than of the gratitude of this extensive community. They have declared, by investing you with the powers of their president, their confidence in you, from their experience of your wisdom and virtues, and they delight to honour you. For your services, in their estimation, will yet far exceed their rewards.

"The union of the states, by a form of government, intended to secure the blessings of liberty, is rendered more perfect under you, as their chief. All the advantages of that government, of our national independence and civil liberty, may be rationally expected under your administration. From you, we shall receive those examples of public and private economy, of prudence, fortitude and patriotism, of justice, morality and religion, which, by the aid of divine providence, insure the welfare of a community.

" To express the voice of our constituents, we join in the congratulations of United America, on this great event, and we earnestly implore the protection of Almighty God upon your person and family ; that he would afford you his divine aid in the duties of your important station, and would long continue you a blessing to the United States."

On the application of the governor, Congress ordered two brass field pieces to be restored to Massachusetts, which were a part of the FOUR that composed the whole American field artillery, at the commencement of the revolutionary war. Congress ordered the following inscription to be put upon them; on one—" HANCOCK—sacred to liberty. This is one of four cannon which constituted the whole train of *field* artillery, possessed by the British colonies of North America, at the commencement of the war, on the 19th of April 1775. This cannon and its fellow, belonging to a number of citizens of Boston, were used in many engagements during the war. The other two, the property of the government of Massachusetts, were taken by the enemy." On the other, the inscription was " ADAMS," with the same explanation and statement as on the former one.

Mr. Hancock was elected governor again in April 1789 ; but received greater opposition than in 1788. There was no particular accusation preferred against him for improper measures, during the former political year, except his conduct with regard to general Lincoln, the lieutenant governor;

which, by many, was considered not only unfriendly to that eminent patriot, but arbitrary in itself, and inconsistent with the nature of the government. His most zealous adherents proposed Mr. Samuel Adams for lieutenant governor, instead of general Lincoln; and this circumstance led the friends of the latter to support Mr. Bowdoin for governor, and to oppose Mr. Hancock and Mr. Adams, with more than ordinary warmth. The various publications in the newspapers, relating to the election, contained personal allusions and bitter criminations, unknown on any former occasion. Mr. Adams was elected lieutenant governor for this political year. Many of his former friends were surprised, that he and Mr. Hancock were on the same ticket, as they had differed on some public measures within a few years. But these were not on material points; their general views and opinions were similar; and they had long been associated in the political affairs of the state and the nation.

The governor in his message,* communicated soon after the General Court was organized, having spoken with great approbation of the federal government, from which he said important and permanent benefits might justly be expected, observed—

"But it ought ever to be remembered that no form of government, or mode of administration can make a vicious people happy; and that therefore the public felicity will in a great measure depend upon the practice of the social and private

---

* Indisposition prevented his attending the legislature in person during this session.

virtues by the people of this extensive republic.—
That this Commonwealth, which constitutes an
important part of the general government, may
increase its own prosperity, while it promotes that
of the Union, we must support and encourage the
means of learning, and all institutions for the education of the rising generation; an equal degree
of intelligence being as necessary to a free government, as laws are for an equal distribution of property.

"Our wise and magnanimous ancestors, impressed with this idea, were very careful and liberal in
the establishment of institutions for this purpose;
among which, that of our university in Cambridge,
and grammar schools in the several towns were believed very important. Every necessary attention
will certainly be paid to the former: and I cannot
but earnestly recommend to your inquiry, the reason
why the latter is so much neglected in the state.*
Should any new laws be wanting on this subject,
you cannot do your country a more essential service than by providing them."

A law was passed at this session, requiring all
towns with two hundred families, to support a
grammar school, agreeably to former usage in the
province. Towns with that number and upwards,
were ordered to employ for instructers of youth,
those who had been educated at some college, and
were able to teach the Latin and Greek languages.
In towns where the inhabitants were less, it was

* It is a matter of regret with many, that, since the time
when governor Hancock gave the above opinion and advice,
the provision by law for grammar schools has been, in a great
measure, virtually annulled.

required, that such as were qualified to teach the English language correctly, should be engaged in the business of education. Great benefits were derived from this and former laws, containing similar provisions, to the people of Massachusetts. In later periods, the laws of the Commonwealth have only required instruction in the English language; which has not only obliged those who desire a knowledge of the Greek or Latin, to go to distant places in order to acquire them; but has lowered the character and qualifications of instructers; the evils of which are apparent to those who compare the present with past times.

The preamble to this law, " providing for the instruction of youth and the promotion of good education," was as follows—" Whereas the constitution of this Commonwealth hath declared it to be the duty of the General Court to provide for the education of youth; and whereas a general dissemination of knowledge and virtue is necessary to the prosperity of every state, and the very existence of a Commonwealth." The governor had expressed similar sentiments in his speech, at the beginning of the session. From the earliest settlement of the country, the benefits arising from affording the means of information to youth of all classes and conditions were acknowledged; and it was also admitted, that, to such as desired it, the opportunity should be furnished of gaining an acquaintance with ancient literature.

During this session (June 1789,) a committee of finance was appointed to " inquire into the several expenditures, and see if any savings can be made; to inquire into the state of all outstanding taxes and of all debts due to the Commonwealth; into the state of the revenue arising from impost and excise; and to see what deductions will be consequent, upon the treasury, by the operation of federal laws: and to devise means for increasing the public revenue." A few days after, this committee reported, " that the debt of the state was 1,400 000*l*., the interest to which the Commonwealth was liable, annually, was somewhat more than 100, 000*l*. This, it was stated, would be reduced by receipts on the sales of the lands in New York 300,000*l*.; by a year's interest, then due on that sum, and by the sale of continental certificates, 90,000*l*.; which had then recently been given by Congress as evidence of claims, to that amount in favour of the Commonwealth, already settled. According to this exhibit, the amount to be provided for was about 1,081,000*l*.; the interest of which was 64,000*l*. To this was to be added 15,000*l*. estimated as necessary for the civil list. It was believed that the excise would give half this sum; and it was recommended, that the other moiety should be raised by a direct tax. And the committee stated, that this amount was less by 10,000*l*. than was assessed upon the province from 1763 to 1770. Several members objected to any direct tax, at this time, on account of the taxes laid in several former years and then required by the General Court to be immediately collected. Some of the representatives appeared to have little concern for the credit of the Commonwealth, and were chiefly anxious for the relief of their constituents, who were still complaining loudly of the public burdens.

The county of Lincoln, which included the easterly part of the district of Maine, a large territory, extending on the sea-coast, two hundred miles, from the river Kennebec* to St. Croix, the boundary between the United States and the British province of New Brunswick, was divided into three shires. The two new ones formed were called Hancock and Washington. The separation of Maine was again proposed by a convention at Portland, in 1788, which presented a petition to the legislature to further the design. The petition was before the General Court some time, but it was not granted; for it did not appear that the majority of the people were desirous of becoming a distinct state. The dispute still continued, as to the true boundary of the state on the east; and the national government being now formed, the legislature requested the governor to make application to the president of the United States to take measures for ascertaining the line of division, according to the treaty with Great Britain in 1783. The dispute was afterwards amicably settled, under the authority of the federal government.

In the month of October of this year, president Washington made a tour through the northern states; and his reception in Boston, the capital of Massachusetts, both by the citizens of the town and by the supreme executive of the Commonwealth, were such as had never before been given to any individual. All classes of people were represented in the procession, formed to meet and escort him into the town; and the highest officers in the state united in this expression of respect to the truly illustrious character of the nation's civil

* The county of Lincoln included some towns on the west of this river.

and military chief. The people were universally animated with all those sentiments of gratitude and veneration for their distinguished benefactor, which a sense of his eminent virtues and services was calculated to inspire; and manifested their feelings by every suitable demonstration of joy and exultation. The visit of Washington gave great satisfaction to the people; but it was scarcely possible to increase the esteem and admiration in which his character was already held. · The lieutenant governor and members of the executive council, the selectmen of Boston and other municipal and state officers, with an immense number of citizens, met the president at the bounds of the town, to bid him welcome, and to accompany him to his place of residence. After his arrival, he received an affectionate and respectful address from the selectmen, in the name and behalf of the inhabitants of Boston; to which he replied, in a style complimentary to the patriotism and virtue of the citizens of that ancient town. The following address was also presented him by the governor and council.

" We meet you, sir, at this time, with our hearts replete with the warmest affection and esteem, to express the high satisfaction we feel in your visit to the Commonwealth of Massachusetts.

" We can never forget the *time*, when, in the earliest stage of the war, and the day of *our* greatest calamity, we saw you at the head of the army of the United States, commanding troops, determined, though then undisciplined, by your wisdom and valour, preventing a sanguinary and well appointed army of our enemies, from spreading devastation through our country, and sooner than we had reason to expect, obliging them to abandon the capital.

"We have since seen you in your high command, superior to the greatest fatigues and hardships, successfully conducting our armies through a long war, until our enemies were compelled to submit to terms of peace; and acknowledged that independence which the United States in Congress assembled, had before asserted and proclaimed.

"We now have the pleasure of seeing you in a still more exalted station, to which you have been elected by the unanimous suffrages of a free, virtuous and grateful country. From that attachment, which you manifestly discovered while in your military command, to the civil liberties of your country, we do assure ourselves, that you will ever retain this great object in your view, and that your administration will be happy and prosperous.

"It is our earnest prayer, that the divine Benediction may attend you here and hereafter; and we do sincerely wish that you may, through this life, continue to enjoy that greatest of earthly blessings, to be accepted by "the multitude of your brethren.""

To which general Washington replied as follows—

"Gentlemen, to communicate the peculiar pleasure which I derive from your affectionate welcome of me to the Commonwealth of Massachusetts, requires a force of expression beyond that which I possess. I am truly grateful for your goodness towards me, and I desire to thank you with the unfeigned sincerity of a feeling heart.

"Your obliging remembrance of my military services, is among the highest compensations they can

receive; and if rectitude of intention may authorize the hope, the favourable anticipation, which
you are pleased to express of my civil administration, will not, I trust, be disappointed. It is your
happiness, gentlemen, to preside in the councils of
a Commonwealth, where the pride of independence is well assimilated with the duties of society ;
and, where the industry of the citizen gives the
fullest assurance of public respect and private prosperity. I have observed too, with singular satisfaction, so becoming an attention to the militia of
the state, as presents the fairest prospect of support to the invaluable objects of national prosperity and peace. Long may these blessings be continued to the Commonwealth of Massachusetts !
And may you, gentlemen, in your individual capa-
cities, experience every satisfaction, which can result from public honour and private happiness."

In appointing to office under the federal government, general Washington selected those who had
been distinguished by their zeal and patriotism during the war of the revolution. And his appoint-
ments were bestowed on none but men of integrity and talents, which fully qualified them for the
stations in which they were placed. This policy
was approved by all impartial men; and yet Mr.
Jefferson, who succeeded to the presidency, some
years after general Washington declined it, removed some of the revolutionary characters from the
offices they held, merely for difference of political
opinions, on subjects or measures of minor consideration, which did not implicate their patriotism or
their republican principles.

A question was long and warmly agitated in the
General Court during this political year, respecting

the eligibility of an officer in the federal government to a seat in the legislature of the state. The judge of a district court, the attorney and marshal of the district, were then members of the legislature of Massachusetts.* A committee was first appointed in the senate, which reported, that the seat of Mr. Jackson, a member of that board, from Essex, in consequence of his receiving and accepting the appointment of marshal of the district, by which he had become an officer of the general government, was vacated: but the report was rejected in the senate, by thirteen votes to eleven.

In the house, the decision was different, on a similar question relating to two of their members; being 137 to 24. The report, however, which gave a full and decided opinion of their ineligibility, like that made in the senate, was not proposed for acceptance; but on the question, substituted for the report, "whether persons holding office under the United States, similar to those declared by the constitution of this Commonwealth incompatible with their holding seats in the legislature thereof, can have a constitutional right to retain their seats in this house?"—after a debate of great length, it was decided in the manner mentioned above.

It was contended, by those in favour of the report, that uniformity and analogy forbid the eligibility of such officers of the federal government to a seat in the legislature, as were similar to those excluded from it, if officers in the state. And that

* David Sewall of Maine, who had been appointed judge of the district court, and Christopher Gore, who had been appointed district attorney, were members of the house; J. Jackson, appointed marshal, was a member of the senate.

there would be an improper and dangerous influence exerted by federal officers, if permitted to be legislators of the Commonwealth. On the other side, it was argued, that the reasons, which rendered it improper for certain public officers of the state to have seats in the legislature, did not hold with regard to officers of the United States; and that, as there was not an express or clear incompatibility in the constitution, they could not be justly excluded. There was a great jealousy of the federal government, at that early period, on the minds of many of the citizens; but, in later years, less fear or hostility towards it have been cherished; and in many instances, men holding office under the general government, have exerted a great influence, in directing the concerns of a single state.

Under the auspicious influence of the federal government, a mutual confidence was strengthened among the citizens of the Commonwealth and of the United States; the common employments and arts of life were encouraged; commercial enterprizes increased; the credit of government was restored, by wise and efficient provisions in the finances of the country, the regulation of foreign commerce and the uniform collection of a revenue; and the nation made rapid advances, from a state of embarrassment and imbecility, to wealth, power and respectability.

APPENDIX.

No. I. *Pages,* 140, 159.

A CONSTITUTION and FORM of GOVERNMENT for the State of MASSACHUSETTS BAY, agreed upon by the CONVENTION of said State, February 28th, 1778; to be laid before the several towns and plantations in said State, for their approbation or disapprobation.

STATE OF MASSACHUSETTS BAY,
IN CONVENTION, February 28th, 1778.

WHEREAS, upon the declaration of independence, made by the representatives of the UNITED STATES, in Congress assembled, by which all connexions between the said states and Great Britain were dissolved, the General Assembly of this state thought it expedient, that a new constitution of government for this state should be formed; and, apprehending that they were not invested with sufficient authority to deliberate and determine upon so interesting a subject, did, on the fifth day of May, 1777, for affecting this valuable purpose, pass the following resolve—

"*Resolved,* That it be, and hereby is recommended to the several towns and places in this state, empowered by the laws thereof, to send members to the General Assembly, that, at their next election of a member ór members to represent them, they make choice of men, in whose integrity and ability they can place the greatest confidence ; and, in addition to the common and ordinary powers of representation, instruct them with full powers, in one body with the council, to form such a constitution of government as they shall judge best calculated to promote the happiness of this state; and when completed, to cause the same to be printed in all the Boston newspapers, and also in handbills, one of which to be transmitted to the selectmen of each town, or the committee of each plantation, to be by them laid before their respective towns or plantations, at a regular meeting of the inhabitants thereof, to be called for that purpose, in order to its being, by each town and plantation, duly considered, and a return of their approbation or disapprobation to be made into the secretary's office of this state, at a reasonable time, to be fixed upon by the General Court; specifying the numbers present at such meeting voting for, and those voting against the same; and, if upon a fair examination of said returns, by the General Court, or such a committee as they shall appoint for that purpose, it shall appear, that the said form of government is approved of by at least two thirds of those who are free, and twenty-one years of age, belonging to this state, and present in the several meetings, then the General Court shall be empowered to establish the same as the constitution and form of government of the state of Massachusetts Bay; according to which the inhabitants thereof shall be governed in all succeeding generations, unless the same shall be altered by their express direction, or at least of two thirds of them. And it is further recommended to the selectmen of the several towns, in the return of their precepts for the choice of representatives, to signify their having considered this resolve, and their doings thereon:"

And whereas the good people of this state, in pursuance of the said resolution, and reposing special trust and confidence in the council and in their representatives, have appointed, authorized and instructed their representatives, in one body with the council, to form such a constitution of government as they shall judge best calculated to promote the happiness of this state, and when completed, to cause the same to be published for their inspection and consideration :

We, therefore, the council and representatives of the people of the state of Massachusetts Bay, in convention assembled, by virtue of the power delegated to us, and acknowledging our dependence upon the all wise Governor of the universe for direction, do agree upon the following form of a constitution of government for this state, to be sent out to the people, that they may act thereon, agreeably to the aforesaid resolve.

I. There shall be convened, held and kept, a General Court, upon the last Wednesday in the month of May of every year, and as many other times as the said General Court shall order and appoint: which General Court shall consist of a Senate and House of Representatives, to be elected as this constitution hereafter directs.

II. There shall be elected annually a governor and lieutenant governor, who shall each have, by virtue of such election, a seat and voice in the senate; and the style and title of the governor shall be His Excellency; and the style and title of the lieutenant governor shall be His Honour.

III. No person shall be considered as qualified to serve as governor, lieutenant governor, senator or representative, unless qualified respectively at the time of their several elections as follows, viz: The governor and lieutenant governor shall have been inhabitants of this state five years immediately preceding the time of their respective election; the governor shall be possessed, in his own right, of an estate of the value of one thousand pounds, whereof five hundred pounds value, at the least, shall be in real estate, within this state; the lieutenant governor shall be possessed, in his own right, of an estate of the value of five hundred pounds, two hundred and fifty pounds thereof, at the least, to be in real estate, within this state : a senator shall be possessed, in his own right, of an estate to the value of four hundred pounds, two hundred pounds thereof, at the least, to be in real estate, lying in the district for which he shall be elected. A representative shall be possessed in his own right, of an estate to the value of two hundred pounds, one hundred pounds thereof, at the least, to be in real estate lying in the town for which he shall be elected. Senators and representatives shall have been inhabitants of districts and towns for which they shall be respectively elected, one full year immediately preceding such election; provided, that when two or more towns join in the choice of a representative, they may choose an inhabitant of either of said towns, being otherwise qualified as this article directs.

IV. The judges of the superior court, secretary, treasurer-general, commissary-general, and settled ministers of the gospel, while in office; also all military officers, while in the pay of this or of the United States, shall be considered as disqualified for holding a seat in the General Court; and the judges and registers of probate, for holding a seat in the senate.

V. Every male inhabitant of any town in this state, being free and twenty-one years of age, excepting negroes, Indians, and mulattoes, shall be entitled to vote for a representative or representatives, as the case may be, in the town where he is resident; provided he has paid taxes in said town (unless by law excused from taxes) and been resident therein one full year, immediately preceding such voting, or that such town has been his known and usual place of abode for that time, or that he is considered as an inhabitant thereof : and every such inhabitant qualified as above, and worth sixty pounds clear of all charges thereon, shall be entitled to put in his vote for governor, lieutenant governor and senators : and all such voting for governor, lieutenant governor, senators or representatives shall be by ballot, and not otherwise.

VI. Every incorporated town within this state shall be entitled to send one representative to the General Court : any town having three hundred voters may send two; having five hundred and twenty voters may send three; having seven hundred and sixty may send four; and so on, making the increasing number necessary for another member, twenty more than the last immediately preceding increasing number, till the whole number of voters in any town are reckoned. And each town shall pay the expense of its own representative or representatives; and the inhabitants of any two or more towns, who do not incline to send a representative for each town, may join in the choice of one, if they shall so agree.

VII. The selectmen of each town shall some time in the month of April, annually, issue their warrant or warrants, under their hands and seals, directed to some constable or constables, within their towns, respectively, requiring him or them to notify the inhabitants qualified to vote for a representative, to assemble in some convenient place in such town, for the choice of some person or persons, as the case may be, to represent them in the General Court the ensuing year : the time and place of meeting to be mentioned in the warrant or warrants for calling such meeting. And the selectmen of each town respectively, or the major part of them, shall make return of the name or names of the person or persons elected by the major part of the voters present, and voting in such meeting, to represent said town in the General Court the ensuing year, into the secretary's office, on or before the last Wednesday of May then next ensuing: and when two or more towns shall agree to join for such choice, the major part of the selectmen of those towns shall, in the manner above directed, warn a meeting to be held in either of the said towns, as they shall judge most convenient, for that purpose, and shall make return as aforesaid, of the person chosen at such meeting.

VIII. The number of senators shall be *twenty-eight* (exclusive of the governor and lieutenant governor) their election shall be annual, and from certain districts, into which the state shall be divided, as follows, viz. : The middle district to contain the counties of Suffolk, Essex and Middlesex, within which ten senators shall be elected : the southern district to contain the counties of Plymouth, Barnstable, Bristol, Dukes county and Nantucket, within which six senators shall be elected : the western district to contain the counties of Hampshire,

Worcester and Berkshire, within which eight senators shall be elected : the northern district to contain the counties of York and Cumberland, within which three shall be elected : the eastern district to contain the county of Lincoln, within which one shall be elected. And as the numbers of inhabitants in the several districts may vary, from time to time, the General Court shall, in the way they shall judge best, some time in the year one thousand seven hundred and ninety, and once in twenty years ever after, order the number of the inhabitants of the several districts to be taken, that the senators may be apportioned anew to the several districts, according to the numbers of the inhabitants therein. And the General Court may, at such new appointment, increase the number of senators to be chosen as they may see fit ; provided that the whole number shall never exceed thirty-six, exclusive of the governor and lieutenant governor.

IX. The inhabitants of the several towns in this state, qualified as this constitution directs, shall, on the first Wednesday in the month of November, annually, give in their votes in their respective towns, at a meeting which the selectmen shall call for that purpose, for senators for the year ensuing the last Wednesday in May then next. The votes shall be given in for the members of each district separately, according to the foregoing apportionment, or such as shall be hereafter ordered ; and the selectmen and town clerk of each town shall sort and count the votes, and, by the third Wednesday in December then next, transmit to the secretary's office, a list certified by the town clerk of all the persons who had votes as senators for each district at such meeting, and the number each person had, affixed to his name. The lists, so sent in, shall be examined by the General Court at their then next sitting, and a list for each district of those voted for, to the amount of double the number assigned such district (if so many shall have votes) taking those who had the highest numbers, shall be made out and sent by the first of March, then next after, to the several towns of this state, as a nomi-

nation list, from which said towns shall, at their meetings for
the choice of governor in the month of May, vote for the senators assigned the respective districts; which votes shall be
counted and sorted and lists certified as before directed, made
out and sent in to the secretary's office, by ten o'clock in the
forenoon of the last Wednesday in said May, and not afterwards;
which lists shall be examined by the house of representatives
for the first time of the election of senators, and ever afterwards by the senate and house of representatives on said last
Wednesday of May, or as soon after as may be; and those
persons in each district, equal to the number assigned such
district, who have the greatest number of votes, shall be senators for the ensuing year, unless it shall appear to the senate
that any member or members thereof were unduly elected
or not legally qualified; of which the senate shall be the
judges. And the senate, when so constituted, shall continue in
being till another senate is chosen, and the members thereof
gone through all the steps necessary to qualify them to enter
on the business assigned them by this constitution.

X. There shall forever hereafter, on the first Wednesday
in the month of May annually, be held, in each town in this
state, a meeting of the inhabitants of such towns respectively, to give or put in their votes for governor, lieutenant governor and senators; which meeting the selectmen shall
cause to be notified in the manner before directed for the
meeting for the choice of representatives: and the town
clerk shall return into the secretary's office by ten o'clock in
the morning of the last Wednesday of said May, and not afterwards, an attested copy of all the persons who had votes for
governor and lieutenant governor respectively, certifying the
number of votes each person so voted for had; which lists shall
be, on said last Wednesday of May, or as soon after as may
be, examined by the senate and house of representatives;
and the persons, who, on such examination, shall appear to
have the greatest number of votes for those offices respectively, provided it be a majority of the whole number, shall

be by the two houses declared governor and lieutenant governor, and entitled to act as such the ensuing year : and if no
person shall have such majority for governor and for lieutenant governor, the senate and house of representatives
shall, as soon as may be, after examining said lists, proceed
by joint ballot to elect a governor or lieutenant governor, or
both, as the case may require, confining themselves to one of
those three who had the greatest number of votes collected
in the several towns for the office to be filled.

XI. If any person chosen governor, lieutenant governor, senator or representative, whose qualifications shall be questioned by any one member of the senate or house of representatives, within twenty-four days after his appearing to
enter upon the execution of his office, shall not make oath
before a senator, the speaker of the house of representatives,
or some justice of the peace, that he is qualified as required by
this constitution, and lodge a certificate thereof in the secretary's office, within ten days after notice given him of such
questioning by the secretary, whose duty it shall be to give
such notice, his election shall be void ; and any person claiming privilege of voting for governor, lieutenant governor,
senators or representatives, and whose qualifications shall be
questioned in town meeting, shall by the selectmen be prevented from voting, unless he shall make oath that he is qualified as this constitution requires ; said oath to be administered by a justice of the peace, or the town clerk, who is hereby
empowered to administer the same, when no justice is present.

XII. Whenever any person who may be chosen a member
of the senate shall decline the office to which he is elected,
or shall resign his place, or die, or remove out of the state,
or be any way disqualified, the house of representatives may,
if they see fit, by ballot, fill up any vacancy occasioned thereby, confining themselves in the choice to the nomination list
for the district to which such member belonged whose place
is to be supplied, if a sufficient number is thereon for the pur-

pose; otherwise the choice may be made at large in said district.

XIII. The General Court shall be the supreme legislative authority of this state, and shall accordingly have full power and authority to erect ar.d constitute judicatories and courts of record, or other courts; and, from time to time, to make and establish all manner of wholesome and reasonable orders, laws and statutes; and also for the necessary support and defence of this government, they shall have full power and authority to levy proportionable and reasonable assessments, rates and taxes; and to do all and every thing they shall judge to be for the good and welfare of the state, and for the government and ordering thereof; provided nevertheless, they shall not have any power to add to, alter, abolish, or infringe any part of this constitution. And the enacting style in making laws shall be " by the senate and house of representatives in General Court assembled, and by the authority of the same."

XIV. The senate and house of representatives shall be two separate and distinct bodies, each to appoint its own officers, and settle its own rules of proceedings; and each shall have an equal right to originate or reject any bill, resolve or order, or to propose amendments to the same, excepting bills and resolves levying and granting money or other property of the state, which shall originate in the house of representatives only, and be concurred or nonconcurred in whole by the senate.

XV. Not less than sixty members shall constitute or make a quorum of the house of representatives; and not less than nine shall make a quorum of the senate.

XVI. The senate and house of representatives shall have power to adjourn themselves respectively; provided such adjournment shall not exceed two days at any one time.

XVII. The governor shall be president of the senate. He shall be general and commander in chief of the militia, and admiral of the navy of this state; and empowered to embody the militia, and cause them to be marched to any part of the state, for the public safety, when he shall think necessary; and in the recess of the General Court, to march the militia, by advice of the senate, out of the state, for the defence of this, or any other of the United States; provided always, that the governor shall exercise the power, given him by this constitution, over the militia and navy of the state, according to the laws thereof, or the resolves of the General Court. He shall, with the advice of the senate, in the recess of the General Court, have power to prorogue the same from time to time, not exceeding forty days in any one recess of said court: and in the sitting of said court, to adjourn or prorogue the said court to any time they shall desire, or to dissolve the same at their request, or to call said court together sooner than the time to which it may be adjourned or prorogued, if the welfare of the state should require the same. He shall have power, at his discretion, to grant reprieves to condemned criminals for a term or terms of time, not exceeding six months. It shall be the duty of the governor to inform the legislature at every session of the General Court, of the condition of the state; and, from time to time, to recommend such matters to their consideration, as shall appear to him to concern its good government, welfare and prosperity.

XVIII. Whenever the person who may be chosen governor shall decline the trust, to which he is thereby elected, or shall resign or die, or remove out of the state, or be otherwise disqualified, the lieutenant governor shall have the like power during the vacancy in the office of governor, as the governor is by this constitution vested with; and in case of a vacancy in the office of governor and lieutenant governor, the major part of the senate shall have authority to exercise all the powers of a governor during such vacancy; and in case both the governor and the lieutenant governor be absent from the senate, the senior or first senator then present shall preside.

XIX. All civil officers annually chosen, with salaries annually granted for their services, shall be appointed by the Ge-

neral Court, by ballot; each branch to have a right to originate or negative the choice. All other civil officers, and also
all general, field and staff officers, both of the militia and of
the troops which may be raised by and be in the pay of this
state, shall be appointed by the governor and senate : captains and subalterns of troops raised by and in the pay of the
state to be also appointed by the governor and senate.

XX. The governor and senate shall be a court for the trial
of all impeachments of any officers of this state, provided that
if any impeachment shall be prosecuted against the governor,
lieutenant governor, or any one of the senate ; in such case,
the person impeached shall not continue one of the court for
that trial. Previous to the trial of any impeachment, the
members of the court shall be respectively sworn, truly and
impartially to try and determine the charge in question, according to evidence ; which oath shall be administered to the
members by the president, and to him by any one of the senate. And no judgment of said court shall be valid, unless it
be assented to by two-thirds of the members of said court present at such trial ; nor shall judgment extend further than to re-
moval of the person tried from office and disqualification to hold
or enjoy any place of honour, trust or profit under the state :
the party so convicted shall nevertheless be liable and subject to indictment, trial, judgment and punishment, according
to the laws of the state : and the power of impeaching all officers of the state for mal-conduct in their respective offices
shall be vested in the house of representatives.

XXI. The governor may, with the advice of the senate, in
the recess of the General Court, lay an embargo, or prohibit
the exportation of any commodity for any term of time, not
exceeding forty days in any one recess of said court.

XXII. The governor shall have no negative, as governor,
in any matter pointed out by this constitution to be done by
the governor and senate, but shall have an equal voice with
any senator on any question before them ; provided that the
governor, or in his absence out of the state, the lieutenant go-

vernor, shall be present in senate to enable them to proceed on the business assigned them by this constitution, as governor and senate.

XXIII. The power of granting pardons shall be vested in the governor, lieutenant governor and speaker of the house of representatives, for the time being, or in either two of them.

XXIV. The justices of the superior court, the justices of the inferior courts of common pleas, judges of probate of wills, judges of the maritime courts, and justices of the peace, shall hold their respective places during good behaviour.

XXV. The secretary, treasurer-general and commissary-general shall be appointed annually.

XXVI. The attorney-general, sheriffs, registers of the courts of probate, coroners, notaries public and naval officers shall be appointed and hold their offices during pleasure.

XXVII. The justices of the superior court, justices of the inferior courts, courts of the general sessions of the peace and judges of the maritime courts, shall appoint their respective clerks.

XXVIII. The delegates for this state to the continental Congress shall be chosen annually by joint ballot of the senate and house of representatives, and may be superseded, in the mean time, in the same manner. If any person holding the office of governor, lieutenant governor, senator, judge of the superior court, secretary, attorney-general, treasurer-general, or commissary-general, shall be chosen a member of Congress and accept the trust, the place which he so held as aforesaid, shall be considered as vacated thereby, and some other person chosen to succeed him therein. And if any person, serving for this state at said Congress, shall be appointed to either of the aforesaid offices, and accept thereof, he shall be considered as resigning his seat in Congress, and some other person shall be chosen in his stead.

XXIX. No person unless of the protestant religion shall be governor, lieutenant governor, a member of the senate or of

the house of representatives or hold any judiciary employment within this state.

XXX. All commissions shall run in the name of the state
of Massachusetts Bay, bear test and be signed by the governor
or commander in chief of the state, for the time being, and
have the seal of the state thereunto affixed, and be attested
by the secretary or his deputy.

XXXI. All writs issuing out of the clerk's office of any of
the courts of law within this state, shall be in the name of the
state of Massachusetts Bay, under the seal of the court from
which they issue, bear test of the chief justice, or senior or
first justice of the court where such writ is returnable, and
be signed by the clerk of such court. Indictments shall conclude "against the peace and dignity of the state."

XXXII. All the statute laws of this state, the common law,
and all such parts of the English and British statute laws, as have
been adopted and usually practised in the courts of law in this
state, shall still remain and be in full force until altered or repealed by a future law or laws of the legislature; and shall
be accordingly observed and obeyed by the people of this
state; such parts only excepted as are repugnant to the rights
and privileges contained in this constitution: and all parts of
such laws as refer to and mention the council shall be construed to extend to the senate. And the inestimable right of
trial by jury shall remain confirmed as part of this constitution
forever.

XXXIII. All monies shall be issued out of the treasury of
this state and disposed of by warrants under the hand of the
governor for the time being, with the advice and consent of
the senate, for the necessary defence and support of the government, and the protection and preservation of the inhabitants thereof, agreeably to the acts and resolves of the General Court.

XXXIV. The free exercise and enjoyment of religious
profession and worship shall forever be allowed to every denomination of protestants within this state.

XXXV. The following oath shall be taken by every person appointed to any office in this state, before his entering on the execution of his office ; viz. *I, A. B. do swear (or affirm, as the case may be) that I will bear faith and true allegiance to the state of Massachusetts; and that I will faithfully execute the business of the office of agreeably to the laws of this state, according to my best skill and judgment, without fear, favour, affection or partiality.*

XXXVI. And whereas it may not be practicable to conform to this constitution in the election of governor, lieutenant governor, senators and representatives for the first year ; therefore,

The present convention, if in being, or the next general assembly, which shall be chosen upon the present constitution, shall determine the time and manner in which the people shall choose said officers for the first year; and upon said choice, the general assembly, then in being, shall be dissolved and give place to the free execution of this constitution.

By order of the convention.,

JEREMIAH POWELL, *President.*

Attest,
SAMUEL FREEMAN, *Clerk.*

No. II.—*Page* 300.

The General Court was to have met on Wednesday 31st January. But a sufficient number of representatives to form a quorum did not attend till Saturday, 3d of February. On receiving official notice, that the two houses were ready to proceed in the public business, the governor immediately proceeded to the senate chamber, and delivered the following speech to both houses then assembled.

" *Gentlemen of the Senate, and*
 Gentlemen of the House of Representatives,

" It was expected by the General Court, that their proceedings at their last session, respecting the insurgents, would have answered the purposes for which they were intended. By those proceedings, there were held forth to them, punishment on the one hand, and pardon on the other.—Punishment, in case of perseverance in their criminal conduct; pardon and indemnity, if they desisted from it; and by a given time, should take the oaths of allegiance. This application to their feelings, and to that actuating principle, a desire of personal safety, it was apprehended, would have had a forcible influence to bring them to their duty. But unhappily, it did not produce any good effect, except upon a very few individuals of them. On the contrary, the lenity and forbearance of government were treated with contempt, and imputed by them to an inability of defending itself; and some of your last acts have been added to their list of grievances.

But the clearest and most unequivocal evidence of their perseverance, in opposition to government, is deduced from their proceedings, respecting the judicial courts, in several of the counties, since the last session of the General Court. They twice, with an armed force, stopped those courts in Worcester; and would not suffer them to open in Hampshire. They attempted it, though unsuccessfully, in Middlesex: and in consequence of that attempt, several of them were taken into custody, by virtue of state warrants; in the execution of which, the sheriff and other persons to whom the warrants were directed, had the aid and support of a number of spirited gentlemen of that county and Suffolk.

At the last time of their assembling in Worcester, there were nearly a thousand of them in arms, who, to the great annoyance and terror of that vicinity, continued embodied for several days after the court had adjourned: meditating, as it was apprehended, further outrages; which were providentially prevented by the continued storms of that week.

These violent and treasonable proceedings of the insurgents were perpetrated after the publication of the last acts of the General Court respecting them; and demonstrated, not only a total disregard of those acts, and the authority by which they were enacted, but a contempt of all constitutional government, and a fixed determination to persevere in measures for subverting it.

This determination, and these measures, were also manifested by their printed declarations; and by some of the private transactions of their leaders, when the main body of the insurgents were last assembled at Worcester: by which it appeared, the insurgents were formed into regiments, and that a committee was appointed for each regiment, to see that it should, without delay, be properly officered and equipped; and completely ready when called upon.

That this was the state of things in the western counties, was further confirmed by letters I received from some of the most respectable characters in those counties; and by the oral testimony of many intelligent persons from thence: who all agreed in the necessity of speedy and vigorous measures being taken, for the effectual suppression of the insurgents: without which the well-affected might, from a principle of self preservation, be obliged to join them; and the insurrection become general.

The safety and well being of the Commonwealth being thus at hazard, and the lenient, conciliating measures of the General Court, having been rejected by the insurgents, I conceived myself under every obligation, of honour and duty, to exert the powers vested in me by law and the constitution, for the protection and defence of the Commonwealth, against the hostile and nefarious attempts of those lawless men.

Pursuant to this idea, I laid before the council all the information and intelligence I had collected, relative to the proceedings and designs of those men; and the council were unanimously of opinion, and accordingly advised, that vigorous measures should be taken to protect the judicial courts, particularly those that were then to be next holden at Worcester; to aid the civil magistrate in executing the laws ; to repel all insurgents against the government; and to apprehend all disturbers of the public peace ; particularly such of them as might be named in any state warrant, or warrants.

For these purposes, upon the effecting of which all good government, and indeed the happy existence of the Commonwealth, do essentially depend, I have called forth from several counties, a respectable body of the militia, the command of which I have given to major general Lincoln, with orders to carry those purposes into effectual execution.

Those orders are now in operation, and will be laid before you, with the general orders, containing the plan of measures, by which the Commonwealth was to be defended against its present assailants.

I congratulate you, gentlemen, on the success of those measures hitherto ; and hope it is a prelude to final success, and to the re-establishment of perfect tranquillity. The despatches concerning it, which I have received from general Lincoln, and general Shepard, will be laid before you.

Thus, gentlemen, from a principle of duty to the Commonwealth, and in conformity to your resolution of the 24th of October, in which you express a full confidence, " that I will still persevere in the exercise of such powers as are vested in me by the constitution, for preventing any attempts to interrupt the administration of law and justice, and for enforcing due obedience to the authority and laws of government," I have taken the measures above represented. I trust they will meet with your entire approbation, and with *that* support, which is naturally to be expected from the guardians of the public safety.

On my part, I have done, in this business, what the duty of my office, and the oath of qualification, indispensably require: and I have the fullest confidence, that on your part nothing will be wanting to carry into complete effect the measures, that have been taken, or that may be further necessary, to suppress the present insurrection; and to ensure a strict obedience to the laws. This is so essential to the peace and safety of the Commonwealth, that it requires your immediate attention; and the speedy application of further means, if those already taken should be deemed insufficient, for that purpose.

Among those means, you may deem it necessary to establish some criterion for discriminating between good citizens and insurgents, that each might be regarded according to their characters: the former as their country's friends, and to be protected; and the latter as public enemies, and to be effectually suppressed. At such a time as the present, every man ought to show his colours, and take his side: no neutral characters should be allowed: nor any one suffered to vibrate between the two.

Vigour, decision, energy, will soon terminate this unnatural, this unprovoked insurrection; and prevent the effusion of blood: but the contrary may involve the Commonwealth in a civil war, and all its dreadful consequences: which may extend, not only to the neighbouring states, but even to the whole confederacy, and finally destroy the fair temple of American liberty: in the erection of which, besides the vast expense of it, many thousands of valuable citizens have been sacrificed.

There are several things, resulting from the measures in operation, which require your immediate attention.

The money immediately wanted for carrying them into execution was supplied by a voluntary loan from a number of gentlemen, and in a manner which does them much honour. I must earnestly recommend to you to provide for its reimbursement, which, upon the principles of policy as well as justice, should be made as speedily as possible. Provision also should be made for defraying the general expense.

Should the time be too short to effect the great purposes, for which the militia were called forth, it may be necessary that general Lincoln should be empowered to continue them in service, by enlistment, until those purposes shall be accomplished. The men being already embodied, and the arrangements for supporting them perfected, the expense of such a continuance will be much less than that of raising a new body for the same service.

There are defects in our militia act, which require an immediate remedy; and which I shall mention to you in a separate message.

These, gentlemen, are matters of importance; but the general subject of this address is of the first magnitude, and demands your immediate and most serious attention. If it be taken up with proper spirit—if the measures in operation be seconded with firmness and decision—and if the powers of the several branches of government be united in a wise and vigorous exertion, we may reasonably expect a speedy and happy issue to the present insurrection: to which happy issue every exertion on my part has been, and shall be, applied.

But, on the contrary, if indecision, languor or disunion should on this occasion pervade our public councils, insurrection, though checked for the present, would gain new strength, and, like a torrent, might sweep away every mound of the constitution; and overwhelm the Commonwealth in every species of calamity. In such a case, if brought on by remissness, or relaxation, on our part, we should be, not only involved—most essentially involved, in that calamity, but justly chargeable with betraying the trust reposed in us by our fellow-citizens; and chargeable with ignominiously deserting the posts assigned us, as guardians of the peace, the safety and happiness of the Commonwealth.

But, very happily—this is only a possible case; for your patriotism, your virtue, your regard for your own liberties and property, and for those of your families and posterity, must induce you to call forth every power of government into vigorous exertion for preventing such a complication, such an accumulation of evils.

On this occasion, it is proper, gentlemen, to inform you, that I have received from several towns, petitions, directed to the governor and council, and also to the General Court, relative to the insurgents. The petitions, being eight in number, do disapprove of the proceedings of government, in regard to those people.

But as the things prayed for, were, for the most part, not cognizable by the governor and council; and such as were so, could not be granted by them, consistently with the duty they owe to the Commonwealth, the petitions will be laid before you, for *your* consideration.

There are other matters, to which your attention, gentlemen, is necessary; and they will be communicated by message.

JAMES BOWDOIN.

Council-Chamber, Feb. 3, 1787.

TO HIS EXCELLENCY JAMES BOWDOIN, ESQUIRE, GOVERNOR OF THE COMMONWEALTH OF MASSACHUSETTS.

" *May it please your Excellency,*

" The senate and house of representatives, in General Court assembled, have read and duly attended to your speech at the opening of this session, and take the earliest opportunity to express their entire satisfaction in the measures you have been pleased to take, pursuant to the powers vested in you by the constitution, for the subduing a turbulent spirit, which has too long insulted the government of this Commonwealth, prostrated the courts of law and justice in divers counties, and threatened even the overthrow of the constitution itself. The General Court congratulate your excellency on the success with which Providence has been pleased hitherto to bless the wise, spirited and prudent measures which you have taken; and they earnestly entreat your excellency, still to encounter, repel, and resist, by all fitting ways, enterprises and means, all and every such person and persons, as attempt or enterprise, in a hostile manner, the destruction, detriment, or annoyance of this Commonwealth ; and to pursue such further constitutional measures as you may think necessary for extirpating the spirit of rebellion : quieting the minds of the good people of the Commonwealth; and establishing the just authority and dignity of government. And in order that your excellency may be possessed of the *full* power of the constitution, to effect these great purposes, the General Court have thought it highly necessary, after mature deliberation, to declare that a rebellion exists within this Commonwealth.

This court are fully persuaded, that by far the greater part of the citizens of this Commonwealth are warmly attached to our present happy constitution : they have a high sense of the merit of a respectable body of the militia, who have with readiness attended your excellency's orders on this pressing emergency, as well as of the patriotic zeal of a number of private citizens, who have cheerfully advanced their money in aid to government ; and you may be assured, sir, that the most speedy and effectual means will be used for the payment of the officers and soldiers who have been, or may be employed in this necessary and most important service ; and for the reimbursement of the monies generously advanced for its support.

It is to be expected, that vigour, decision and energy, under the direction and blessing of Heaven, will soon terminate this unnatural, unprovoked rebellion, prevent the effusion of blood, and the fatal consequences to be dreaded from a civil war; and it is the determination of this court to establish a criterion for discriminating between good citizens and others, that each may be regarded according to their characters and deserts.

If it should appear to your excellency, that the time for which the militia, under the command of major general Lincoln, are enlisted, is too short to effect the great objects in view, it is the request of this court, that you would be pleased to direct the commanding general to reinlist the same men, or enlist others, for such further time as you may think necessary, or to replace them by detachments from the militia; and, if you shall think it expedient, to increase their numbers, and continue them in service until those purposes shall be completely accomplished.

The General Court will give the most ready attention to your message of the third instant, and every other communication you shall be pleased to lay before them. They will vigorously pursue every measure that may be calculated to support the constitution, and will still continue to redress any real grievances, if such shall be found to exist—humbly beseeching Almighty God to preserve union and harmony among the several powers of government, as well as among the honest and virtuous citizens of the Commonwealth, and to restore to us the inestimable blessings of peace and liberty, under a wise and righteous administration of government.

In Senate, *4th February,* 1787.

Read, and unanimously accepted—and ordered, That Samuel Adams, Caleb Strong, annd Seth Washburne, Esquires, with such as the honourable house may join, be a committee to wait upon his excellency the governor with the foregoing address.

Sent down for concurrence.

SAMUEL PHILLIPS, jun. *President.*

In the House *of* Representatives, *Feb. 4th,* 1787.

Read and concurred, and Mr. Shepard, Mr. Brooks, Mr. Beckford, and Mr. Davis are joined.

ARTEMAS WARD, *Speaker.*

Commonwealth of Massachusetts.

Whereas many persons who now are, or have been, in arms against the government, may not have considered the evil nature and tendency of their crime; and might not have been apprized that an opposition to the legal authority of the state, with force of arms, is treason and rebellion: *And whereas* General Lincoln has given to a particular description of the insurgents his assurances of recommending them to the clemency of the government on certain conditions therein mentioned:

Resolved, That this court approve of general Lincoln's conduct in his overtures of recommending certain descriptions of insurgents to the clemency of government, and that the governor be, and he hereby is, authorised and empowered, in the name of the General Court, to promise a pardon, under such disqualifications as may hereafter be provided, to such private soldiers and others, who act in the capacity of non-commissioned officers, as have been, or now are, in arms against the Commonwealth, with such exceptions as he or the general officer commanding the troops may judge necessary; *provided*, they shall deliver up their arms, and take and subscribe the oath of allegiance to this Commonwealth, within such time as shall or may be limited by his excellency for that purpose.

In SENATE, *4th February*, 1787.

Read, and unanimously accepted.

Sent down for concurrence.

SAMUEL PHILLIPS, jun. *President.*

In the HOUSE *of* REPRESENTATIVES, *Feb.* 4, 1787.

Read and concurred:

ARTEMAS WARD, *Speaker.*

Approved.

JAMES BOWDOIN.

━ ━

No. III.—*Page* 300.

DECLARATION OF REBELLION.

WHEREAS the doings of the General Court at their last session, relative to the insurgents against the government and the authority of the state, in several counties within this Commonwealth, were lenient and merciful, were intended to quiet the minds of the disaffected, and ought to have had the effect they were designed to produce :

And whereas every complaint of grievance was carefully attended to, with a disposition to grant all that relief which could be afforded consistent with equal justice and the dignity of government; and the General Court, so far as they were able, adopted measures accordingly, and gave full and clear information, to the insurgents as well as others, of the general situation of public affairs :

And whereas a full and free pardon, for all the outrageous proceedings against the government, whereof the insurgents had been guilty, was tendered them upon this mild condition alone, that they should be guilty of such outrages no more ; and as evidence of their intentions to demean themselves, in future, as good and faithful citizens, should, before the first day of January, A. D. 1787, take and subscribe the oath of allegiance; it manifestly appears, from the subsequent con- duct of the leaders of the insurgents, that their opposition to government has not arisen from a misapprehension as to the views and disposition of government, or from a temporary irritation, arising from the pressure of supposed grievances, or from a misguided zeal to promote the public happiness, as has been insidiously asserted ; but from a settled determina- tion to subvert the constitution, and put an end to the govern- ment of this Commonwealth: it is also abundantly manifest, that the conduct of the insurgents, in stopping the courts of justice in the counties of Worcester and Hampshire—in as- sembling in arms, avowedly to commit the same outrages in the county of Middlesex—in calling upon the towns in some counties to furnish themselves with arms and ammunition—in appointing committees to form their adherents into regular military companies, properly officered, thereby to establish within this Commonwealth a standing force, beyond the con- trol of, and for the express purpose of opposing, in arms, the constitutional government of the state—in endeavouring to increase the commotions in the counties aforesaid, by publicly inviting and alluring others to throw off their allegiance and join their body; is subversive of all order and government, absolutely incompatible with the public safety and happiness; and is an open, unnatural, unprovoked and wicked rebellion, against the dignity, authority and government of this Commonwealth:—and the legislature, in duty to their constituents, in conformity to their oaths, and by virtue of the authority vested in them by the constitution, (having ineffectually tried every lenient measure to reclaim them) Do HEREBY SOLEMNLY DECLARE, *That a horrid and unnatural* REBELLION *and WAR has been openly and traitorously raised and levied against this Commonwealth, and is still continued, and now exists within the same,* with design to subvert and overthrow the constitution and form of government thereof, which has been most solemnly agreed to, and established by the citizens of this Commonwealth; and that government ought and will, with the greatest energy and force, exert and bring forth all the power of the Commonwealth for the suppression thereof: and all the horrors and evils, that may follow in consequence of this rebellion, must be imputed to those men who have, contrary to the duty of their allegiance, and every principle of law and justice, been the fomenters, abettors and supporters of the same.

In SENATE, *4th February,* 1787.

Read, and unanimously accepted.

Sent down for concurrence.

SAMUEL PHILLIPS, jun. *President.*

In the HOUSE *of* REPRESENTATIVES, *Feb.* 4. 1787.

Read and concurred:

ARTEMAS WARD, *Speaker.*

No. IV. *Page* 321.

THE following letter was addressed by Hon. E. Gerry, who was one of the delegates from Massachusetts to the general convention, to the senate and house of representatives. A copy of the constitution had been previously forwarded by Congress to the governor, to be laid before the legislature of the state. Mr. Gerry was the only delegate from Massachusetts, who declined signing the constitution; his reasons for which appear in the letter. It contains, in substance, the principal objections to the constitution. It is therefore proper to be preserved, in reference to the discussion on the subject stated in this volume.

New York, October 18, 1787.

Gentlemen—I have the honour to inclose, pursuant to my commission, the constitution proposed by the federal convention.

To this system, I gave my dissent, and shall submit my objections to the honorable legislature.

It was painful for me, on a subject of such national importance, to differ from the respectable members who signed the constitution. But, conceiving as I did, that the liberties of America were not secured by the system, it was my duty to oppose it.

My principal objections to the plan are, that there is no *adequate* provision for a *representation of the people;* that they have *no security for the right of election;* that some of the powers of the legislature are *ambiguous,* and others *indefinite* and *dangerous;* that the executive is *blended* with, and will have an *undue* influence over, the legislature; that the judicial department will be *oppressive;* that treaties of the highest importance may be formed by the president, with the advice of *two thirds* of a quorum of the senate; and that the system is without the security of a *bill of rights.* These are objections which are not local; but apply equally to all the states.

As the convention was called for " the sole and express purpose of revising the articles of confederation, and report=

ing to Congress and to the several legislatures, such alterations and provisions as shall render the federal constitution adequate to the exigences of government, and the preservation of the union," I did not conceive that these powers extended to the formation of the plan proposed ; but the convention being of a different opinion, I acquiesced in it ; being fully convinced, that, to preserve the union, an *efficient government was indispensably necessary ; and that it would be difficult to make proper amendments to the articles of confederation.*

The constitution proposed has *few,* if any *federal* features ; but is rather a system of *national* government : nevertheless, in many respects, I think it has great merit ; and by proper amendments, may be adapted to " the exigences of government," and the preservation of liberty.

The question on this plan involves others of the highest importance—First, whether there shall be a *dissolution* of the federal government? Secondly, whether the several state governments shall be so altered, as, in effect, to be dissolved ? And thirdly, whether, in lieu of the *federal* and *state* governments, the *national* constitution, now proposed, shall be substituted without amendment ? Never, perhaps, were a people called on to decide a question of greater magnitude. Should the citizens of America adopt the plan as it now stands, their liberties may be lost. Or should they reject it altogether, anarchy may ensue. It is evident, therefore, that they should not be precipitate in their decisions ; that the subject should be well understood, lest they should refuse to support the government, after having hastily adopted it.

If those who are in favour of the constitution, as well as those who are against it, should preserve moderation, their discussions may afford much information, and finally direct to a happy issue.

It may be urged by some, that an implicit confidence should be placed in the convention. But, however respectable the members may be who signed the constitution, it must be admitted that a free people are the proper guardians of their rights and liberties; that the greatest men may err; and that their errors are sometimes of the greatest magnitude.

Others may suppose, that the constitution may be safely adopted, because therein provision is made to *amend* it. But cannot this object be better obtained before a ratification, than after it? And should a free people adopt a form of government, under conviction that it wants amendment?

And some may conceive, that, if the plan is not accepted by the people, they will not unite in another. But surely, while they have the power to amend, they are not under the necessity of rejecting it.

I shall only add, that, as the welfare of the union requires a better constitution than the confederation, I shall think it my duty, as a citizen of Massachusetts, to support that which shall be finally adopted; sincerely hoping it will secure the liberty and happiness of America.

(Signed)   E. GERRY.

To Hon. S. Adams,
         President of the Senate, and
Hon. James Warren,
         Speaker of the House of Representatives.

A

PARTICULAR ACCOUNT

OF THE

BATTLE

OF

Bunker, or Breed's Hill,

ON THE

17TH OF JUNE, 1775.

BY A CITIZEN OF BOSTON.

Second Edition.

◆

BOSTON:

PUBLISHED BY CUMMINGS, HILLIARD, & COMPANY.

—

PRINTED BY MUNROE AND FRANCIS.

1825.

ADVERTISEMENT.

As there have been several accounts, heretofore given, of the Battle of Bunker Hill, it may be thought unnecessary again to bring the subject before the public, and impossible to say any thing of importance, not to be found in former narratives. It may be observed, that some of those accounts have been found to be partial and incomplete ; and that some were written, not so much for the purpose of giving a correct view of *all* the events, as to establish particular facts, before denied or doubted. It has been suggested that a more *particular* yet brief statement of that enterprize would be acceptable to the public at this time. Inquiries are often made on the subject, and are likely to be repeated, as a formal celebration of that ever-memorable event is soon to take place.

The most correct and perfect account, which has been given, was by Colonel S. SWETT, by way of Appendix to a second edition of the Life of General ISRAEL PUTNAM, published about seven years ago. The design of the writer of the following narrative is to give a *concise* statement, and yet to record whatever is material and important. Having examined and compared all former accounts with diligence, and received some additional statements, he believes that it will not be considered a mere *republication* of other and earlier accounts. He has confined himself to the transactions of the day and the event, with reference only to some circumstances closely connected therewith ; nor has he indulged in any remarks which belong more properly to the historian or to the orator.

Boston, May 20th, 1825.

BATTLE

OF

BUNKER OR BREED'S HILL.

The battle in Charlestown, Massachusetts, which was fought between the British and Americans, on the 17th of June, 1775, was an event of great interest, and importance. It was the *first* real trial of strength and courage between the troops of the parent country and of the provinces. The affair at *Lexington* and *Concord*, on the 19th of April preceding, could hardly be called a *battle*. Though a few guns were fired by the militia assembled under arms at Lexington, after they were attacked, yet no attempt was made by them to oppose the march of the British, who were *ten* times more numerous.* And at

---

* General *Heath* says, " The British advanced towards the militia, *ordered* them to disperse, huzzaed, and fired upon them. Several were killed and wounded, and the rest dispersed." Gordon says, " The huzzaing and firing produced an *immediate* dispersion ; though some of the milita fired before, or as they were dispersing." The British account was, "that the militia, when ordered to disperse, immediately retired in *confusion* ; but that several guns were fired upon the king's troops from behind the stone wall ; by which one man was wounded, and Major Pitcairn's horse was shot." Mrs. Warren says, " The British made an attack upon the *defenceless* peasants at Lexington—that Colonel Smith *ordered* them to lay down their arms and disperse ; at the same time ordered his troops to fire, and proceeded without molestation to Concord."

Concord Bridge, where a part of the British troops was opposed with much spirit and bravery, there was nothing really deserving the name of a *formal battle*. The British were pursued, indeed, on their return to Boston, but in a very irregular manner, as the militia collected on the occasion were not sufficiently numerous to justify them in offering a serious contest. But that at *Breed's* Hill was a hard-fought battle. Large detachments of American and British troops were closely engaged in martial combat for *several hours*.* The contest was most severe and bloody. A fair trial was exhibited of the military *powers* of each.

It would seem that a battle must have been expected by the Americans ; yet so little was done by way of previous preparation, and so unequal were they in discipline, in arms, and in numbers, to meet the British, that it may be considered by some as a rash and imprudent measure to *challenge* an engagement as they did. The event indeed, proved their courage and heroism, notwithstanding their final defeat. They contended against the enemy with a *desperate* résolution, as if the liberties of their country depended upon the issue of that single battle. And, perhaps, it is not too much to say, that it did so in a great degree.

The British received a formidable check. They had melancholy evidence of the resolution and brave-

---

* The first attack was made between two and three o'clock ! and the Americans did not retreat till after six o'clock. It is said, in a letter from a British officer, that the battle continued nearly *four* hours.

ry of the provincial troops. From that battle, they learned to appreciate aright the character of Americans. They were convinced of the great suffering and bloodshed which would attend the contest in which they were engaged. And, from that day, they feared to attempt (what, if they had attempted, *might* have proved most disastrous to the American cause) an attack upon our undisciplined troops, and which, as a regular army, furnished with all necessary military stores and arms, they ought to have done.

We have suggested, that the battle of Breed's Hill was a *rash* affair on the part of the Americans. It was so considered, at the time, by many judicious men in the Provincial Congress and Committee of Safety, though the majority of the *latter* did finally sanction the enterprise. Even *Warren*, ardent and resolute as he was, considered it a desperate undertaking. No reasonable man could have supposed that the Americans would maintain their position so near Boston, where the British had 10,000 regular troops, and when they had command of the waters of Charles river by their ships of war. Had the latter been as successful as they had reason to calculate, they would, with the troops* they landed at Charlestown, have

---

* There are different accounts of the number of British troops engaged in this battle. Some have stated them to be three, and others, five thousand. General Gage, in his official account, said there were about 2000. By comparing several early statements, it appears that somewhat more than 3000 first landed at Charlestown, and made two attacks upon the Americans; and that about 1000 passed over, afterwards, as a reinforcement; and, joining those of the first detachment who survived, made the third attack, when the redoubt was carried.

driven the Americans† from their works (which afforded but a partial shelter, almost destitute as they were
of cannon as well as of powder;) and pursued them
to Cambridge, where General *Ward* was stationed
with the main body of the provincial troops; who
would probably have been routed by such a powerful
force.

The plan of taking possession of the heights of
Charlestown was adopted, in consequence of intelligence that the British general intended to occupy that
position, and also the high land on Dorchester Neck,
on the south of Boston, in order to extend his situation, and to take advantage of possessing these commanding places, to attack the provincials at Cambridge
or Roxbury, whenever he might think it proper.*   It

---

† The whole number of provincials engaged did not, probably, much exceed 2000. Some, indeed, have supposed there were only about 1500.
Those who went on to Breed's Hill the evening of the 16th, have usually been
estimated at 1000 : being *Prescott's*, parts of *Bridge's* and *Frye's* regiments,
a detachment of 120, with four lieutenants, from General *Putnam's* regiment,
under command of Captain *Knowlton ;* and one artillery company.
The regiments, at this time, consisted of ten companies of sixty men each ; but very *few* of them were *full*.   The reinforcements, which
were sent on the next day, though belonging to several regiments, did not
probably exceed 12 or 1300, (and some of these arrived only in time to
protect and cover the retreat.)   These consisted of two regiments from New
Hampshire, under *Stark* and *Reed ;* two more companies of *Putnam's* regiment, commanded by *Chester* and *Clark ;* parts of *Little's*, *Whitcomb's*, *Brewer's*, *Nixon's*, *Gerrish's*, and *Gardner's* regiments, the latter of which was not
ordered on to the field till a late hour, and after the first attack of the British, though its brave commander was anxious to march at the first alarm.
There is proof that only parts, even of these incomplete regiments, were in
the battle.

* Soon after the affair at Lexington and Concord, of the 19th of April,
the " minute men" (so called) and others, to the number of about 15,000
assembled in the vicinity of Boston.   Many of them were without efficient

was not until the 15th of June that the Americans determined to occupy the former spot. Why more time was not allowed for preparation is not known. It is probable there was an apprehension that the British intended to take immediate possession.*

The detachments ordered upon this most hazardous enterprise consisted of about 1000 men, under the particular and immediate command of Colonel *William*

---

and complete equipments. In powder they were very deficient. And as to artillery, it was little more than a *name*. Of these men, nearly 10,000 belonged to Massachusetts; Connecticut, New Hampshire, and Rhode Island furnished the residue. General Ward was appointed commander in chief by the Provincial Congress of Massachusetts; General Thomas was second in command, and was stationed at Roxbury. Washington had not taken the chief command. He was appointed, about the middle of June, by the Continental Congress, and arrived at Cambridge on the 3d of July; when the troops were soon organized as a *national* army. It is probable, however, that, before he took the command, *all* the troops collected acknowledged General Ward as chief; and that there was an understanding to act in concert, and with some regularity and system, though the organization of the troops was not *perfect*. A contrary supposition would imply extreme inattention or want of military knowledge, both in the Committee of Safety and in the officers assembled; several of whom had been in the campaigns of 1756, 1757, and 1758.

* It is said by those who were then living, and in a situation to know all the circumstances connected with the enterprise, that it was undertaken at the particular instance of *General Putnam*, and that Colonel Prescott requested to have the post, in which he so bravely distinguished himself. *Putnam* expressed the opinion, that something must be done (unprepared as they then were for offensive operations), to employ the men and to accustom them to military service. He conducted the expedition to Noddle's and Hog Islands, in Boston harbour, the last of May, to prevent a large quantity of sheep from falling into the hands of the British, in which he discovered great activity and courage; and on the 10th of June he marched from Cambridge to Charlestown, with most of the provincial troops collected at the former place. This was done in full sight of the British in Boston, and with a view to excite the spirit of emulation and courage in the militia, who were then assembled in arms for the defence of the country.

Prescott of Pepperell in the county of Middlesex. Far the greater part of the detachment belonged to Massachusetts, and chiefly to that county, and included a part of Colonel *Ebenezer Bridge's* and a part of *Frye's* regiments, with about 120 from General † *Israel Putnam's* regiment (from Connecticut,) with Captain *Knowlton*, as their chief officer.* *Putnam* accompanied this detachment, and, according to the testimony of several respectable witnesses who were in the expedition, had the superintendance of it ; or gave direction and advice, which, even if he attended as a volunteer, must have had much influence. That

---

† Though called *General*, he had *then* command only of a regiment, which was the case with several general officers in Massachusetts at that time. The other Connecticut troops were stationed at Roxbury.

* Judge *Grosvenor*, now living, was a lieutenant in this corps, and was wounded the next day at the rail fence. The statement lately made by him is as follows :—" I was one of the detachment from General Putnam's regiment, posted at Cambridge. On the evening of the 16th June, Captain Knowlton, with four subalterns and 120 men, were detached and marched to Breed's Hill, with others of Massachusetts. General Putnam was with us and attended to laying out the ground for erecting the redoubt. He returned to Cambridge that night, and attended early the next morning. He was on the hill repeatedly during the day ; and particularly at the *posting of the troops in the redoubt, and at the arm of the ditch leading north towards Mystic River, and at the rail fence adjoining the river.* Colonel Prescott was constantly with the troops ; but General Putnam was backwards and forwards from Cambridge during the day, to bring on reinforcements. He commanded and ordered the troops engaged with regularity and satisfaction, so far as I know."—" When the British landed at Moreton's Point, the detachment under Knowlton, from Putnam's regiment, was ordered by the General to take post at a rail fence on the left of the breastwork. This was promptly executed. Each man was furnished with a pound of powder and forty-eight balls. *No corps was posted at the rail fence, save our own, at the time the fire began.*"

he had the *official* and *authorized command*,† may be difficult to prove by direct evidence. The orderly-book of General *Ward* is silent on the subject. *Putnam* was a very active as well as brave officer, and had seen much military service in a former war between France and England. Colonel *Gridley* was also with the detachment, and acted as engineer.

This detachment of provincial troops proceeded to the peninsula of Charlestown late in the evening of the 16th of June. They paused on Bunker Hill; but

---

† Different opinions have prevailed on this point. But on comparing all the circumstances and transactions of the occasion, by recollecting the conduct of Putnam, as stated by several persons in the battle, and by other citizens who were on Charlestown heights as volunteers, and by assuming that such an important enterprise would not have been undertaken by advice of the Council of War or Committee of Safety, without some system (although the short time there was to make arrangement, and the imperfect organization of the American troops prevented it being entirely regular and complete,) it will appear that he was, in *fact*, the commander in chief. He evidently *acted as such ;* and either had the appointment by General Ward, or by designation and consent of the Council of War. He superintended the works the night of the 16th; was there again early on the morning of the 17th; directed Knowlton to the rail fence, when the enemy landed at Moreton's Point; advised to carry the entrenching tools to Bunker's Hill, and there ordered another breastwork to be thrown up, though when the enemy advanced to the attack, he relinquished it, and marched his men to the lines; was seen riding along the lines, directing and animating the troops; often rode to the Neck and beyond, to urge on the recruits; and, in company with Prescott, covered the rear of the Americans on their retreat. Still, perhaps he had not that entire and complete command which would have been given, if the army had been perfectly organized, and the expedition regularly and maturely prepared. That he was often on Bunker Hill, where he could take a full view of the whole ground and of all the troops engaged, both British and American, and rode to the Neck to hasten and urge on the reinforcements, instead of remaining posted either at the redoubt or at the rail fence, go to prove rather that he was commander of the expedition, than that he was *inactive or out of place.*

after some consultation they concluded to advance to Breed's Hill, which lies nearer to Boston by about 120 rods, and is about the same distance from the banks of Charles River.* It was nearly midnight when they began to throw up a redoubt (as had been previously ordered by a Council of War at Cambridge,) for a partial defence against the British, who they could not but believe would soon attack them. As a fortress, of which they were to retain permanent possession, they could not have proposed it; for, without more cannon and a greater supply of ammunition, they must have known that they could not long hold out against the superior and formidable force of the British in Boston. Such was the opinion even of the sanguine and heroic Putnam, expressly given by him to General *Warren*, when he came on the field, just before the enemy first advanced to the attack.

In the course of the night, when the works were in forwardness and the men industriously engaged in completing them, General Putnam returned to his quarters in Cambridge. But early in the morning, on hearing the cannonade of the British, which began soon after the dawn of day, from their fort at the northern part of Boston, and their ships of war in Charles River, he repaired again with great alacrity to Charlestown. During the night, Colonel *Prescott*,

---

* In a direct line, Copps' Hill, at the northern part of Boston, where the British had a fortress, is about half a mile from Breed's Hill in Charlestown. No reason can be given why the Americans chose to fortify Breed's rather than Bunker Hill, but that it was nearer to Boston. Bunker Hill is much more elevated, and would have been more difficult to attack by the enemy.

attended by Major *Brooks*,* proceeded to the margin of the river, to ascertain whether the British were alarmed, and were preparing to attack them ; but all appeared quiet. At an early hour of the morning, Prescott sent to General Ward,† at Cambridge, for provisions and reinforcements. His men were fatigued, and the works were not finished. No answer and no supplies were received. At nine o'clock, Major Brooks, as a confidential officer, was despatched to head quarters, with an urgent request for more supplies and men. But on this message, requiring the greatest despatch, he was obliged to travel on foot. No horse was to be procured. It was nearly ten when he arrived at Cambridge. A consultation was immediately had between General Ward and oth-

---

* Brooks was major of Bridge's regiment. He commanded a battalion of minute men in the affair at Concord on the 19th of April. During the war of the revolution, he held a colonel's commission, and was repeatedly distinguished for acts of bravery, and in high estimation as a correct disciplinarian. Afterwards he was major general of militia, and governor of Massachusetts. He died the first of March last, universally respected and beloved, sincerely and deeply lamented.

† It is argued, that if General Putnam had the regular and official command of the expedition, *he* would have made the request to Ward for provisions and recruits ; and that Prescott would have applied to Putnam, and not to Ward, for any assistance he needed. That Putnam was on the field early, there is full proof ; and it also appears that he was active at the redoubt, and in his endeavours to bring on more men. It is not improbable that he joined with Prescott in the message to Ward for reinforcements. It is evident that there was a want of *perfect* organization and system in the military movements of the day. But this does not disprove that Putnam was considered and acted as commander in chief. And we cannot but believe that, as there were commanders of companies and of regiments, and as Prescott was stationed at the redoubt, there was a commander in chief of the whole, who superintended and directed the movements of all the troops concerned in the expedition.

ers, as to the propriety of sending more troops from the main body at that place. It was believed the British would avail of the circumstance of a great portion of the provincials being at Charlestown, to make an attack on Cambridge, by passing directly over the bay from the western part of Boston,† disperse the men retained there, and destroy the scanty stores collected; which would prove a disaster that it would be almost impossible to repair. It was considered necessary, therefore, to retain a large force at Cambridge, notwithstanding the perilous situation and urgent request of Putnam and Prescott.

The remainder of Putnam's regiment, stationed in the easterly part of Cambridge, near Inman's farm, so called, were very desirous of marching to Charlestown; but General Ward believed their service would be more important in checking the British, should they come out from Boston and make an attack upon head quarters.* At a later hour, however, they were permitted to proceed to Charlestown, for the support of their fellow citizens there engaged. These were commanded by Captains Chester, Coit, and Clark, and reached the rail fence, where Knowlton was stationed, just as the engagement began.

---

† At this time the British had not landed at Charlestown, and it was uncertain where they would make an attack.

* For a similar reason, no doubt, the provincial troops at Roxbury were not ordered to reinforce those at Charlestown. It would have left the American camp, in that place, wholly exposed to the British; who might have easily marched from Boston and made an attack upon it.

At an early hour in the forenoon, Gardner's regiment was ordered to proceed down the Charlestown road, near the foot of Prospect Hill, and there to remain till further orders should be given them.† In this situation they remained until after one o'clock; when, seeing the enemy's boats pass over to Charlestown, the Colonel consulted with his officers, and it was agreed to march immediately to the heights of Charlestown.

In the meantime, it had been concluded by General Ward to send to Medford for some New Hampshire militia, under Colonels Stark and Reed,‡ who were ordered to Bunker Hill, for a support to the men already there. It was between ten and eleven o'clock when the messenger was despatched from Cambridge with these orders. The brave New Hampshire men soon prepared to obey. But it was about one o'clock when they left Medford; and must, therefore, have been two o'clock, or later, when they reached Bunker Hill. They were in season, however, to repair to the lines on the left of the redoubt, at the breastwork and rail fence (where the Connecticut troops, under Captain Knowlton, were, by the special direction of General Putnam, already stationed,) when the attack was first made by the enemy.

Putnam, who rode to Bunker Hill, and even to the Neck, or still farther, to hasten on the reinforcements,

---

† Scammons' regiment was ordered to Lechmere's Point, and Little's still nearer to the Neck.

‡ This proves that Ward had the command of all the men in the vicinity, even from other colonies; or that there was a disposition to act in concert,

which were requested and expected as soon as the British landed at Moreton's Point, met the New Hampshire troops, and entreated their immediate presence at the lines ; with which they as readily complied. He also probably directed or advised the position most suitable for them to take. Parts of Little's regiment, sent on from Cambridge, and of Gardner's, already mentioned, arrived on Bunker Hill just before or about this time, and were directed chiefly to the rail fence, but some to the redoubt. At this time also it was, or a few moments earlier (for it was just before the British made the first attack,) that Judge Winthrop saw Putnam and Warren conversing together a little in the rear of the eastern part of the breastwork, on the left of the fort. A soldier in Knowlton's company also states, "that, just as the battle began, he saw General Putnam earnestly engaged in rallying some men, who were retreating towards Bunker Hill; and that, after he had drove back as many as he could, he rode towards the redoubt."

In the course of the forenoon, notwithstanding the heavy fire of the British from their ships of war, and their fort in Boston, a redoubt was thrown up by the Americans of about eight rods square, and a breastwork, on the left of it, extending down the eastern declivity of the hill, about seventy feet. East of this breastwork, and a little northerly in the rear of it, was the rail fence, at which the few Connecticut men were first placed, and afterwards the New Hampshire troops and two more companies of the Connecticut forces, as well as some belonging to Massachusetts,

who came on about the same time.* The rail
fence stretched almost to Mystick River; and an effort was made by the Connecticut troops, under
Knowlton, to render it something like a protection,
by adding another fence in the vicinity, and throwing
up some grass recently mown against it.

Colonel Prescott commanded in and at the redoubt
which had just been finished under his inspection.
He had sent two companies down into the street towards the ferry way to reconnoitre, but they were
soon recalled and placed in and near the fort. Some
of the men, with Prescott, were on the exterior of the
redoubt, but near it, on the right and left. He seems
to have had the sole command of this important post,
while Putnam was urging on the recruits and inspecting the troops in other parts of the peninsula.

Not only was the detachment, under Captain
Knowlton, ordered to the rail fence on the left, but
most of the fresh troops which came on to the field,
as reinforcements, were directed to take the same
position. The redoubt was sufficiently furnished with
men to act with effect, though deficient in cannon,
ammunition, and bayonets, to enable them to repel
the British who were superior both in numbers and
equipments. A part of *Little's* regiment seems to
have been the only troops ordered to the redoubt, in
addition to those stationed there at an earlier hour.

* It appears, from some accounts, that a part of the New Hampshire militia, and those of Massachusetts, were placed at the breastwork, in the low
land between the redoubt and the rail fence.

3

On the left, at the breastwork and rail fence, a large force became indispensable. The movements of the British, soon after they formed for the attack, fully indicated their purpose to march a large detachment near the margin of Mystic River, at a considerable distance northeast of the redoubt, and then to make an attack in the rear of it. A great portion of their troops were so disposed of as soon to render this plan most evident; while another party of them prepared to advance directly in front of the redoubt. Prescott was in full preparation to receive them at the fort; and all the attention and activity of Putnam were put in requisition to meet them on the left, and to prevent their advancing in that direction. Accordingly we find, from all the testimony given at the time and subsequently, that General Putnam was making every possible effort to forward fresh troops to that quarter. For this purpose, soon after the British landed, he rode to the Neck and beyond, and urged the scattered companies and parts of regiments, which he found, to proceed with the greatest despatch to the rail fence and to the breastwork on the left of the fort.

The British were some time in determining upon the particular mode of attack, and in forming after they had decided ;* it was between two and three o'clock when they first advanced to the bloody contest.† This was done in two separate bodies ; one

* They landed near Moreton's Point, S. E. from Breed's Hill.

† *Botta* says the Americans laboured at their entrenchments during the *whole* day ; and that the British did not make the attack till *towards* night. He is not entirely correct in this statement. He is also mistaken, in saying,

directed towards the redoubt of Breed's Hill, and the other towards the rail fence on the left and near Mystic River. The British began the fire upon the provincials when at a considerable distance, and without much effect. But the latter reserved their fire, by the express orders of *Putnam* and *Prescott*, no doubt by previous agreement, until the enemy had approached within about eight rods ; when they poured forth a most destructive volley of small arms, and continued it for some minutes (as rank after rank of the British succeeded,) by which a great number of the assailants were cut to pieces, while comparatively few of the Americans received any injury. The British troops were soon thrown into confusion, and retreated to the margin of the river, where they first landed.

The British officers soon rallied their men, and formed anew for a second attack ; during which General *Putnam* rode to the Neck to press on such of the militia as might have advanced thus far, and some of whom were reluctant to march nearer to the place of slaughter. The incessant firing of a sloop of war and of several floating batteries in Charles River,* rendered it extremely dangerous to pass on to the peninsula. *Putnam* rode over the Neck repeatedly, to show that

---

that the British had floating batteries in Mystic River, and the Americans a *competent* artillery.

* It has been supposed by some that there were floating batteries in Mystic River also ; but this was a mistake.

himself was without fear, and that it was possible to pass unhurt.

The British soon advanced a second time as before; a portion towards the redoubt, and others to the breastwork and rail fence on the east.† The Americans were prepared to receive them with equal resolution as at the first assault; and orders were again given by *Putnam*, *Prescott*, and other officers, to withhold their fire until the enemy should approach even nearer than before. The enemy were again repulsed with great slaughter. They soon shrunk from the tremendous fire of the provincials;‡ and a second time retreated to the banks of the river. The British soldiers were discouraged, and were not led on again to the attack, but by repeated orders and threats, and until a reinforcement arrived from Boston. The Americans, on the contrary, were elated by their repeated success; though the officers must have perceived the difficulty of long maintaining their position, unless they could receive a new supply of ammunition and large reinforcements of men.

The third attack was not made by the British without considerable delay. They sent to Boston for more troops; which were forwarded, indeed, with all possible despatch, accompanied by several officers of high rank and great military skill and experience. During this interval, it appears that

---

† It was at this period that the town of Charlestown was set on fire by the British, and the whole burnt, consisting of about 500 buildings.

‡ The British officers said the Americans fought like " devils."

General Putnam again rode to the Neck, and to a short distance beyond, where some provincials had assembled from the neighbouring towns. Some of these were unwilling to proceed, as it was very dangerous passing the Neck, and as they expected the troops on the Heights must soon retreat. At this time, also, unfortunately, a part of the artillery, from a defect in the apparatus of their guns, or some great error in judgment, retired from the field of action; which served to discourage the militia from advancing.

These men belonged to Massachusetts, were imperfectly organized, and unaccustomed to military discipline. The resolute and brave, however, readily hastened to the relief of those who had already been long engaged. Having urged the advance of these troops, *Putnam* returned to those he had left at the lines, with the great despatch for which he was always distinguished; and arrived some time before the reinforcements came up, to encourage the men and to direct their movements on the renewed attack of the British, which was then expected.

In the third and last attack the enemy conducted with much deliberation. They were convinced of the great importance of their field artillery; and particular care was taken to have it accompany the troops. It was taken to the eastern declivity of Breed's Hill, between the rail fence and the breastwork, where it was directed along the line of the Americans at the latter position, and a part pointed also into the opening or gate-way of the redoubt, which was on the north-eastern corner. The redoubt was now attacked also on the south-eastern and south-western sides by the enemy with fixed bayonets. At the same time, a column of the British advanced against the provincials posted at the rail fence on the extreme left.

Those in the redoubt were destitute of bayonets, and their powder also was soon expended. In this situation, after having made a most resolute resistance for some time, but without a possibility of maintaining their ground, and in hopes of saving the lives of his brave men, the intrepid *Prescott* ordered a retreat. To effect this, surrounded as he was by the British, was a difficult task. The troops on the left were ordered to cover them as they retired.* And this important service was performed with ability and despatch. *Putnam* and *Prescott*, having braved the enemy as long as hope remained, were very active in conducting the retreat.† Though many of the Americans were killed or wounded by the British

---

* The troops at the rail fence were closely engaged with a column of the British, when those at the redoubt were obliged to retreat. They fought with great bravery, and had hitherto prevented the advance of the enemy, whose plan was to force their way and turn this flank of the provincials. Here the New Hampshire men under Colonels Stark and Reed, and the Connecticut men under Captains Knowlton, Chester, Clark, and Lieutenant Grosvenor, gave proofs of a firmness and courage, which richly entitled them to the glory of a victory.

† According to the statement of several persons who were in this battle, *Putnam* and *Prescott* kept in the rear of the provincials as they retreated, and were much exposed to the fire of the British troops, who pursued them to Bunker Hill.

troops, who pursued them to Bunker Hill, a great degree of regularity and order was maintained by the attention and activity of the officers,‡ assisted by some fresh troops, who arrived at this time. This was between six and seven o'clock. Here General *Putnam* proposed to make a stand and fortify; but the plan was too desperate to meet the approbation of any other officers. " He wished, at least, to face the enemy and give them one more fire before they left the peninsula." But the men were too much exhausted and too destitute of ammunition to comply with his proposal. The provincials, therefore, passed over the Neck; and some posted themselves at Winter and Prospect Hills, within a mile and a half of Bunker Hill, and others proceeded to *Ward's* head quarters, at Cambridge, a distance of about three miles.

Just at the moment the word was given to retreat, General *Warren*, who was near the redoubt, received a musket ball in the head, and immediately expired. He was President of the Provincial Congress and of the Committee of Safety at this time; and three days before had been appointed a Major General of the Massachusetts troops. On this occasion, he was

---

‡ It is stated, in a report of a committee of the Provincial Congress, " that the retreat was conducted with more regularity, than could be expected of troops, who had been no longer under discipline, and many of whom never before saw an engagement; and that the retreat of the men from the redoubt would have been effectually cut off, had it not happened that the flanking party of the enemy was checked by a party of our men, at the rail fence, who fought with the utmost bravery." These belonged chiefly to Connecticut and New Hampshire.

merely a volunteer. His ardent and patriotic feelings led him to the scene of danger, as soon as he heard of the threatened attack. He was among the most eminent of the *many* brave men, who, at that critical period, were ready to sacrifice every thing for the liberties of the country.

The slaughter, on this occasion, was very great. The British had nearly 1500 killed and wounded; and the Americans estimated theirs at about 350. Some statements have given different numbers. But the above may be considered as very near the truth. Governor Gage's account, prepared soon after the battle, gave only 3000 in the engagement; and 1100 killed and wounded. It was his policy to make a favourable report. From the most accurate calculation, it is evident that the whole number of the British engaged could not have been less than 4500 (some suppose about 5000;) and soon after the battle it was reported and generally believed, that the whole number of the enemy killed and wounded amounted to 1492; ninety of which were commissioned officers. Of the provincials, 250 were wounded and 136 killed and missing; thirty of the latter were afterwards known to have returned to their respective homes the night following the battle.

Of the officers killed or mortally wounded in the provincial regiments, the principal were General Joseph Warren, Colonel Thomas Gardner, who survived a few days: Lieutenant Colonel Parker, who was mortally wounded, and died the week after in prison in Boston; Majors M'Clary and Moore. The numbers of men killed or wounded in the several regiments engaged, were as follows. In *Prescott's*, 42 killed and 28 wounded; In *Bridge's*, 16 killed and 30 wounded; in *Frye's*, 15 killed and 31 wounded;* in the detachment from Putnam's regiment, consisting of about 250, 15 were killed and 30 wounded. Of the two New Hampshire regiments, under Stark and Reed (the latter of which was not full,) 15 were killed and 45 wounded; in Little's, 7 killed and 23 wounded; in Brewer's, 7 killed and 11 wounded; in Gardner's, 6 killed and 7 wounded; in Whitcomb's, 5 killed and 8 wounded: and a few belonging to Nixon's and Gerrish's regiments.

In referring to the officers, who particularly distinguished themselves on this ever-memorable occasion, by their activity, their zeal, and courage, we may justly name General Israel Putnam of Connecticut; Colonels William Prescott, Ebenezer Bridge, James Frye, and Moses Little; Colonels John Stark and James Reed, both of New Hampshire; General Pomeroy, Lieutenant Colonels John Robinson and William Buckminster, Major Henry Wood, (General Warren, Colonel Gardner, Lieutenant Colonel Parker, and Majors M'Clary and Moore, who were slain or mortally wounded in the action,) Captains Knowlton, Chester, Coit, and

---

* Only parts of Bridge's and Frye's regiments were in battle.

CLARK, Lieutenants GROSVENOR, KEYES, DANA, and HILLS, all of Connecticut; Captain HENRY DEARBORN of New Hampshire; and Captains BURNHAM, TREVETT, FORD, WALKER, BANCROFT, and Ensign THOMAS MILLER,* &c. Many others exhibited great proofs of patriotism and courage, whose names it is not in our power particularly to mention.

The survivors of that brave and heroic band of freemen, who made such a resolute stand against the British troops, on this occasion, which are recollected are General HENRY DEARBORN, Major JOHN BURNHAM, Captain R. TREVETT, Judge GROSVENOR, General JOHN KEYES,* Colonel J. CLARK, General BENJAMIN PIERCE, Deacon THOMAS MILLER, Major DANIEL JACKSON, Captain BENJAMIN DANA, PHILIP JACKSON, Esq. JOHN BRAZER, Esq. and Mr. TIMOTHY THOMPSON.

The Americans justly considered this defeat a great disaster, but they did not despond. It taught them the courage of their men, and the necessity of greater discipline and preparation. The want of system and of military subordination was fully perceived. To this, in part, was attributed the final failure of that glorious enterprise. It would be unjust, perhaps, to accuse any one, then in *high* civil or military authority, of inactivity or want of spirit and

---

* Those not of Connecticut or New Hampshire belonged to Massachusetts.

† General Keyes was living in the state of New York a short time since.

zeal.† The contest was a glorious one to the Americans'; for, unprepared and unfurnished as they were with military stores and implements, a different result could not have been justly expected. That greater reinforcements were not provided, was perhaps the fault of no individual. But had they been furnished, the British would probably have been checked and repulsed, in their third attack, as they were in the two former. The enemy could boast only of having gained possession of the field for which they contended. But it was not without double the number of men to those whom they engaged. And they were convinced, by melancholy facts, that the provincials were too brave to be despised, or to be attacked except by superior numbers, and with every advantage of a competent artillery and a full supply of military stores. Though the American troops remained for several months almost wholly without cannon, and deficient, to an alarming degree, of the essential article of powder, the British made no attack upon their lines, nor attempted any offensive operations.

---

† Two colonels and a major of artillery were censured for remissness of duty. The artillery was in a very imperfect state, which furnished some apology for the inefficiency of the officers, though one of them was justly blamed. The two colonels were evidently deficient in that zeal and activity, by which all the others engaged were distinguished.